Literacy and Advocacy in Adolescent Family, Gang, School, and Juvenile Court Communities

"CRIP 4 LIFE"

Literacy and Advocacy in Adolescent Family, Gang, School, and Juvenile Court Communities

"CRIP 4 LIFE"

Debbie Smith
Northeastern State University

Kathryn F. Whitmore
The University of Iowa

LAWRENCE ERLBAUM ASSOCIATES, PUBLISHERS

2006   Mahwah, New Jersey   London

Lawrence Erlbaum Associates, Inc., Publishers
10 Industrial Avenue
Mahwah, New Jersey 07430
www.erlbaum.com

Cover design by Kathryn Houghtaling Lacey

Library of Congress Cataloging-in-Publication Data

Smith, Debra, 1955 Jan. 24– Literacy and advocacy in adolescent family, gang, school, and juvenile court communities : "Crip 4 life" / Debra Smith, Kathryn F. Whitmore.
    p. cm.
    Includes bibliographical references and index.
ISBN 0-8058-5598-X (cloth : alk. paper)
ISBN 0-8058-5599-8 (paper. : alk. paper)
1. Gang members—United States—Case studies. 2. Juvenile delinquents—United States—Case Studies. 3. Mexican American youth—Case studies. 4. Teacher-student relationships—United States—Case studies. 5. Gangs—United States. 6. Gang members—Education—United States. 7. Literacy—United States. 8. Marginality, Social—United States. I. Whitmore, Kathryn F., 1959– II. Title.
HV6439.U5S615   2005
362.74—dc22   2005050709
                                                       CIP

Books published by Lawrence Erlbaum Associates are printed on acid-free paper, and their bindings are chosen for strength and durability.

Printed in the United States of America
10 9 8 7 6 5 4 3 2 1

To my current and past students, and ones I have yet to meet,
who are forced to live on the margins of school and society
and whose voices are unheard.

To Nathan Hale Smith. Grandpa, you believed in me and my
dreams. You loved and respected me for me. With you I always felt
I could do anything. Thanks for being in my corner.
—debbie

As always, to Martin, Monica, and Kaeli Nieves, without whom
my work would have no meaning. And to my parents, Dill and Kay
Whitmore, without whom my work would not be possible.
I always want to make you proud.
—kathy

Contents

List of Figures

Foreword

Debbie Smith and Kathy Whitmore have produced a remarkable book. In *Literacy and Advocacy in Adolescent Family, Gang, School, and Juvenile Court Communities: "CRIP 4 LIFE"* we meet Lil Boy Blue, Smurf, Juice, and Lil Garfield and learn that even when their lives are torn apart by their gang membership there is a coherence and a reasonableness to their participation. To understand what happens to them we need to know why Lil Boy Blue says his life as a CRIP is quite average, why Smurf writes that he is from "dat insane wicced ass westside Manzanita Lynch Mob," why Juice says "If you are a gangster they really don't want you for school," and why Lil Garfield dreams of being a rapper.

Gang participation is not viewed favorably by society. Our ideas of the Crips are shaped by the media, by our reactions to news reports on TV and to stories we read in newspapers. Prejudicial stereotypes are difficult to avoid. Gang participation is problematic: lives are lost, literally. Death is often the consequence of gang participation. In this time of societal fragmentation, avoidance of the complexities of these young men's everyday lives leaves us reliant on stereotypic images and information that positions them in negative ways. Lives are also lost metaphorically. Deaths are encoded politically and reported officially. We rarely have an opportunity to know the names of the young men who are gang members. We know very little about their families or the communities in which they live. We know almost nothing about their experiences in school, or what happens to them when they enter the juvenile justice system. We make no allowances. We accept the official version of their lives without ever coming to understand their gang existence. There is no public conversation about the ways in which we as a society contribute to their exclusion, discrimination and alienation.

In *Literacy and Advocacy in Adolescent Family, Gang, School, and Juvenile Court Communities: "CRIP 4 LIFE,"* Debbie and Kathy help us understand how our society mores set the conditions for injustice to thrive. They help us understand how the fragmentation of their everyday lives echos the general state of societal fragmentation. Gang membership helps Lil Boy Blue, Smurf, Juice, and Lil Garfield make sense of their lives, providing them with a coherence that is otherwise denied. Vachel Lindsay's poem "The Leaden-Eyed" echos their plight. Lindsay pleads with us not to let young souls be smothered out before they flaunt their pride or let our poor children grow dull and leaden-eyed. Lil Boy Blue, Smurf, Juice, and Lil Garfield get this. They know how they are positioned by society and what their lives will be if they survive and so they flaunt their pride.

Debbie and Kathy invite us as readers to meet these young men and to get to know them. They encourage us to ask ourselves about our own participation in their exclusion from society and how we can support them in ways that bring them to full citizenry rather than othering them in ways that deepen their alienation and position them as an outcast minority.

The task that Debbie and Kathy set for themselves is fraught with difficulty and has taken them many years to achieve. They have not only had to revisit Debbie's original research study over and over again but they have also had to think deeply of the ways in which they interact with the reader. I was with Debbie when she presented her data at a conference at the University of Arizona. A man in the audience stood up and shouted at her. He was angry that she working with the young men in her study, that she was trying to help them and that she cared for them. Yetta Goodman and I both spoke with the man but he was too annoyed to listen and he left without actually engaging in conversation with us. We protect ourselves in the anonymity of alienated youth. "Dissing" the other takes away the possibility that we have any responsibility for what happens to them or what they do. Clearly, we are learning both nationally and internationally, that we have a lot to learn about excluded and alienated youth.

But, before you turn the page and meet Lil Boy Blue, Smurf, Juice, and Lil Garfield it is important that you meet the authors of this timely work. Theirs has been an original collaboration unlike any other that I have known. Debbie and Kathy have worked together for many years revisiting the ethnographic data of Debbie's doctoral research as they searched for insights into the fragmented lives of the young men in her study. The research began with Debbie's own courageous struggle to become a scholar and to advocate for disenfranchised youth.

I first met Debbie Smith when I went to Tucson in 1991 to teach at the University of Arizona. She was a doctoral student in the Department of Language Reading and Culture and she was already working with Kathy Whitmore. Kathy had just finished her doctorate with Ken and Yetta Goodman. I remember talking with Debbie on the first night of the doctoral class that I was teaching. She was concerned about taking ethnographic notes. Looking back, I think I remember the conversation because Debbie made it so clear to me how important writing was to her and that just the thought of my reading her notes was extremely painful. I tried to reassure her. I promised to write back and after the first "to and fro" Debbie wrote daily; observational notes, analytic memos, reflections on conversations, responses to the books she was reading, and questions—endless questions and the questions behind the questions, livid questions about social and political inequities. I wrote back but not as much as I should have written. Sometimes I did not know what to write. I had no answers. Debbie's questions resonated with my own questions leaving me deeply contemplative but without commentary or explanation.

My meetings with Kathy in the fall of 1991 were more casual, between classes at the University of Arizona, dinner at Ken and Yetta Goodman's house, and lunch with Rick Meyer (who was finishing up his doctoral dissertation and now teaches at the University of New Mexico). Kathy was teaching in the Department of Language Reading and Culture while she worked on a book based on her doctoral dissertation with Caryl Crowell, the teacher in her study. Debbie talked a lot about working with Kathy. It was clear that Kathy was challenging her thinking, getting her to read deeply, and encouraging her to write. Debbie was never without a note book. Kathy read her notes and wrote back to her on a regular basis.

"Hmmm what can I tell you?" Kathy says when I ask her to reflect on working with Debbie. "I've been a behind-the-scenes collaborator with Debbie on her study since its inception. Debbie was a student in the first course I taught at the University of Arizona. The first time I met her she wanted to know about course requirements and she about keeled over when I said she would need to keep a journal that I would read. We negotiated a contract of sorts and she took big risks in that class. It turned out that she loved my response and I loved the content of her writing! From that moment forward I was a support for her as a student, writer, thinker, researcher, and eventually—friend. Debbie took three courses with me before I left the University of Arizona, and during which time she wrote volumes in her beloved journal and I wrote back to her regularly."

"What is the nature of the teacher–learner relationship when they collaborate?" Debbie asks when she reflects on working with Kathy. "We can teach writing but there is so much more to writing than putting one's thoughts on paper. It's the focus on words, the rereading of the stories, the talking and the teaching."

"I've always been fascinated by writing," Debbie says, "It's as if there was a secret about writing and sometimes while writing in my notebooks, or when Kathy wrote back to me, I would get a glimpse of the secret." She explains, "Kathy was first my professor in my doctoral program. We became friends, but more than anything she was my teacher. Often I found myself at times getting frustrated with myself and this thing called writing. She is first and foremost a teacher."

"By the time she got to the point of dissertation I was in Iowa," Kathy tells me, "but she called frequently and we talked through design, method, everything as the study progressed. I read through and edited each chapter of Debbie's dissertation before she turned it in to Dana Fox who was her chair. I never changed the ideas, mostly helped with organization and provided the support Debbie needs so much as a writer."

"After she graduated I continued to provide that role for her as she wrote a couple of pieces for publication," Kathy continues and Debbie adds that by that time she was reading and commenting on the pieces that Kathy was writing for publication.

"At first when I started talking with Kathy about the book I was envisioning a shorter version of my dissertation," Debbie says. "But the book is very different from my dissertation. Even the writing is different. At first I would work on a chapter and send it to Kathy. She would read it and we would talk on the phone. Eventually the book took the form it now has. It is a story with dialogue that readers can hear instead reading interviews."

"I knew Kathy was giving up a lot of her free time to help me with the book," Debbie continues, "And so I asked her to co-author the book with me."

"I originally intended to be a 'with' author," Kathy continues, "but Debbie was pleased to have me as a co-author and we began to carve out a structure that would retain the strength of her primary voice, but allow me to write more directly and analytically, as well. I think what we came up with works. I suggested that we construct a community of practice frame and extend the concept of critical ethnography into advocacy, particularly as we saw more clearly that the literacy in the boys' school and court communities was so toxic. So after years of examining the data and talking about the events in the boys' lives we read *Situated Learning*, by Jean Lave and Etienne Wenger, *I Won't Learn from You*, by Herbert Kohl, *The Book of*

Learning and Forgetting, by Frank Smith, and *Toxic Literacies*," Kathy smiles, "by Denny Taylor."

"Kathy also had us rereading the manuscript all the time," Debbie adds. "I think I can safely say I have read this book, either chapter by chapter or as the whole book hundreds of times. By rereading one chapter at a time or reading the whole book the stories grow."

From their years of conversation Debbie and Kathy have developed a unique writing collaborative. Their hesitation and tentativeness encourages the reader to co-construct the stories first approaching at a distance and then close up. We get to know Lil Boy Blue, Smurf, Juice, and Lil Garfield and their families and we care about them. Eventually, their very survival seems to depend upon our reading, and perhaps our own survival depends on it too. For the story does not end on the last page of the book. In this age of fragmentation when the alienation of youth has reached such an extreme Debbie and Kathy have provided us not only with an opportunity for reflection but also for direct action in our classrooms and in our communities to reach out and change the conditions of those who grow up disenfranchised and dispossessed.

—*Denny Taylor*
New York, July 2005

Preface

For most teachers and the general public the word "gang" conjures up a picture of a bunch of male juvenile delinquents doing "drive-bys," firing guns at innocent kids who are wearing the wrong color or walking in the wrong neighborhood. Some people picture these same young men armed with spray paint cans destroying the city's walls and buildings with graffiti. In classrooms, these boys are predictably the "trouble makers." They are in school for a couple of weeks and they are out again either suspended, expelled, or they just quit coming. Groups such as The Crime Prevention League and gang task forces associated with local police forces promote descriptions like these. The media, too, through documentaries and local news reports, play a role in the formation of society's perception of gangs. The general public accepts the media portrayal as fact, without questioning sources or reliability. As a result, teachers, neighbors, and store owners treat gang members as if they are responsible for many, if not all, of the problems found in some neighborhoods.

School systems create new polices under the guise of preventing gang phenomena from entering schools and infecting the "good" students. Many schools have forbidden the wearing of certain colors or styles of clothes or have instituted school uniforms. In some schools, displaying gang hand signs can result in suspension. As members of an "illegal group," students associated with gangs can be punished accordingly. Some schools have created zones of "zero tolerance." These policies are typically created without efforts to really get to know the students who are affected by them.

In this book, you will come to know four Mexican American male adolescents who were active members of a gang and the first author's students in an alternative high school program. The boys are referred to by their street names: Lil Boy Blue, Smurf, Juice, and Lil Garfield. As you become acquainted with the boys, you will see that gang members live in multiple worlds. As sons and teenage parents they live in a Family Community; as taggers and gangbangers they live in a Gang Community; as "at-risk" students and dropouts they live in a School Community; and due to their illegal activities, they live in a Juvenile Court Community. You will discover, perhaps with surprise, that literacy is found in each of these worlds. You will hear how the boys perceive their own literacy and how literacy affects their lives. By becoming acquainted with these stories, you are invited to revalue boys like Lil Boy Blue, Smurf, Juice, and Lil Garfield, challenged to reformulate your assumptions about gang kids, and invited to develop ideas about ways to "do school" that will help students like them be successful.

The stories found in *Literacy and Advocacy in Adolescent Family, Gang, School, and Juvenile Court Communities: CRIP 4 LIFE* were constructed from ethnographic case studies. Each case study was originally created by the first author (Debbie Smith). She took field notes in the alternative classroom setting, in the boys' homes, and in their neighborhood. She conducted in-depth interviews and collected artifacts from school settings, the families, the courts, and the boys. Debbie played on a co-ed softball team with the boys, sat in court with them, cried with them as they buried classmates and friends, was invited to and expected to show up to family parties, garage sales, and casual visits, wrote letters to the welfare department on the families' behalf, and helped file taxes. She was the boys' teacher, mentor, and friend, and they were her guides, teachers, and friends.

We have decided to write this book for several reasons, with researchers, classroom teachers, and other people who work with marginalized adolescents in mind. First, sharing stories is one way we make meaning in our world. Schaafsma (1993) sees "storytelling as a way we learn from each other" (p. xvi). Wells (1986) says "storying ... is one of the most fundamental means of making meaning; as such, it is an activity that pervades all aspects of learning" (p. 194). He writes, "The important criteria in judging the worth of a story are: does it fit the facts as I have observed them and does it provide a helpful basis for future action?" (p. xiii). When the events we tell as stories transpired, Debbie questioned why some of her students were not successful in school even when they wanted to earn a diploma. While accumulating their stories, she came to know the complexity of their lives as readers, writers, and students, as well as gang members. She came to see their world(s) as they do and their decisions began to make sense. You will learn in this book, as we did through Debbie's experiences, that many students don't choose to quit school—they are forced out.

Another goal for writing this book is to validate these particular four young men's stories. The voices of many students who never reached their academic goals haunt the halls of our nation's schools (Hagood, Stevens, & Reinking, 2002). Their voices are silenced and then forgotten. Our goal is to put four of these voices on paper so that their stories are documented and readers may become witness to the heartache schools can cause in the lives of students that don't fit the picture of "typical student."

This book is greatly about Debbie and how she developed as a teacher, a teacher researcher, an advocate, a critical theorist, and a person. Debbie and her co-author, Kathryn Whitmore, have been theorizing about these stories for as long as they have been happening in real time. Kathy was the professor in Debbie's first course in her doctoral program and worked closely with her as a committee member as Debbie collected and analyzed the data for this study as a dissertation. Post-graduation, Debbie asked Kathy to collaborate on a new telling of these stories, and the now years-long conversation continued.

We know we will never "figure out" the issues that fill these pages: intersections of families, gangs, schools, courts, and literacy, and we are comfortable—even insistent—knowing that a linear, rational "solution" will never and should never be found. More important than answers to the research questions that initiated this book are more questions—we hope the boys' problematized stories and the questions that have troubled our thinking for years will do the same for a wider audience of readers.

ORGANIZATION OF THE BOOK

The majority of the chapters in this book are stories about Lil Boy Blue, Smurf, Juice, Lil Garfield, and Debbie. The stories are narrated by Debbie from the anthropological stance of the ethnographer and focus solely on the people and events that occur. Our intent is to draw you into the scenes of the classrooms, the homes, the neighborhoods, and the courts where the four boys live, so the stories include a lot of details about people, their histories, and the events that they experienced. In the introductory and final section of chapters 1 through 8 and the entirety of chapter 9, Kathy joins Debbie to explore the theoretical issues that ground our interpretation of the stories. We have a sociocultural and critical position regarding issues of school, community, literacy, and learning, and we borrow from several theorists to ponder the boys' lives in each of their worlds.

An introduction of the characters in this story (Lil Boy Blue, Smurf, Juice, Lil Garfield, and Debbie) is the content of chapter 1. Chapter 2 reveals a complete picture of the boys' Family Community, including their families when they were children and the families they are building as adults with children of their own. Chapter 3, about the Gang Community, lends insight into the Manzanita Lynch Mob Crip gang that is often denied to outsiders. It includes stories of how the boys loved each other and stories of heartache as they buried four of their best friends. It explores how literacy functions within the gang world, specifically, the characteristics and functions of tagging (graffiti) used by Crip gang members.

The School Community is described over the course of two chapters because two overlapping experiences occurred for the boys. Part I, in chapter 4, tells stories from the boys' early school years and explains their struggles in the traditional public secondary school setting before they worked with Debbie. Lil Boy Blue, Smurf, Juice, and Lil Garfield's desire to gain an education is paired with their inability to navigate the school system. Chapter 5 focuses on Part II of the School Community in the alternative program, called Nuestra Casa, where Debbie made learning as unlike "school" as possible.

Chapter 6 presents how each of the boys became acquainted with the Juvenile Court Community due to their gang-related behavior. It shows how court decisions and probation often clashed with Lil Boy Blue, Smurf, Juice, and Lil Garfield's successes and failures in school. The stories in this chapter demonstrate what results when an institutional community ignores the voices of the students on the boundaries.

Chapter 7 is a discussion of the images of gangs and gang members that are available in the media and existing research. Gang members are often viewed simplistically as damaged and needing to be fixed or locked up, and as the cause of many of the evils in society. However, some research is more holistic, authentic, and inclusive of the gang members' voices. In these portrayals, blame is not placed nor is the researcher's/author's primary goal to fix gang members. These researchers try to understand. This chapter situates *CRIP 4 LIFE* in the existing literature.

In chapter 8, Debbie describes her experiences as an official advocate for the boys in their schools and the court system. Teachers and researchers alike can learn from her experiences. They were not always successful. Debbie and Kathy join voices for the final section of the chapter to suggest that advocacy is a particularly effective form of critical ethnography.

By chapter 9 you will have heard Lil Boy Blue, Smurf, Juice, and Lil Garfield's provocative stories, as well as Debbie's challenges as an advocate. The last chapter elaborates on the research analysis and situates the narratives and the case studies in the larger educational system. We see literacy as ideological, related to power, and embedded in a sociocultural context (Street, 1995). We examine the role of literacy across the four communities to suggest that literacy hinders or facilitates the boys' roles in each. Our discussion reveals how the boys perceive their own literacy and how literacy functions differently across communities. We suggest that each community's literacy includes or excludes, facilitates or denies, Lil Boy Blue, Smurf, Juice and Lil Garfield's successful *membership*. We argue that until schools, as communities of practice, create peripheries that enable children and adolescents to retain identities from their other communities where they are full members, frightening numbers of students are destined to fail. We borrow from the theories bulleted below to understand the stories of chapters 1 through 8:

- We examine each of these worlds as a *community of practice* (Lave & Wenger, 1991) in order to understand the role identity plays in group membership and situated learning.
- We consider the notion of the *literacy club* (F. Smith, 1988, 1998), which complements the theory of communities of practice in helpful ways.
- We recognize that schools are construction sites where particular identities are built around particular images and expectations related to success and *failure* (McDermott, 1997) and where many children intentionally claim *to not learn* (Kohl, 1991).
- We suggest that literacy is not only a critical element in community participation and membership, failure, and not-learning, but that literacy is in fact *toxic* in some communities (Taylor, 1996) and actively constructs failure *identity* to keep gang members from legitimate participation or success in school.

In the Family and Gang, as well as School (II) Communities, the boys are full members of the community. In the School (I) and the Juvenile Court Communities, the boys never attain membership. They remain, because of their limited access to knowledge and power, participants who are on the margins. Literacy keeps gang kids, and other marginalized children, on boundaries of the school.

HELPFUL TOOLS

We invite you to access helpful supportive information in several places in this book. Vivid examples of conversation, art, tagging, rap, poetry, and other language and literacy events bring the narratives to life in figures and photographs in all the chapters. These images, and the explanations that accompany them, serve to indirectly teach some basics about gangs: how to read a tag, how to understand gang vocabulary, how to recognize gang-specific marks in clothing and other symbol systems. Appendix A is a time line that provides an overview of the complex events told. Appendix B is a family tree of sorts that identifies the primary characters and their relationships to one another. Appendix C is a glossary of gang terminology that is also marked by italics within the narratives. The terms and definitions are those used by the boys, with recognition that they are locally constructed and may differ from gang language in other groups and areas of the country. Finally, if you are particularly interested in the theoretical frame of this study, you might select to read the last chapter first.

A NOTE TO READERS

When we have shared copies of this manuscript and made presentations about the boys and their stories and experiences, Debbie has been accused several times of promoting violence and supporting the students' behavior. "Why do you condone gangs and gang activity?" is a common question. Debbie's typical answer is something like the following excerpt of an e-mail message she sent to Kathy as we corresponded about these challenges:

> What is so crazy about that is I know the pain of losing someone through violent acts. It is true Plucy, Murder, and Guero were my students and not blood relatives, but I cared for them, and their deaths hurt deeply. I don't believe in any type of violence. In a simple, probably naive way, I wish people would just be nice to each other. I feel this because of what I learned from my boys. Watching a mother pat her son's cheek, straighten his tie, and then shut the casket lid leaves you ... well, there is no way I condone the gang lifestyle .... I have seen and felt the hurt that comes from it.

> The thing is, people don't acknowledge the hurt and pain that the boys feel when they are kicked out of school or judged wrongly. Like Smurf told his mom once when he was on probation, "I'm still just a kid."

> I don't condone their behavior, I try to understand it. There is a difference. How can we help or teach if we don't understand? I wanted to see their world from their eyes and then I saw something completely different from what we read or see on TV. The gap isn't just about my gang kids, but all my students who have been marginalized by school and society. When we talk about violence and the dangerous behavior such as the

lives of the boys ... we never question the violence that has happened to them ... the way school and society treats them. I wonder why?

Literacy and Advocacy in Adolescent Family, Gang, School, and Juvenile Court Communities: CRIP4LIFE encourages you to ponder this question.

ACKNOWLEDGMENTS

We are most indebted to the Espinoza and Alvarez families, who were willing to let us retell their stories and teach others through their experiences. Lil Boy Blue, Smurf, Juice, and Lil Garfield—you should know that through your stories you are teachers to many. We thank you for allowing us to spend hours of time with you, learning from you and working hard to understand your lives and literacy.

Many people have helped in making this book a reality. We are appreciative of the early readers of this manuscript who encouraged us to continue; the editors and production staff at Lawrence Erlbaum Associates, in particular Naomi Silverman; Bobbie Bevins, for her constant and patient smile as she agreed over and over again to accomplish necessary tasks large and small, but always important. And Debra Goodman, Associate Professor at Hofstra University, whose review of the manuscript was deeply appreciated.

From Debbie

Many people have helped in making this book a reality. My family were my first teachers. My father, no matter what was happening in his world, never quit but got up every morning and did those things that were expected of him. From him I have learned to keep putting one foot in front of the other. My little sister, Lucy, picked up the pieces when times were hard and frustrating and kept me on my journey.

As a graduate student, I was lucky enough to have teachers who went beyond their job and opened my eyes to worlds I could never have imagined. Dr. Carole Edelsky started me on the road I travel today; she helped me discover that there are multiple realities which should be heard and respected.

The members of my dissertation committee, Dana Fox, Yetta Goodman, Ken Goodman, Luis Moll, and Kathy Whitmore, saw the possibilities within me and encouraged me to question my world and not settle for the simple answers but continually search for understanding and meaning.

I offer a special thanks to Kathy, my co-author, for her support, her help, and her belief in me and my students. This book would never have become a reality without her. The voices in the book that were never heard can now be heard.

—debbie smith

1

Introducing the Characters: Lil Boy Blue, Smurf, Juice, Lil Garfield, and Debbie

Lil Boy Blue, Smurf, Juice, and Lil Garfield are the street names of four boys who grew up together in the same neighborhood, called Manzanita. They attended the same middle and high schools. They liked to break dance, go to parties, and play baseball. They stayed overnight at each other's homes when they were younger. They got interested in girls at about the same time and struggled with the normal issues of adolescence. Lil Boy Blue and Smurf are brothers, and Juice and Lil Garfield are half-brothers. Over the course of the 4-year study reported in this book, these boys developed from young teenagers to young men with children of their own. They were learners together in an alternative high school program, called Nuestra Casa, where Debbie was their teacher. They were also active members of the gang known as the Manzanita Lynch Mob Crips (MLMC).

This book presents how four Latino adolescent boys construct their literacy and education identities in and out of school in the context of four multiple worlds in which they live and learn. As sons and teenage parents the boys live in a Family Community; as taggers and gangbangers they live in a Gang Community; as "at-risk" students and dropouts they live in a School Community; and due to their illegal activities, they live in the Juvenile Court Community.

Moje (2000) cautions that literacy researchers have examined literacy in "communities" without acknowledging their complex nature, especially the ways they overlap, converge, and conflict. Her critical review of the reference to "community" in literacy research highlights the difficulty of defining community and the likelihood that community be romanticized, oversimplified, and essentialized, particularly in regards to marginalized groups.

The four communities we discuss in this study (of the many in which the boys participate) are "complex entities that overlap with one another and that change and grow" (Moje, 2000, p. 102). They align with Moje's description of community as "the enactment of many different kinds of relationships ... within a given geographical and physical space that makes available particular tools for making sense of and participating in social practices" (p. 104). They are examples of "circles of kinship, friendship, position and power" (p. 106) in the geographic space of the westside neighborhood.

It may be surprising to some readers that literacy is found in each of these communities. We offer Lil Boy Blue, Smurf, Juice and Lil Garfield's stories about their literacy lives in each community in order to revalue them as learners and students and to reformulate assumptions about gang kids and their families. We view all of the boys' communities as clubs (F. Smith, 1998) and communities of practice (Lave & Wenger, 1991). We argue that Lil Boy Blue, Smurf, Juice, and Lil Garfield are successful members of some communities of practice but marginalized participants in others, in part because each community's literacy includes or excludes—in other words, facilitates or denies—their membership. Stated more succinctly, literacy constructs the boys' failure identities.

The primary narratives throughout the book are told in first person by Debbie, as she experienced them. Kathy's voice joins Debbie's for the introductions and conclusions of Chapters 1 through 8 and in the discussion that is presented in Chapter 9.

LIL BOY BLUE:
"MY TEENAGE LIFE IS QUIET, AVERAGE. I'M A CRIP."

Lil Boy Blue is a tall, thin young man. When I first met him, he was 17 years old. For a long time, I never knew if Lil Boy Blue really had hair because his Dallas Cowboys baseball hat never left his head. All I saw was a long *tail* (a chunk of hair going down the back of the head lower than the hair line) that hung 12–15 inches below his cap. Lil Boy Blue's dad, Felipé, once offered to pay Lil Boy Blue $150.00 to cut it off.

Lil Boy Blue is a private person, sometimes so quiet that he can fade into the walls. There are times when he speaks up, but even then he is soft-spoken and reserved. He is very caring. His *homies* (friends) are important to him. He often brags about how in the *hood* (the neighborhood in which the gang is located) everyone knows each other.

I asked Lil Boy Blue to describe himself. He wrote, "I am ... a father, a Chicano, a student, a smoker, a Crip. I have a Blue heart. A heart for family and *locs* (friends in the gang)." In a letter to a pen pal Lil Boy Blue said, "I'm Mexican American, we call ourselves Chicanos. I am 5'9" with light brown hair and light brown eyes. My teenage life is quiet, average. I'm a Crip." [Any oral language represented via quotation marks was audiotaped and transcribed. Nonverbatim language is not represented with quotation marks.]

As a ninth grader, Lil Boy Blue was a typical high school student. He got into trouble for such things as talking too much in class, forgetting homework, being tardy and, a couple of times, for ditching class. In his sophomore year, Lil Boy Blue was suspended or expelled (this distinction was never clear in his school records) for having a gun in his locker. Lil Boy Blue developed a negative view of school. According to Lil Boy Blue's mother, Kristina, Lil Boy Blue had always talked about going to college, but the negative experiences he had in high school caused him to give up on the idea.

Before the birth of his daughter when he was 17, Lil Boy Blue was a *gangbanger* (worked for the gang). After his daughter was born, another side of Lil Boy Blue emerged. He wrote about his daughter, "She's so special to me. She changed my life in a lot of ways." He believed that God sent his little girl to him so he would quit ganghanging. Getting a job and supporting his new daughter were now Lil Boy Blue's priorities. He knew he had to complete school to get a good job. With this in mind, I knew it was important to structure Lil Boy Blue's schooling so that he could work full time and still attend school and graduate.

While he was completing the final requirements for high school graduation, Lil Boy Blue worked close to 50 hours a week at a bottling company where, within his first year, he was promoted in the company structure several times. He attended two high schools and three alternative schools or programs over a 2-year period before he graduated with a high school diploma in May, 1996.

SMURF:
"I'M ... FROM DAT INSANE WICCED ASS WESTSIDE MANZANITA LYNCH MOB CRIP."

When I first met Smurf, he was 14 years old and small for his age. Later, at 17, Smurf had grown into a well-built young man. Smurf is darker than his brother and has black hair that he combed straight back when it was long. Against his mother's wishes, he sometimes wore his hair very short, almost shaved. Smurf has long eyelashes and a cute twinkle in his eyes. His mother shared with me that when Smurf was in seventh grade, they couldn't afford to order school pictures for Smurf. The girls in his class got together and collected enough money for Smurf's picture! Once the picture was taken, an 8 × 10 was given to Smurf's mother, and the girls kept the rest.

Smurf was a natural leader, both in the classroom and in the gang. Even though he was a *peewee* (the youngest boys in the gang) at the beginning of the study, he seemed to have a status not given to the other peewees.

I asked Smurf to describe himself. He wrote, "I'm short. I wear nothing but blue and gray clothes. I don't know how I feel inside. I don't know what makes me hurt. I worry about dying. It seems everybody dies in the gang. My dreams are to become a rapper and make lots of money." In a letter to his pen pal, Smurf said, "I'm a gang member on da streets of ... I'm a Crip gang member from dat insane wicced ass westside Manzanita Lynch Mob Crip. I'm short and have black hair and I'm always dressed in blue. I like to rap."

Smurf dropped out of traditional high school about 1 month into his freshman year. He transferred to Nuestra Casa, the alternative program, with his brother, Lil Boy Blue. Because of the policy which states students can only attend 2 years of school in a community-based alternative program, Smurf had to return to traditional school his junior and senior years. He wasn't happy. He didn't like traditional school. He was afraid he would mess up. His mom and I spent a whole summer convincing Smurf he could be successful in traditional school. He lasted about 1 month.

During the study, Smurf became the father of a baby girl and, like his brother, he took his responsibility as a parent seriously. He worked full-time in a yo-yo factory, which meant he was unable to return to school. He moved into an apartment with his daughter and girlfriend. He had been writing raps since he was young, and his dream was still to become a rapper. He didn't want to work at the yo-yo factory forever, yet he hesitated about going back to school because he needed to work to support his family. He asked me to search for a program he could attend while continuing to work full-time, but most of the time he believed he would never make it at school. He told me, "School and I don't mix." Smurf never finished school.

JUICE:
"IF YOU'RE A GANGSTER THEY REALLY DON'T WANT YOU FOR SCHOOL."

I first met Juice the day I interviewed for a teaching position at the alternative program. Juice and I were the lone San Francisco 49ers fans present at a table of administrators and students. Juice is a charmer. His engaging smile and sweet talk put me instantly at ease, and I immediately felt like I'd known him for a long time. Juice was completely bald when I first met him and later I learned this was a physiological result of stress. Juice dressed in oversized clothes like all gangsters, but Juice's pants were big enough to hold three of him! He pinned the bottom of his pants to his socks so they wouldn't drag on the floor. During the time he was a student at Nuestra Casa, Juice's girlfriend had a baby girl. He worried about how he could support his daughter and whether or not he wanted a long-term commitment to her mother.

Juice had been enrolled in two traditional high schools and two alternative high school programs. He worked at a neighborhood organization designed to provide service such as counseling and GED classes for the surrounding community. By the end of the study, he quit that job and began working at a telemarketing company. During this time he was also a student.

Juice only attended the Nuestra program for one semester before he transferred back to traditional high school. He soon had attendance problems and was suspended. His safety was uncertain after a fellow gang member was killed and Juice was removed from school. After that, he came to my class to visit. Because he was a member of MLMC, Juice was part of the community of my students and involved in many of my students' activities. This made him an unofficial part of the classroom community. During 1996-97, when I was no longer the teacher, Juice returned officially to Nuestra Casa, but he wasn't really happy and asked me to make sure he was taking the right classes. Within 2 months, Juice dropped out of the program. The second semester of the 1996-97 school year, I helped Juice register again for traditional high school. That semester was a turning point for him. He completed the semester and passed four of his classes; it was the first semester he had ever completed out of six semesters at any school. Although he quit school again soon after, Juice did successfully graduate in May, 2001.

LIL GARFIELD:
"I WOULD LOVE TO BE A RAPPER."

I met Lil Garfield when he was 13. He was serving community service at Nuestra Casa. Lil Garfield was in eighth grade and therefore not old enough to attend Nuestra Casa, which was for ninth through twelfth graders. Given his membership in the MLMC, Lil Garfield was a member of the classroom community, however, with full access to our classroom as an unofficial student. Lil Garfield was the biggest, but the youngest of the *peewees*. He

came across as a tough *gangsta*. He had a close relationship with his grandfather and looks a lot like him. Lil Garfield was shy and at times very quiet.
He pondered things at a deep level. When his homie was killed, Lil Garfield
broke down and cried in front of the other homies. He didn't try to hold
back. He has a heart that feels to the extreme, yet he can be very angry and
tough on the outside.

It wasn't easy for Lil Garfield to describe himself. After a long silent
pause, he finally said, "I don't know, just a Crip."

Our conversation continued. I asked, "What are your dreams?"

He answered, "To be successful, to be wealthy, have a nice house and a
good family, barbecue on Sunday."

"What type of job would you like to have?"

Lil Garfield said; "I would love to be a rapper …. I don't think it will
happen."

I asked, "Let's say you couldn't be a rapper …. What would you be?"

"Probably if that happened a lawyer, or doctor or maybe an architect."

Lil Garfield reminded me of a big teddy bear. He wanted people to hear
his growl and see how tough he was, but in the quiet moments when he
smiled and joked—his strong caring heart was revealed. Sadly, the year after I moved away from the area, Lil Garfield was shot in the head in a
drive-by. Although he survived, he was left with brain damage and physical
disabilities. A teacher from the neighborhood high school is supposed to
visit Lil Garfield at home once a week, and he has great difficulty learning.
Lil Garfield graduated in May, 2002.

THE FAMILY COMMUNITY

Lil Boy Blue, Smurf, Juice, and Lil Garfield had known each other for a
long time when I became acquainted with them. They attended the same
middle school located on the westside of the city. They call themselves
third generation "American Mexicans." Even though they were all born in
the same city and English is their first language, they were exposed to Spanish since birth in all family activities. Lil Boy Blue and Smurf were raised
Catholic. Juice and Lil Garfield were raised outside of a church but have
studied the Catholic religion.

Like fingerprints, families are unique and different. Lil Boy Blue and
Smurf's family, the Espinozas, is working class. Both parents work to meet
the family's needs. Their mother, Kristina, works in a yo-yo factory and
their father, Felipé, is a manager of a refrigeration store. The Espinoza family are die-hard Dallas Cowboys fans. Their home is a virtual Cowboys

shrine during the football season. Lil Boy Blue is the middle child in the Espinoza family, and Smurf is the youngest. They have an older sister, named Sylvia. Both boys have lived on the west side of town all of their lives. Both are natural athletes. Kristina shares many stories of the boys' successes in sports. They competed in little league baseball. Lil Boy Blue ran track in eighth grade. In a state track meet he won three ribbons—first, second, and third place. When I played on a co-ed softball team with both Lil Boy Blue and Smurf, I watched Lil Boy Blue run from center field to shallow right field and catch a fly ball. Smurf can hit a slow grounder to the pitcher and outrun the throw to first base to be safe.

Juice and Lil Garfield are half brothers in a single-parent family that lived on welfare and food stamps when they were young. Juice is the older brother. When I first met them I could hardly believe they were brothers, because they look nothing alike. Their mother, Diane Alvarez, worked at a menial job and put in overtime trying to provide some extras for the boys. Juice and Lil Garfield's first language is English, but their family also speaks Spanish. At family gatherings both languages bounce around the room as children and adults converse. Most of their young lives, the boys lived with relatives: aunts, uncles, and grandparents. Juice shared with me that they lived with their mother when she wanted to "play mom."

The Family Community was the first community to which Lil Boy Blue, Smurf, Juice, and Lil Garfield belonged. It was the community where they were successful as they learned to talk, read, and write, as will be explained in chapter 2. As they became adolescents, Lil Boy Blue, Smurf, Juice, and Lil Garfield chose to become members of a second community, the gang known as MLMC.

THE GANG COMMUNITY

Lil Boy Blue, Smurf, Juice, and Lil Garfield were members of a gang known as Manzanita Lynch Mob Crip (MLMC). Smurf wrote on a poster what Crip stands for—Community Revolutionary Inter-Party Service. Crip is one of the two nationally known gangs in the U.S.—the Crips and the Bloods. Crip is associated with the color blue; Blood is associated with the color red. There are several versions of the history or origin of these two gangs. One story about the Crip comes from a police report on a group of young men who were harassing some older people. As the older people were retelling the incident to the police, one elderly lady reported there was a young man who was crippled. The police picked up the word "cripple," referred to the group of boys as "Crips," and a gang name was born. Another story about the origin of the Crip claims the name came from a comic book, *Tales of the Crypt*. Yet another story claims the gangs came from rival schools whose colors were red and blue. I also heard the gang was started by a crippled Vietnam veteran. This veteran allegedly recruited young men to steal for him, and they would shoot the kneecap of anyone who resisted or caused trouble, thereby crippling the victim.

After reading and hearing several stories concerning the origin of Crip, I decided to accept the version found in *Source* magazine, which contains the name of "Tookie" Williams, a cofounder of the Crip who is now on death row (Williams, 1996). The article claims both gangs were founded in the 1960s and were neighborhood activist groups. They were designed to help young parents who didn't have jobs and to provide for after-school programs. The economy took a turn for the worse, drugs moved into the neighborhood, and the gang became what we see today.

Lil Boy Blue, Smurf, Juice, and Lil Garfield dressed in what is referred to as gangster style. They wore oversized, baggy clothes that *sagged* (pants riding low on the hips). Figure 1.1 is Lil Boy Blue's self-portrait, drawn to illustrate how a *gangbanger* dresses. Clockwise, beginning at the top right, the text reads: Crip hat, teardrop for dead homies, gangster belt, baggy pants, blue Nikes, tagg on shoe, tatoo, Mi viva loca (My crazy life).

Chapter 3 elaborates on the Gang Community. It explains the role of tagging as a socially constructed written language system and how gang members' specific use of oral language, hand signs, and other symbols served as multiple ways that Lil Boy Blue, Smurf, Juice, and Lil Garfield represented who they are to the broader community. Next, however, it's important to introduce the School Community.

THE SCHOOL COMMUNITY

Lil Boy Blue, Smurf, Juice, and Lil Garfield's stories concerning school were familiar. They consisted of dropping out of traditional high school, registering in an alternative program or school, dropping out of the alternative program or school, re-entering a new traditional school and dropping out again, and, in some cases, registering for a new alternative program. I once heard a school office worker refer to such students as "revolving door students" because they keep registering for school, dropping out, re-registering—a process which my students knew all too well. Smurf, for example, spent 4 weeks in the ninth grade at a traditional high school. He then dropped out and registered in the Nuestra Casa alternative program where he studied with me for four semesters; then he moved back into his home

FIG. 1.1.   Lil Boy Blue's
self-portrait drawn to
illustrate how a gang-
banger dresses.

high school where he was dropped in 4 weeks. Lil Garfield started his
school experiences in a traditional high school and quit within 4 weeks after
school started. Lil Boy Blue and Juice were veterans of the system; they re-
volved in and out of traditional and alternative settings for years before they
graduated.

Smurf explained one reason for this process from his point of view: "I
was constantly called into the office and padded down. How can I do school
work? I was never in classes long enough to do any work." School officials
regularly took the boys' belts, belt buckles, shoes, shoe strings, hats, and
shirts—anything that the school associated with gangs or gang membership. The boys were sometimes asked to change their shirts or shoes, or to
go home. The school told them they couldn't wear blue. For these kids no
blue meant a whole new wardrobe—a new way to think. The four boys
rarely had anything good to say about school, and they all had many bad
memories associated with school learning.

It's significant however, that I also heard the boys say they wanted to be
successful and graduate, to receive their diplomas. Their stories indicated

that they did value an education. They wrote about school: "I feel schools are very important. They provide education and knowledge." "It's very good to have an education." "School is important." Yet they were unable to navigate the school system—unable to be successful. School didn't accept them. It was a place where they were harassed—a place that didn't welcome them. In the words of Smurf, "School sucks." This tension—hating school and knowing it is important—is well illustrated by a poem Lil Boy Blue wrote (see Fig. 1.2). He wrote that school is "sorry, succs, stinks," but he also believed school can provide "opportunity."

School was only one part of Lil Boy Blue, Smurf, Juice, and Lil Garfield's lives. It was, however, the context that provided me the opportunity to get to know them and to learn to see their worlds through their eyes. The School Community is described in two chapters. School Community (I), in chapter 4, narrates the boys' experiences in traditional public school, from the elementary grades until the boys and I met at Nuestra Casa. School Community (II), in chapter 5, narrates the school experiences that we

FIG. 1.2.   Lil Boy Blue's poem about school.

shared at Nuestra Casa and what occurred related to school thereafter. These chapters demonstrate that the School Community was one of the predominate contexts for the bureaucratic literacy that pushed these students to the boundaries. The other was the Juvenile Court Community.

THE JUVENILE COURT COMMUNITY

As a result of their gang activities, my students became participants in the Juvenile Court Community. Over time, Lil Boy Blue, Smurf, Juice, and Lil Garfield were charged with participating in a drive-by, using drugs and alcohol, possession of a firearm, committing domestic violence, and driving under the influence. In the Juvenile Court Community, my students were assigned public defenders, probation officers, and surveillance officers to monitor their behavior both in and outside of the courts. All of these individuals were afforded official standing in the broader community because of their position in the judicial court.

Entering the Juvenile Court Community meant literally entering a physical facility. When I entered the building with one of the boys and his family for a hearing, we were required to pass through a metal detector and report to a clerk stationed behind a counter. She would direct us to proceed to a common area where everyone sat while waiting for their time to meet with the judge. Once Lil Boy Blue, Smurf, Juice, or Lil Garfield was arrested, he received a court date and time to appear before the judge in the mail, but the schedule was often behind. It was the boys' responsibility to arrive early and to sit and wait until they heard their name called. The process of being accused, found guilty, and sentenced was often a long, drawn-out procedure which involved several trips to the courts.

The boys' membership in the Juvenile Court Community necessitated that their families became part of the community, as well. At the same time, once one of the boys was part of the juvenile court system the official members of the Juvenile Court Community automatically received access to their Family and School Communities. Suddenly, for example, at any time of any day, a surveillance officer could enter the home to search for drugs or weapons. Probation officers had access to all school records and could remove the students from the classroom or school grounds without school or parental permission.

In the following section I share the story of how my relationship with Lil Boy Blue, Smurf, Juice, and Lil Garfield moved beyond the typical teacher–student relationship in the classroom. After I resigned my teaching position at Nuestra Casa I took on the role of the boys' official advocate.

This meant our relationship grew to be co-learners, co-researchers, and friends extending beyond the classroom walls. I advocated for about 12 students. Many families talked with friends about my work so that the numbers of students for whom I advocated grew. My advocating story with Lil Boy Blue, Smurf, Lil Garfield, and Juice is introduced here and continues through the narratives about the School and Juvenile Court Communities. The focus of chapter 8 is a reflection that summarizes my data collection and analysis procedures used in the study and explains how advocacy was a particular form of critical ethnography.

WE BECAME CO-RESEARCHERS: "WE'VE GOT YOUR BACK, MISS."

By now readers may be wondering how I got involved with, and gained access to, such a group of boys. I have often asked that question myself. I come from a religiously conservative, working-class, Caucasian family. Everyone around me as I grew up looked, acted, and sounded just like me. As a child I was taught that people in the world who faced the challenges of homelessness, unemployment, or other hardships had made decisions that placed them there. In other words, anyone in our society could be anything they wanted to be; if they were not successful the blame was theirs alone. The values I was taught as a child dictated that gang members, dropouts, and at-risk students were at fault and deserved their consequences. Although as an adult I had come to question this ideology long before I met Lil Boy Blue, Smurf, Juice, and Lil Garfield, as I came to see the world through their eyes, ears, and experiences, I also came to understand that the world is not black and white or right and wrong. With each new conversation or interview we shared, and with each success and failure in my work as their advocate, the worlds of my students gradually made more sense to me. I learned it was often the dictates of others that governed the choices my students were allowed to make.

Perhaps the only thing I had in common with these four boys was negative school memories. In fact, I have very few good memories associated with school. Graduating from high school wasn't a choice; it was something I was expected to do—but I was always an outsider. I sat in remedial classes being accused of not having the necessary skills to succeed in school. I often sabotaged the teacher's agenda with smart remarks and "acting up." Like my students, I never felt I was a part of the School Community. Frank Smith (1988) would say I didn't have access to "the literacy club."

Joining the School Community

This study began in January 1995, when I started a new job as a teacher in the alternative high school program. The only thing I knew about my new students was that they had been removed from traditional school by the school or had chosen themselves to leave. They were all members of a gang and a ready-made community. I was an outsider—a stranger to their community. In their own words, they were *down* (with support, help) for each other, meaning they had proven worthy of each other's loyalty. I, however, had to earn their loyalty. They seemed to be saying to me, "This is our classroom. You may come in, but we have the control."

I spent the first 2 weeks watching and listening to my new students. Listening to their stories stirred many emotions with in me. I was excited. There were so many things I wanted to do for the kids. At the beginning I was going save them from the gang. But I was also sad and angry. My mixed feelings surfaced in my personal journal writing:

> Teaching at this alternative program is so exciting, but my heart is also heavy—so sad. One minute I want to scream. The next minute I want to cry. Both seem to come from anger/mad, almost a hatred, because the students are being abused with worksheets and a false hope. And then a heavy sadness as I look into their eyes—the eyes that still seem to sparkle with the child-like innocence for learning—for being valued. These kids, for whatever reason, cannot or will not attend "traditional" school. So we now have an "alternative" school/program. What does "alternative" mean? Well, this school isn't an alternative. It is a warehouse for kids that are not wanted in the "real" school. I think right now trying to get the kids to come and participate in active learning—to dialogue—inquiry—discovery would be nice, but realistically the goal is to just get the kids to come!!! To realize they are valued as learners. That they are learners. (Feb 5 & 12, 1995)

One day I brought in poems from *Barrio Warrior: Homebody of Peace*, by Gus Friar (1982). Smurf read the poems aloud to the other students who sat stoically with no expression or comment. Perplexed, I asked them, "Why will you not talk to me about how you feel about the poems?"

Smurf replied, "Miss, we don't like things that tell us gangs are bad. People are always saying things like that."

I asked, "Do you feel this poem was saying that?"

"Yes."

My thought was, I know the fact is they are in gangs. It is their way of life. Why do I have a right to point out all the negatives?

I learned a lesson on that day: I must first view and respect my students for what they are and not for what I think they should be. It wasn't my place to judge or to try and save them. I decided I wouldn't use poems, articles, or my own questions and statements that dealt with the negativity of gangs or urging them to "say no" to gangs. They knew what life was like in the gang. They certainly didn't need me to tell them.

I consistently negotiated with and learned from my students. As a result, my teaching changed. The curriculum I planned became more project oriented. We built the solar system and solar ovens. The texts we used frequently came from popular culture. We discussed history after watching the movie *Forrest Gump*. We examined the role of gangs in movies that the kids felt would help *me* better understand gangs. The students taught me about tagging and what life in a gang was like. They shared what it was like being them in "school." I brought in magazines filled with articles and photographs about rap and rap artists and gangs and the life of gangsters. The kids skimmed through the magazines until they found what they wanted to read. I watched as they shared what they read with their homies, and saw how their talk nudged the kids who didn't want to read toward reading. Everything was done in groups. No one was left alone. Everyone supported each other.

I eventually realized and believed that my students' resistance to reading and school was a manifestation of their negative schooling histories, particularly those in their recent pasts. In order to be successful I knew I had to make my lessons seem less like conventional "school." I also had to venture out of my more comfortable and familiar classroom context and learn about their families. Little did I know at the time that years later I would feel as comfortable and knowledgeable about the boys' Family, Gang, and Juvenile Court Communities as their School Community.

Joining the Family Community

One weekend, I went to a barbeque at Lil Boy Blue and Smurf's home. Kristina, Lil Boy Blue and Smurf's mother, informed me that since this was my second visit to the home I was no longer a guest but part of the family and therefore I had to serve myself. This was my first indication that I was joining my students' Family Community.

Another time, at Juice's little girl's first birthday party, I went to the kitchen to serve myself and returned to find someone sitting in the chair I was using. Jokingly, I stated, "You took my spot." I was told the rule of the family: to save a spot you have to say "safety pin." My answer was, "I did. I come from a large family and know how that works." We all laughed. When the uncle left the party, he reminded me of the two main rules of the family: first come first served, and to save a place say "safety pin." I was part of the family and was expected to act accordingly. I was invited and expected to participate in birthday parties, garage sales, and any family gatherings. On one occasion I was referred to as a student's second mother because I worried about him so much.

Joining the Gang Community

As I worked with these kids, I felt I was flying by the seat of my pants. I often sat and listened to stories about their life in the gang. I needed to understand their ways of knowing and see their world through their eyes. As they taught me and as my understanding grew I gained entrance into the Gang Community.

Two events took place that showed me I was becoming accepted. The second year I taught at Nuestra Casa one of the gang members who wasn't officially enrolled in the program was having a hard time with school and my students asked me to help their *homie*. I heard Sad Boy (a student) explain to his homic that I was okay because I was an *OG* (old gangster). Although I never was actually initiated into the gang, this label indicated that the gang members accepted me.

The second confirmation of my acceptance was the appearance of a blue rag (Crip color) over the rear-view mirror in my truck. This was the class's way of showing me respect. I was part of them. They took me to their *hood*, they showed me the parts of town and what happened there in terms of gang history, and they took me to the *rock house* (a partially torn down house made of rocks) which was their place to hang out. We went to movies and to amusement parks together.

My acceptance was mutually negotiated, however. The boys knew I didn't agree with some of their behavior and we had many class discussions about drugs, alcohol, and violence. I was frequently invited to parties or meetings the gang was having, but I often chose not to go because of what might take place. On one occasion, we talked about loyalty. They were teaching me about gangs and how they look out for each other. I tried to explain to them that I was there for them, too. One student said, "Do you want us to *jump you in* (initiation for membership in the gang)?" We all laughed. Finally, we had achieved a mutual sense of loyalty and respect. My students understood and respected my feelings, but they also knew I "had their backs," so I was never denied access.

Since my students took me into their world, I took them into my world, including my academic community at the university. On more than one occasion the students participated on panel presentations in my graduate classes. I introduced them to my professors and colleagues. After one such event Smurf asked, "Did we do good enough for you to get an A?"

Our relationship grew especially strong as the boys, their families, and I mourned the loss of friends and students to tragic deaths. My students were concerned about how I would take the news of the death of a student. They worried about me, and I worried about them.

Because I was willing to "cover their backs," I became confidante, counselor, chauffeur, friend, mentor, and advocate. This carried over as the students returned to traditional school. Many times I answered phone calls requesting me to pick them up for school. We frequently went to breakfast and then to school or we'd eat out to celebrate the end of a day when they went to school. The relationship we developed allowed me to move beyond observer or participant-observer to an advocate who was an active member of their individual communities.

THE CHARACTERS

As their teacher, Debbie was an active member of the school community. She had access to their records and counselors. However, after she started to advocate, she was quickly pushed to the margin where she began to live the stories her students were sharing with her.

You have been introduced to Lil Boy Blue, Smurf, Juice, and Lil Garfield. In chapter 2, you will become acquainted with Lil Boy Blue's, Smurf's, Juice's, and Lil Garfield's families and some of the rituals that are a part of the Family Community. Lil Boy Blue, Smurf, Juice, and Lil Garfield are full members of the Family Community with all rights and privileges, and they use literacy to accomplish the events of the community.

Family Community:
Mi Familia

This chapter describes the Family Community that Lil Boy Blue, Smurf, Juice, and Lil Garfield were members of as Debbie came to know it. Family Community is the first community experienced by Lil Boy Blue, Smurf, Juice, and Lil Garfield. This community is where many of their beliefs about the world are formed, and where they develop a sense of self and place. The family is also the first place where they come in contact with literacy. Debbie introduces Lil Boy Blue's and Smurf's parents, sister, and grandparents first, followed by Juice and Lil Garfield's mother and grandparents. Next, she describes Lil Boy Blue, Smurf, and Juice's new families, meaning their girlfriends (who became their wives) and their daughters. Debbie shares the rituals and events that she was able to be a part of as a newcomer to the boys' Family Community, tells stories that would be hidden when casual visitors might enter the families' homes, and highlights the literacy found in each household. The chapter concludes as we consider the Family Community through a theoretical lens.

GENERATIONS OF THE FAMILY COMMUNITY

One day at Nuestra Casa I was helping Lil Boy Blue and Bad Boy with a math assignment when they started to talk about the death of Oso, an older member in the gang who had been killed in a drive-by shooting. The boys talked about how Oso was in their thoughts all the time. "We wake up in the morning thinking about Oso. On the way to school, we look up at the mountain to see the cross" (which was placed there by the gang members). I informed them they were grieving. I explained that they may have days when they are sad, days that would proceed normally as if Oso didn't die, days they would feel guilty because they are not sad, and days they may even be angry because Oso left them. They continued to share memories of Oso with me.

As they talked, I took the opportunity to share my concerns about Smurf, the student who I thought of as my best worker and the one who kept things going in the classroom. He had recently stopped working and frequently tagged *EBK* (everybody killa). Lil Boy Blue said, "Smurf was locked up for three months accused of Oso's death." I realized he hadn't had an opportunity to formally grieve with his homies because he was locked up in Juvenile Detention. He hadn't even been allowed to attend the funeral. Given this information, I saw that Smurf's anger and hurt was emerging in his classroom behaviors.

I decided to call Smurf's mother. This telephone call was the beginning of a new role for me as the boys' teacher; my first conversation with Kristina led to another, and another. I soon found myself calling and visiting with many of my students' families. My relationships with these families allowed me a new understanding of my students and their lives.

LIL BOY BLUE AND SMURF'S PARENTS
AND GRANDPARENTS

Lil Boy Blue and Smurf are third-generation, as they say, "American Mexicans." Their father, Felipé, was raised on the southwest side of Tucson. According to Lil Boy Blue and Smurf's mother, Kristina, Felipé is a "typical Mexican." He is short with dark hair and has a goatee. He is a devoted husband, father, and grandfather. His children and grandchildren come first in his life. Lil Boy Blue and Smurf claim their dad is a softy. When they wanted something when they were children they approached their dad first. Their mom was the disciplinarian. Kristina's family lived on the west side of Tucson, but moved to the southwest side when she was young. Kristina is a short woman with light brown hair she wears at shoulder length. Kristina has a big heart. Her door is always open to people who need help. Lil Boy Blue and Smurf's friends were often found sleeping on the couch. She worries about her children and wishes she could protect them from the harms of the world. In her words, she admitted, "I'm a controller." She wants to control her kids so she can make sure they don't get hurt. She also knows this can never be.

I asked Kristina when her family immigrated to America. She said, "My grandma's ... marriage was having a hard time so they decided to come to America. [The marriage] didn't work out and [my grandfather] left her and a daughter. This all took place during the Depression. My grandma earned money by cleaning house. She got $1.00 per house. She would rush and clean one house then rush and clean another. She was also a seamstress. My mother was the oldest. My father was abandoned by his parents. He and his sister and I think another sister lived under the St. Mary Bridge in a cardboard box. They got married at a young age—18 years old."

Felipé also told me about his family. "I don't know much about my family. My grandfather worked for the railroad. I'm not sure where he was from. He fought in the Mexican war. My grandmother is still alive. My mother was born in Tombstone. My father was born here and lived his whole life in Tucson. My father was in a gang—pachucos, zoot suits. But now he is really religious."

Kristina and Felipé lived two blocks from each other during their high school years and met during Felipé's senior year. Felipé narrated their story. "I decided I was going to my senior prom, so I had to pick the best looking chick I could find. I saw her coming down the hall. I said, 'Haven't I met you somewhere?' Kristina said, 'You can't try that line on me I don't think so, I don't go out.' Two weeks later I bought her a watch for her birthday and asked her out."

Kristina was raised very strictly and wasn't allowed out of house without permission. According to Kristina, "We couldn't even look out the window if someone drove by and honked. That wasn't what nice girls did." After the prom Felipé and Kristina continued to date. They had to take Kristina's cousin with them as a chaperone and Kristina had to be in by 9:00 p.m.

Felipé and Kristina had been married for 26 years when I met them. Kristina claimed that Felipé never really proposed. He would say, "when we get married," but never made an official proposal. He did promise her that when they got married he would have a house for her to move into. Kristina went from her parents' house to her own house.

Kristina, Felipé, and I talked about Lil Boy Blue and Smurf constantly. Kristina said, "Lil Boy Blue was a typical middle child. He just went along with everything. He would be pulled from one side to the other. 'You are a boy so you're on my side,' Smurf would argue. Sylvia, the older sister, would contradict, 'He's a brat, you're on my side, you're closer to my age.'"

Smurf is the youngest child, the youngest grandchild, the baby of the entire family. According to Kristina, Smurf is very spoiled. When Smurf was small, Kristina's mom, Smurf's grandma, had a special drawer full of candy just for Smurf and she still keeps the drawer full for him today.

There is a cul-de-sac on the Espinoza's street where the older boys in the neighborhood gathered to play baseball. There was no one Smurf's age to play with. Kristina explained, "The only kid close to Smurf was a little boy across the street. [The family across the street] was really religious and was always at church. I mean they go to private school and they go to church. Whenever Smurf got a chance he'd go play with him, but that was very rare. Smurf always tagged along with Lil Boy Blue and his friends. That's how Smurf started hanging around with older kids."

As Kristina and I talked, Lil Boy Blue came into the family room and said he needed some money for gas. Marisela, the granddaughter, gave him three pennies. Kristina looked at Felipé and said, "What does that remind you of huh?" They smiled and Kristina shared, "One time we were ... I don't know where we were going. We were in the car. [The kids] were all sitting in the back seat. Felipé and I were discussing bills and Felipé goes, 'I don't even have money for gas.' He goes like that to me, you know, and then Lil Boy Blue pops his little head and he pulls out a nickel, a dime and a penny. 'Here Dad, I got money.' He gives him his money." This story illustrated a side of Lil Boy Blue I saw in class. He was the one who helped whenever possible.

To Kristina the boys were just typical boys. When they were younger, Kristina explained, "They all had chores to do: like one had to set the table, the other one had to clean the table, and the other one had to sweep, and they would rotate. When they got older one had dishes one day, the other one had to clean the living room, the other one had to clean the company bathroom. That's what they called it. They used to hate that one and the dishes. I think they hated the dishes more than anything else and vacuuming. They all had to take turns vacuuming. They all know how to wash and cook and clean." Along with the chores Kristina kept a close watch over them. They weren't allowed outside to play unless she could see them. When company came, they knew not to interrupt the conversation and played quietly in another room. As Kristina shared this information her eyes gleamed with pride.

Like many "typical boys," Lil Boy Blue and Smurf got involved with sports. "Baseball was their favorite," said Kristina. "Lil Boy Blue is the one that liked baseball. Every year you know he came home [from school] with a flyer yelling, 'Look, Mom, they're going to have baseball at the park.' My dad was a real baseball fan and [Lil Boy Blue] used to go and watch the baseball game with my dad on TV."

Felipé interrupted, "I put Lil Boy Blue in cause that's what he wanted."

Kristina continued, "Then Smurf just followed along and would say, 'I don't want to play baseball this year. I don't want to.' [But] at the first game, Smurf would see his friends and say, 'I want to play baseball all my friends are on that team I want to be on that team.' We would sign him up."

The boys who played baseball in the neighborhood also joined and the cul-de-sac team became an official city recreational sports program baseball team. Felipé either coached or was an assistant coach. Kristina and Felipé laughed as they thought back to attempting to coach Smurf. Felipé explained, "I would try and teach him to throw the ball this way. Smurf would say, 'I know how, I know how.' I said, 'Let me just show you the way I want you to try.' He would say, 'No I already know I already know .... '"

Kristina said, "Felipé would come home upset."

Kristina believed Smurf always had an advantage because of Lil Boy Blue. She told me, "Lil Boy Blue was playing ball, Smurf would go with him to all practices. So by the time Smurf got to t-ball he had it made and he even played one time on Lil Boy Blue's team. Lil Boy Blue's team was short a player. They had to forfeit. Smurf joined in at that point. He was playing in the minors. Lil Boy Blue was in the majors. [The team] decided to play for fun and Smurf played with them." Kristina believed Smurf was a better player because he hung out with Lil Boy Blue and his friends. Lil Boy Blue and Smurf were very close growing up.

I played with Lil Boy Blue and Smurf on a co-ed softball team that Kristina and Felipé organized. I saw that Lil Boy Blue and Smurf were talented athletes. I wondered if the boys had ever played school sports. I asked Kristina, "Did Lil Boy Blue or Smurf play on any school teams?"

"No."

Smurf said, " We never did play anything for school."

Lil Boy Blue, however, participated on the middle school track team. "He did really well," explained Kristina. In a state track meet Lil Boy Blue took first place in the 100-yard relay, second in the 100-yard sprint and third in the mile relay. I kept asking about school sports because as a high school track and field coach I would certainly have asked Lil Boy Blue to try out for the team. Lil Boy Blue was never approached to run track by the coach. Lil Boy Blue told me he wanted to, but he claimed he never knew where to sign up.

Events, Rituals, and Celebrations

I was invited to many different family activities over the years I worked with the boys. The first activity was a garage sale. Kristina's parents were preparing to celebrate their 50th anniversary and the family had decided to hold several garage sales to earn money. I had some things to contribute so on a bright Saturday morning, I loaded my truck and nervously drove to the aunt's house. After unloading the truck, I was invited into the house to eat breakfast and soon noticed that this was more than a garage sale. All the relatives showed up. Aunts, uncles, grandparents, and the kids, including Lil Boy Blue and Smurf, came by. This was a family social event! Everyone took part. The family members talked and shared stories, family news, and news of things happening in the community, in English and Spanish. We all ate and laughed together. The garage sale took place in the background.

I toured the grandparents' small home while I was there. In the bedroom, Kristina showed me the drawer that had candy and toys just for Smurf. Next, Kristina's mother took me into a room located on the side of the house that was swarming with religious artifacts. There was an altar with candles, statues, and written prayers. As she pointed out different artifacts, she told me the stories behind them. She remembered how all the boys (Lil Boy Blue and Smurf's friends) came over after the death of Oso and prayed for their friend and for Smurf who was locked up.

I found the same social setting on each visit. Things were sold from the garage sale on both weekends and stories and news were shared among family and friends. I never heard how much money was made or if the garage sale was considered a success. The success was the coming together of the family and friends.

The next type of social event I was invited to was birthday parties. Kristina said, "Birthdays are a big thing" and I soon learned just how big. "I always used to make [the kids] their favorite French toast or pancakes or whatever. I always used to stick little candles in there and sing, 'Happy Birthday,' then I would wrap their birthday outfit and put it on their beds at night so in the morning they'd wake up and they knew they were going to get a new outfit for school. When it was my birthday they would do the same thing. Sylvia learned how to make breakfast. The very first time they started doing this, Sylvia made me scrambled eggs and Lil Boy Blue made the toast and Smurf [said], 'I passed the food to Lil Boy Blue and Sylvia. Sylvia the eggs and Lil Boy Blue the butter.'"

Once the kids grew older with their own families, the special birthdays were celebrated for the grandkids with a party attended by the extended family and friends. The first birthday party I was invited to was one of Kristina's granddaughters. The house was decorated, and crowds of people gathered in different locations. We munched on snacks and socialized while we waited for dinner.

Everywhere I went in the house I heard dialogue and again, I found myself in a setting where people code-switched between Spanish and English with ease. I asked Kristina and her mother why they switched between the two languages. Kristina's mother explained that when her children started school they brought friends home who spoke only English. The family had friends that spoke only English and friends that spoke only Spanish. Kristina's family decided to use both languages so everyone would feel included.

Another family event I was lucky enough to be a part of was the Christmas season. On Thanksgiving, names of relatives and friends were placed in a bowl. It was my responsibility to buy a gift for less than $5.00 for the person whose name I drew. Next, the family (grandkids, great grandkids, uncles, and aunts) and friends got together on the first Saturday in December to decorate the grandparents' house for Christmas. Hundreds of lights were strung around the outside of the house, and many decorations were hung inside. After all the decorations were in place, the family ate dinner and we gave our presents to the person whose name we had drawn.

Tamale making, the next event in the Christmas season, was a tradition passed from generation to generation, and once again I was invited to participate. Although the tamale-making ritual historically involved the women in the family community, the men were occasionally asked to mix the *maza* (dough), particularly when a large quantity of *maza* was being manipulated. The *maza* was mixed by hand in a large pan. At one moment, I noted that there were four generations, from great grandma to great granddaughter, gathered around the table making tamales (see Fig. 2.1). As we spread the *maza* on the corn husks and watched Nana expertly place the

FIG. 2.1. Four generations making tamales.

meat on the *maza* (she was the only one allowed to complete this step of the process), family stories were shared.

The youngest tamale maker was 4-year-old Marisela, Sylvia's daughter. Marisela was placed on a chair and given the tools needed. She watched and did what everyone else was doing. No one corrected her. She was a member of the tamale-making family. I was taught the same way. At times the boys' grandma would gently show me an easier way, like how to set the corn husk on the table while spreading the *maza* if it was too difficult to hold it in my hand, but she never let me feel as though what I did was wrong. Marisela and I learned by watching and doing. I'm not sure who made the biggest mess, Marisela or me! According to Kristina, I had more *maza* on me. I learned that the twelve dozen tamales we made (see Fig. 2.2) was a fraction of what was made in the past when selling tamales was a second income.

While we waited for the tamales to cook, Kristina's mom brought out the newspaper and turned to the section where word games are located. She quickly completed the seek-and-find word puzzle. When I learned that she is also the family's champion Scrabble player, I realized the origin of Lil Boy Blue's ability to play and win the word games we played in class.

It was finally time to taste the tamales. After everyone was served, Kristina's mother sat down at the head of the table. As she settled in she informed me that this house is a "matriarchal" house. We laughed.

FIG. 2.2.   Twelve dozen tamales were made.

The next big event was Christmas Eve. The whole family—cousins, aunts, uncles, grandkids, and friends—came together at the home of Kristina's parents. When I arrived Kristina's father greeted me with, "I'm sick, I think I ate one of the tamales you made." As I ate the tamales, however, I teased, "Mmmm, good, I must have made it," and if anyone else commented how good the tamales were, I quickly claimed them as mine. Lil Boy Blue and Smurf laughed as they confessed to me they heard how I had tamale maza all over myself. Kristina reminded me I did the same thing making cookies the year before at Christmas time.

At midnight we gathered in the living room in a big circle. Kristina's mother expressed how grateful she was for her family and friends. Everyone gave each other a Christmas hug and gifts were distributed. No one was left out. Kristina explained that this tradition came about because as kids were married holidays were often split between in-laws and their immediate family. Coming together and exchanging gifts on Christmas Eve meant Christmas Day was available for immediate family celebration and time to visit in-laws.

Literacy in the Home

The kitchen table at Grandma Espinoza's home was a place where everyone gathered to talk. After several visits, I started to notice the print in the house. On the kitchen table was a holder full of personal letters and bills that needed to be paid. The refrigerator was covered with magnets that were pictures or quotes, and these magnets displayed work done by the grandkids and great grandkids. The women passed different catalogs around the table as they chatted. Newspapers and magazines were in the living room. Always present in the home was oral dialogue.

Kristina and Felipé's home was no different when it came to literacy. The refrigerator magnets held pictures, notes, and bills. On one occasion when the grandkids were there, Kristina opened a cabinet to a shelf full of children books. She explained that these books were Lil Boy Blue's, Smurf's, and Sylvia's when they were little, and now they were for the grandkids. There were greeting cards located on the counter, and full bookshelves. There were newspapers, magazines, and catalogues in the living room. One time, Felipé brought in his briefcase; it contained all the important papers for the family, such as W-2 forms, tax documents, and important school papers.

Kristina said her sons each had their own library card; she helped them select their own books about once a month. Smurf's favorite book was *Curious George* (Rey, 1941). During the month the books were checked out,

Kristina and the children had conversations about what they read. When they got older and in school, she felt the school library would be there for the kids to check out books.

Lil Boy Blue and Smurf were raised in a home that valued literacy. Books were a part of their lives as children. Important documents were saved. Messages were used to remember important dates and to communicate with members of the family. Literacy was a regular feature of daily family life.

JUICE AND LIL GARFIELD'S MOM AND GRANDPARENTS

Juice and Lil Garfield come from a single-parent family that struggles every day to maintain the family structure. Gaining access so that I could understand their story was not easy. Juice and Lil Garfield seldom talked about their past. Several times I asked Diane, Juice and Lil Garfield's mother, what the boys were like when they were little. She reminded me that she was high most of the time Juice and Lil Garfield were young kids. However, by asking questions at the right moments, I put together a small part of this family's story.

Juice and Lil Garfield never talked about their fathers, and as far as I could tell their fathers were not part of their lives. Juice had one memory associated with his father, when his father's mother gave him some jewelry. Lil Garfield never spoke about his father. The only family Juice and Lil Garfield knew was their mother and her side of the family.

Grandparents are central in the lives of many children of single parents. Juice and Lil Garfield's grandparents played such a major role in their lives that their childhood was divided between living with their mother and living with their grandparents. Juice once told me that when his mom felt like being a mother they would live with her.

Their grandmother, who the boys called Nana, was from Kansas and their grandfather, who the boys called Tata, was from Tucson, Arizona. Often I waited in the living room in Tata's house for the boys to get dressed for school. As I waited I admired a picture of a young soldier and his many military awards that hung on the wall. After gaining some courage, one day I asked Tata about the picture, and he said that it was him.

I asked, "What war did you serve in?"

"World War II."

Tata joined the army at the age of 16, serving in the Rangers. I became excited to hear stories about the "war to end all wars"; however, to my disappointment he didn't like to talk about the war. I could only imagine the sadness and hurt he must have felt. I discovered that he had earned a purple heart and was wounded several times. He received veteran's disability. The boys never heard him talk about the war.

After World War II, Tata went to a plumbing school in Kansas on the GI bill, and there he met his wife. The home he lives in today was the house he and his new bride turned into a home. Before Nana passed away, I had several opportunities to visit with her. The first time was at a car wash the kids had organized for Plucy, a homie killed in a drive-by shooting. She came to get her car washed and to check on her grandkids. Juice introduced me. She talked about her daughter, who was a teacher, and how much she worried about her grandkids and the other boys in the gang. Nana also made sure to remind me that all the boys were good kids.

The next time I met Nana she was very sick. I learned from the boys that she had cancer and was dying. She passed away in December, 1996. Her death was a hard time for both Juice and Lil Garfield. After the funeral, Lil Garfield wrote in his personal journal about his grandmother and grandfather: "Today my Tata for the first time I ever heard him speak out of his heart and not the cold man society made him." Diane shared with me that Lil Garfield and Tata had a special relationship. He was Tata's favorite, and I believe Tata was Lil Garfield's favorite.

During early August, 1997, the courts were deciding if a live-in treatment center for alcohol and drug abuse would be best for Lil Garfield. He kept telling his probation officer, "I can't leave Tata." Lil Garfield feared that while he was gone his Tata would die. He wrote about his grandparents and how they had given him everything—"love, a house, food ... and so much more. And also the tools that I need to live and to be the successful person I want to be." On the following page in his journal was a picture of his Nana with the words "I miss you." On the top of the page in big print were the words "I HOPE U CAN HEAR ME."

Juice also wrote about his grandmother in his journal. Juice told how important Nana was to him in the first sentence (see Fig. 2.3). "My Nana was like a mother to me." Diane shared, "Juice was Nana's favorite." Juice's journal entry reveals just how much Nana meant to Juice: "When I was small before I went to bed we would pray the Our Father together. But now that she's dead I feel lost I can't talk to nobody because I have no trust so I write in my journals to myself about how I feel inside." Both Lil Garfield and Juice wrote to understand their feelings during the death of their Nana. Juice and Lil Garfield's deep love for their grandparents was obvious.

12/30/96   about my nana

my nana was like a mother to
me. when I was sick to the
time to when I was not. Ill
allways Remember when she
used Ask me when I was laying
down on the sofa do want a
pillow mijo I Would say no
nana its all Right But hear she
comes with a pillow or when
I was small Before I went to
Bed we would pray the our
father to gether. But now
that she's dead I feal lost
I cant talk to noBody Because
I have no trust so I write
in my journale to myself aBout
how I feal inside and mayBe
write aBout the dark parts
of myself inthis Book But for now
I Just write. this.

FIG. 2.3. Juice's journal entry about his grandma.

Diane was very much aware that she wasn't a real mother to her boys. She knew that her mother was more of a mother to her children then she was. Diane said, "I walked into being a mother at their teenage years, which is extremely hard. I wasn't the mother from the beginning, my mother was the mother."

When the boys were young, Diane decided to work toward a GED. I asked about the classes and the test. With a smile she said, "Oh yeah, I went back and this is how [the school teachers] led me to believe I was stupid that I couldn't, but when I went back I didn't even try the test I just went in and boom—boom I took the test. [The GED class] was all welfare mothers. I lived two blocks from there. All we ever done was go to the house to get high. I never study or nothing, but [school teachers] had me believe and I had such fear cause I was stupid, but I passed them. I can comprehend better. When I went back the lady told me the key is read, read, read books. Anything you can get and as long as you can comprehend you can pass. That's what I done. I read everything I could read, mostly junk: *Inquiry* and true romances, dirty books. I went in there and I passed. The whole time thinking I was going to flunk, 'cause I was so stupid. I had the attitude 'I'm still going to flunk anyway.'"

As she shared her story, I could tell she was happy and had pride in her accomplishments. She informed me that, "I want to go back to school one day when my Lil Garfield is 18. Right now, my thing is more trying to get him ready for society."

While getting ready for the GED, Diane discovered the joy of reading. I asked her if the boys had books and if she read to them when they were young. She replied, "They didn't do a lot of reading. They had books. They wanted me to read, but I was in my own thing. I never did those things."

When Juice was in seventh grade and Lil Garfield was in fifth grade, Diane went to jail for possession of marijuana. The time in jail was hard for Diane and the boys. As Diane shared this part of her story, I could tell she was having a hard time. I informed her she didn't have to tell me the story if remembering hurt too much. She continued, "They started out living with my sister and Lil Garfield lived with my brother. Then my brother kicked Lil Garfield out and Lil Garfield came by [the house] riding the bike twelve midnight over here. He was little. He was just going on twelve late at night on the bike."

"What was your brother's reason for doing that?"

Diane took a deep breath. "He wouldn't do what [the uncle] said. Juice went to live with my sister, and they weren't very fair to them. They made them clean the yard, this and that. They would be punished and yet her kids wouldn't have to do the work, and my kids have to do the work. I think that's why my kids have a real problem with that sister. They love my other sister but this sister they can take her or leave her. They can't stand her kids."

Diane went to prison for 2 years, and according to her "those two years, it seemed like 50 years." She served her time in a prison located about 4 hours from the boys. The family had to rent a van to go visit her, which was an all-day trip. Diane said the hardest time was when the family would leave and she was left alone.

Both Juice and Lil Garfield have stated that when their mom went to prison, their lives changed. They started to have problems and get into trouble. Juice felt like he had no one to talk to and no one he could trust. When Juice was in ninth grade and Lil Garfield was in eighth grade, Diane was released from prison and placed on probation for 5 years. Her probation officer could come into the home at any time.

Because I wanted a better understanding of Diane's world and her boys' early life, I asked her to share a little of her background. She grew up on the south side of Tucson and attended Brighton High School, the same school her kids attended. This meant that when Diane tried to help her boys at Brighton High School, she had to deal with people who had been her teachers. On several occasions as we sat at the school and waited for an appointment with a school official, she reminisced about when she was a student.

High school was not friendly to Diane. With disappointment and sadness she stated, "It wasn't good. I didn't comprehend a lot, and I came from a time when they would throw erasers at you. You know, it was legal. It wasn't like now, they can't touch you. It was like you get in trouble, you got paddled or you got an eraser thrown at you. I couldn't comprehend as far as junior high. I didn't really like school. I think it was because the teacher would have favorites, and they would help their favorites and the rest, oh well. I couldn't really comprehend a lot. I really couldn't read. I wasn't happy in school. I was overweight. I seen a lot of people you know doing what you do in high school. I wasn't included in that, so I was like a sore thumb I guess, and umm the teachers never made it easier. I was in trouble all the time, because I wasn't happy at school, you know, I couldn't learn. Teachers didn't really, didn't help you, and so I just started ditching." Diane was unhappy in high school. She felt she didn't belong and teachers didn't care.

Diane's biggest regret was not being a mother to her kids. However, today she is doing everything in her power to be their mom and to be there for them. As Diane and I talked about her kids and their future, she cried several times. She didn't know how to help Juice and Lil Garfield. For Diane, everyday life was hard. She worked 40 to 50 hours a week to support her family. She had to deal with government bureaucracy as she tried to maintain her family. She asked me to write letters to the welfare agency verifying that she lived alone with her sons. The first time she asked, she concluded the conversation with, "I didn't have anyone else to ask."

In late December, 1997, I had the opportunity to help Diane move into her father's home. She made this move so her son, Juice, could have her little house for his new family. As I helped her move all her possessions into a back bedroom, I became more aware of Diane's simple life and the fears and struggles she faced each day to make her world work. Through understanding the struggles of this family I found a mother who cared.

This was evident when the courts ordered Lil Garfield to attend a live-in treatment center for teenagers with drinking and drug problems. Diane asked me to take him to the center, because she had to go to work. If Diane missed work, she wouldn't get paid which would result in not being able to pay the bills. After dropping Lil Garfield off at the home and checking to make sure everything was right, I drove home to report back to Diane. On the phone I described the home and explained the program. She said, crying, "I felt like I couldn't take him. I wasn't sure I would be able to leave him." Lil Garfield had never been away from the family. Diane did in fact have to work, but the real problem was that she couldn't bear to leave her son at the center in the hands of strangers. While in the treatment center, Lil Garfield wrote about how his mom sacrificed, stating, (see Fig. 2.4) she "makes sure me and my brother don't go without …."

Keeping Diane's own life going was hard and discouraging. Diane confessed, "I've done my booze, I've done my drugs, and I've done my men." When Juice and Lil Garfield were young and lived with their mom, this lifestyle was their world. Later, even though Diane's life was different it still was a struggle. Several times when I visited Juice and Lil Garfield, I arrived during a huge, loud argument with both mother and son yelling at each other.

Lil Garfield wrote in his journal about one incident when he got into a fight with his cousins and then the family. Lil Garfield wrote that when he got home he and his cousin started *trippen* (fighting). This soon included the aunt, mom, and everybody. He continued, "I felt real bad, sad, confused, betrayed, bewildered, nervous, and scared. At the same time I wanted to fight somebody but I didn't. I went outside and prayed. But I still didn't feel right so I got my clothes ready and went to Sunday mass." After mass Lil

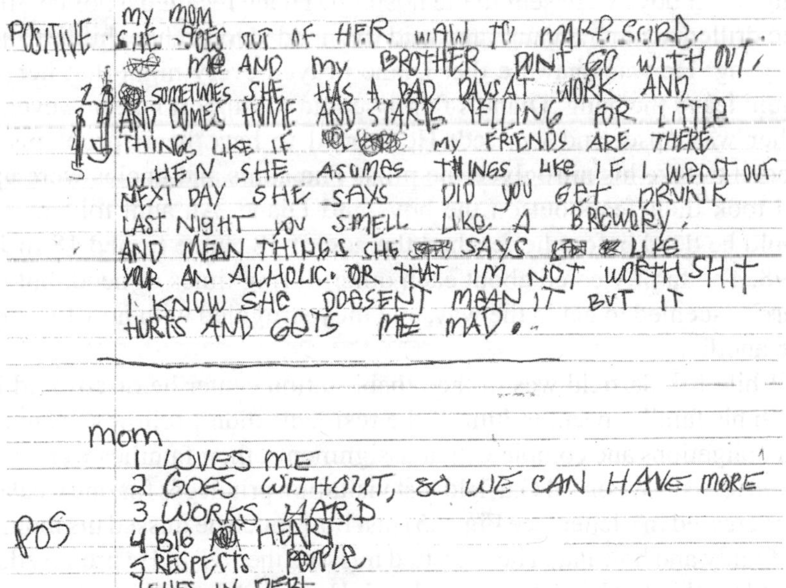
my mom
POSITIVE SHE GOES OUT OF HER WAY TO MAKE SURE
me AND my BROTHER DONT GO WITHOUT,
2 SOMETIMES SHE HAS A BAD DAYS AT WORK AND
3 AND COMES HOME AND STARTS YELLING FOR LITTLE
4 THINGS LIKE IF my FRIENDS ARE THERE
WHEN SHE ASUMES THINGS LIKE IF I WENT OUT
NEXT DAY SHE SAYS DID YOU GET DRUNK
LAST NIGHT YOU SMELL LIKE A BREWERY.
AND MEAN THINGS SHE SAYS LIKE
YOUR AN ALCHOLIC OR THAT IM NOT WORTH SHIT
I KNOW SHE DOESENT MEAN IT BUT IT
HURTS AND GETS ME MAD.

mom
1 LOVES ME
2 GOES WITHOUT, SO WE CAN HAVE MORE
POS 3 WORKS HARD
4 BIG HEART
5 RESPECTS PEOPLE
1 SHES IN DEBT
2 SHE JUMPS TO CONCLUSIONS
NEG. 3 SHE DOESENT LIKE TO GO PLACES TO HAVE FUN
4 DEPREST
5 ALWAYS STRESSES

FIG. 2.4. Lil Garfield's writing about his mom.

Garfield claimed he "felt good" and even though he was angry and mad, he wanted to apologize to his aunt. At the end of the journal entry, Lil Garfield wrote, "Maybe U don't understand or maybe shocked that I have feelings but whoever reads this I want them to know I love my family no matter what." Even amidst the fighting, a caring family did exist.

I observed a mother and son's love during a teacher-parent conference meeting at Brighton High School with Diane and Juice. Juice held his mother's hand and laid his head on her shoulder. He seemed to feel safe in this room with his mother.

Diane stood with Juice and Lil Garfield in court, and she picked them up from the juvenile detention center. When they were in trouble, they knew that all they had to do was call their mom and she would be there to fight for them. When the school was willing to "throw them aside," Diane came to their side.

On several occasions I observed the Alvarez family struggle to maintain the integrity of the family. One such incident was when Juice and Lil Garfield were beaten so badly they ended up in the hospital. The boys had gone to a party and were *jumped* (beaten up) by 15 other boys from a rival gang. Both boys were sent to the hospital. Diane recalled a police officer who drilled her about gangs and said she needed to get her children out of the gang. He was unaware that Diane prayed every night that her sons would leave the gang. Diane's family came to support her; however, her father was upset and worried. He started to have heart problems and needed to take his nitroglycerine pills. The aunts and uncles were upset and took their fears out on the boys and Diane. An aunt told Juice he would be dead before he reached the age of 18. Juice turned 18 in July, 1998. The family cared about each other during times of need, but their worries seemed to get in the way, and they struggled with how to support one another.

While Lil Garfield was in the rehabilitation center he discovered how much his family meant to him. If the residents didn't follow certain rules and obligations and complete their assignments, their families were not allowed to visit. When Lil Garfield lost visitation privileges for one weekend, he expressed in a letter (see Fig. 2.5) just how much he missed his mom and the family and how much he regretted missing their visit. He promised they would be able to visit the next weekend. He ended the letter with, "I'm doing real good except the fact I haven't seen the family, so that sucks. I really miss everybody and Tata most importantly." He even reminded them to bring the baby. Diane, Juice, and Lil Garfield were a fragile family, a family that struggled to survive each day.

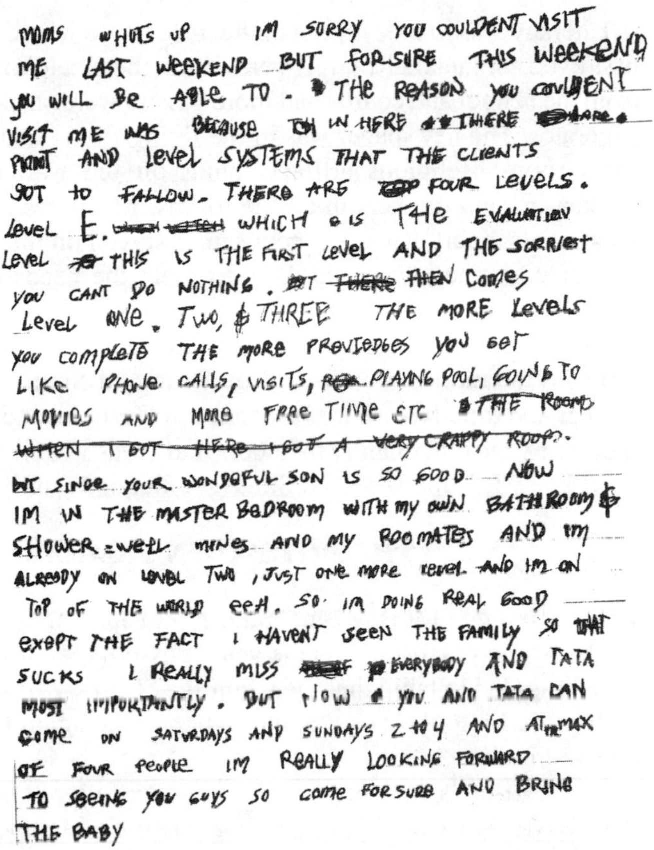

MOMS WHATS UP IM SORRY YOU COULDENT VISIT
ME LAST WEEKEND BUT FOR SURE THIS WEEKEND
YOU WILL BE ABLE TO. THE REASON YOU COULDENT
VISIT ME WAS BECAUSE IM IN HERE THERE ARE
POINT AND LEVEL SYSTEMS THAT THE CLIENTS
GOT TO FALLOW. THERE ARE FOUR LEVELS.
LEVEL E. WHICH IS THE EVALUATION
LEVEL THIS IS THE FIRST LEVEL AND THE SORRIEST
YOU CANT DO NOTHING. THEN COMES
LEVEL ONE, TWO, & THREE THE MORE LEVELS
YOU COMPLETE THE MORE PREVIEDGES YOU GET
LIKE PHONE CALLS, VISITS, PLAYING POOL, GOING TO
MOVIES AND MORE FREE TIME ETC ~~THE ROOM~~
~~WHEN I GOT HERE I GOT A VERY CRAPPY ROOM.~~
BUT SINCE YOUR WONDERFUL SON IS SO GOOD NOW
IM IN THE MASTER BEDROOM WITH MY OWN BATHROOM &
SHOWER = WELL MINES AND MY ROOMATES AND IM
ALREADY ON LEVEL TWO, JUST ONE MORE LEVEL AND IM ON
TOP OF THE WORLD EEH. SO IM DOING REAL GOOD
EXEPT THE FACT I HAVENT SEEN THE FAMILY SO THAT
SUCKS I REALLY MISS EVERYBODY AND TATA
MOST IMPORTANTLY. BUT NOW YOU AND TATA CAN
COME ON SATURDAYS AND SUNDAYS 2 TO 4 AND AT THE MAX
OF FOUR PEOPLE IM REALLY LOOKING FORWARD
TO SEEING YOU GUYS SO COME FOR SURE AND BRING
THE BABY

FIG. 2.5. Lil Garfield's letter to his mom while in rehabilitation.

Literacy in the Home

After several visits, I attended more carefully to the print in this family's homes. The newspaper and the TV guide were always on the grandfather's table or couch. There were bills and notes stuck to the refrigerator door in the kitchen. On the door frame between the kitchen and living room was a container for paper and pencils used to take phone messages or to leave messages to each other. The boys claimed, "[Mom and Tata] read the newspaper all the time." Lil Garfield said, "My Tata is always reading books such as western books before he goes to bed. My mom used to read a lot." Their Nana had loved to write letters to her brothers who lived out of state. In Lil Garfield's room, there were Play Station magazines, CD inserts, and religious artifacts on the walls. On the walls, Lil Garfield's tags signified who he was and *represented* (built respect and a reputation for the gang) to all who entered his room.

Literacy was in every room in the little home where Diane and the boys first lived. In the kitchen, refrigerator magnets held important documents from the school and courts, and more papers were stacked on top of the refrigerator. The newspaper was in the living room, and books were in Diane's room. Religious artifacts hung on the wall and sat on tables, bookcases, and dressers in all the rooms. Messages about important appointments, court dates, and counseling stayed on the kitchen table as reminders. Literacy was used daily to meet the needs of the family, both formally and informally.

My relationship with Juice and Lil Garfield's family was quite different from my relationship with Lil Boy Blue and Smurf's family. I was the teacher and the advocate for Juice and Lil Garfield, and as a result I was respected by the other family members, but I wasn't able to get to know them like I knew Lil Boy Blue and Smurf's extended family.

THE BOYS' OWN FAMILIES

When I first met Lil Boy Blue, Smurf, and Juice they were sons, cousins, brothers, and grandsons. As the years passed, they became young fathers who struggled to build their new families. Lil Boy Blue, Smurf, and Juice each moved into their own homes where once again I found caring, supportive families.

Lil Boy Blue's daughter was born 2 weeks after I started teaching at the alternative high school program. In a writing assignment, I asked my students to describe a person who had changed their life. Lil Boy Blue wrote about his daughter (see Fig. 2.6). He stated, "… my daughter because she's so special to me. She changed my life in a lot of ways." He continued, "And remember no one said it was easy, but it's the greatest thing that will happen to you."

When Lil Boy Blue's daughter was born, he lived at home and spent the evenings and night with his daughter and girlfriend at his girlfriend's home. When the girlfriend's father moved out of his trailer, Lil Boy Blue had a place he could afford and the family moved in.

Lil Boy Blue and his girlfriend, Teresa, met in middle school. According to Teresa, she was the one that arranged to meet him. They were each other's first and only girlfriend and boyfriend. As they shared their story, I could tell they still cared very much for each other.

Lil Boy Blue worked an evening shift in a bottling company which allowed him the opportunity to care for his daughter during the day, and his girlfriend (soon to be wife) worked in the daytime as a medical receptionist.

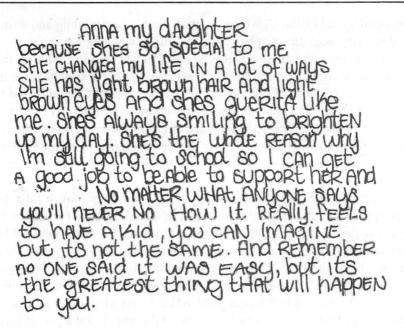

Anna my daughter because shes so special to me. She changed my life in a lot of ways. She has light brown hair and light brown eyes and shes querita like me. Shes always smiling to brighten up my day. Shes the whole reason why I'm still going to school so I can get a good job to be able to support her and

No matter what anyone says you'll never no how it really feels to have a kid, you can imagine but its not the same. And remember no one said it was easy, but its the greatest thing that will happen to you.

FIG. 2.6.   Lil Boy Blue's writing about his daughter.

When I watched him with his daughter, I could tell she was the "greatest thing" to him. He was a proud father.

On my first visit to Lil Boy Blue's home, I observed Anna, Lil Boy Blue's 3-year-old daughter, bring books for her daddy to read. She climbed up next to him and turned the pages, telling him the story. Anna held the book correctly and turned the pages left to right. She was aware of the social structure around reading books. Lil Boy Blue said, "She knows the stories so well that when I try to skip parts of the story or change the story in some way, she corrects me." Within Anna's collection of books were copies I gave her that were signed by authors and illustrators. Every time I gave her a book, she immediately sat down and read or found her mother to read to her. Lil Boy Blue and Teresa read to Anna every night.

After one reading, Anna wanted some cereal. Lil Boy Blue told her to get her favorite cereal. I asked Anna to bring the box of cereal over to me. "Where does it say Frosted Flakes?" She pointed to the big print on the front of the box. Anna understood that print has meaning. She developed this awareness as part of a family that values literacy.

In Lil Boy Blue's home, I noticed the newspaper and magazines on the coffee table. Lil Boy Blue read the *Dallas Cowboys Weekly*, a newspaper published by the Dallas Cowboys football team. I saw reading and writing used in many activities that helped build this new young family.

Smurf sounded a little shocked as he discussed his family: "I have a family, now everything changes. I never knew I was going to change. I mean it has completely changed my whole life. I never thought I could have fun with my own family, and everything you know like Mom and everybody else. I never thought I could have fun, but I only thought I could have fun with my *locs* [homies] and shit, and now I have a family and Dea [Smurf's girlfriend and the mother of his daughter], and the baby, they bring me closer to my family you know …."

Smurf was 17 years old and Dea was 16 when they moved into their own apartment. Smurf's mom had to sign all documents for Smurf and Dea to acquire a lease and have the utilities turned on. As Smurf and Dea learned to be a family, their arguments often ended with one of them leaving, but the desire to be a family brought them back together. They were both proud of their daughter and wanted the best for her. Smurf's young daughter, Sabrina, was 8 months old when I first visited his new apartment. I watched Smurf interact with his daughter. I saw a proud father who wanted everyone else to know that his daughter was wonderful. While I was there Smurf paid bills for the first time. He said with excitement and wonderment, "Did you know they give you envelopes [return envelopes for the payment of bills]?" He carefully read the statement then filled out the check. As he sealed the envelope, a proud look came over Smurf's face. He was taking care of his family.

When I visited Smurf, I noticed CDS, the *Source*, a hip hop magazine that was delivered to the house, an article on the Internet, and the newspaper. Smurf spent hours on my computer searching for information about his favorite football team, the Dallas Cowboys, and for sites that were about Crips, his gang. He spent time in a chat room dialoguing with several other young men. Smurf celebrated his ability to take care of his family, and he used literacy as a tool to meet their needs.

When Diane moved out of her little house so that Juice and his new family could move in and become more of a family, they struggled. In his journal (Fig. 2.3) he wrote, "I just don't feel the same for [Melinda, his girlfriend]." Yet he also wrote, "But I love her with all my heart and our baby." He struggled with all the pain inside. He felt "stopped up by the pain," and. was tired of it. He wrote, "I feel like crying."

I was invited to Juice's little daughter, Julia's, first birthday party. I watched Juice play with her and unwrap the gifts. Even though they were struggling trying to make a family, Juice and Melinda were devoted to their little girl. I saw him feed her and dress her, read to her, and lie beside her, comforting her. He loved his little girl and wanted to be a good father.

In Juice's little home, children's books lay on the bed, and Juice said he read to his daughter all the time. On one visit he cuddled on the couch with his daughter, each with a book on their lap. She looked at the pictures as he read the story. This was a group of three young people who struggled to become a family. The love they had for their daughter helped Juice and Melinda take the steps needed to be a family. Literacy was evident in their home as it was in every other household in the study.

THE FAMILY COMMUNITY

Lil Boy Blue, Smurf, Juice, and Lil Garfield loved and cared for their families, and their families loved and cared for them. The families struggled to provide the best they knew how for their children and each other. They celebrated successes like weddings, birthdays, and the births of new members in the Family Community. They gathered in times of need. When Smurf was in the Juvenile Detention Center, the extended family comforted and supported Felipé and Kristina. Kristina once said, "My mom feels like when there is a tragedy in the family that is when the family should be the closest. Nothing is going to break that or take that. My family is really close." This quote describes the Espinoza family. In the years Debbie worked with them, nothing seemed to be able to break their strength. Similarly, although the Alvarez family was challenged to be strong, they supported each other. It was his family Lil Garfield wanted to see while in rehabilitation.

The boys were full members in the Family Community with all its rights and privileges. They chose to participate or not, they had access to the resources and information they needed to participate, and they had equal, reciprocal relationships with other members. They belonged (Wenger, 1998). These are elements of a community of practice *(Lave & Wenger, 1991).*

In the Family Community, Lil Boy Blue, Smurf, Juice, and Lil Garfield initiated and participated in numerous literacy events. As young children, they observed and interacted with their parents and grandparents while they read and wrote numerous texts. As adults, they used literacy to structure and make sense of their world and to maintain family and social relations. Even when they lacked experience or specific knowledge they weren't kept from accessing information. Smurf was not chastised or judged when he wasn't aware that many companies provide the envelopes needed to pay bills. The boys weren't "taught" in a formal way; they were "helped." They were accepted for who they are and as a result gained confidence and secu-

rity. These are elements of membership in a literacy club *(F. Smith, 1998). The concepts of community of practice and the literacy club offer theoretical frames for the descriptions of each of the boys' communities in the next chapters and are discussed at greater length in chapter 9.*

Although the Family Community was the first community in which Lil Boy Blue, Smurf, Juice, and Lil Garfield found membership, it is one of many overlapping communities they were part of as they grew up. The community the boys joined as young teenagers was the Gang Community, where they experienced the tension that is part of gang membership. It was a place to belong and to stay loyal to the friends of their childhoods, but it was also the community that resulted in the loss of those childhood friends.

Gang Community: "West Up Cuzz"

There are no easy explanations for why an adolescent chooses to join the Gang Community, but it is clear that if adolescents didn't receive something from membership, they wouldn't join. It is hard for outsiders to imagine what gang life is like. In this chapter, Debbie provides a glimpse into what Lil Boy Blue, Smurf, Juice, and Lil Garfield's lives were like as gangbangers (gang members). We also describe the literacy found in this community, including tagging, oral language, rap, and other forms of representing that the boys engaged in regularly and that facilitated their membership in the community.

A GLIMPSE INTO THE GANG COMMUNITY

The co-ed softball team the boys and I played on was celebrating the end of the season at a pizza joint. After munching one last slice of pepperoni pizza, I announced it was time for me to leave. I said my good-byes and slowly walked out to the parking lot. Lil Boy Blue, Smurf, and the rest of the boys were already outside and challenging another group of boys. Both groups were name calling and flashing their gang colors to disrespect the other gang. I stood listening, hoping my presence would discourage them from fighting. I remember thinking, "Felipé, hurry up and get out here." I was scared! I wasn't sure what I would do if the two groups decided to fight. Finally, Felipé came out and ushered the boys to the cars. I was relieved.

As I reached my car, I decided to take one more look at the other group of boys. I'm not sure what happened, but the boys were fighting. I stood in a daze. I started to run after my boys. I just wanted the fight to stop. The manager of the pizza parlor came out and hollered, "The police are on their way."

Because no one wanted to get arrested, Lil Boy Blue, Smurf, and the rest of the boys ran to the cars and drove off as the police arrived. I followed Felipé. From the back of Felipé's truck, the boys mouthed the message that one boy was stabbed, but nothing serious. I went on my way and Felipé took the boys to their individual homes.

Back at my apartment, the reality of what happened hit me. Two gangs were fighting—a gun could have been pulled. Someone could have been badly hurt. The next day, the boys came into class bragging. I couldn't be silent any longer. I looked at them and asked, "How could you? There were young kids there. Your own daughters."

No one wanted to hear that. I informed the kids I wasn't judging them and I tried not to. I needed to understand. They talked about respect and not letting the other gang disrespect them. No matter what I said they kept telling me, "We couldn't let them disrespect us." The fight was all about pride and honor.

For Lil Boy Blue, Smurf, Juice, and Lil Garfield the gang was about staying together as friends. I asked Lil Boy Blue to define gangs. His response was simple, "A group of kids that grew up together."

A little discouraged by his short answer, I commented, "You know that most people in the community think that gangs are really bad."

"Yeah, but everybody grew up with a gang, think about it. They grew up in the neighborhood. They have friends. They grew up close. I guess nowadays it turns more … to more of a rival of neighborhoods."

Lil Boy Blue believed everyone who grew up in a neighborhood full of friends grew up in a gang. A gang is a group of friends. His group of friends all lived on the westside and at first represented "the westside." Later they adopted the name of their neighborhood, Manzanita, as their gang name.

Smurf's concept of the gang was similar to Lil Boy Blue's. Joining the gang for Little Boy Blue and Smurf was no different than being part of the neighborhood friends who played t-ball and became skaters together. Smurf insisted, "To me it's something like, I grew up in my neighborhood all my life since I was a little baby. You know, I did everything in my neighborhood. I grew up around everybody in my neighborhood from elementary and everything. Just growing up, and it happened to be that my neighborhood was a Crip neighborhood. So you know I seen everybody around me, Crips. So you know I learned that was my neighborhood thing. So I mean just like … it was like everybody was skaters, into skateboarding, so we were skateboarding. It wasn't really about being a follower. It was about, it was like a crew. Like you know, it was like just … like the thing we should do then. Everybody got into baseball and everybody was into sports and then, boom, everybody got into gangs, and gangs became a big part of our lives. I mean it was like a family to me. I mean I didn't really know anything else. I was young when I got into it. I had a lot of fun with my home boys. I had a lot of love for them." In a research paper for his English class during the 1996 school year, Juice wrote that the MLMC gang originated in 1985 by a Hawaiian boy known as Kilo G:

> [H]e was talking to a vato who decided to start up a gang called Manzanita Lynch Mob Crip. Manzanita came from the name of the neighborhood, Manzanita Terrace. This gang became popular in the hood with the other teens. The teens in the hood were looking for something to do so as a friendship, they all joined the gang. There were at least 350 heads but now there's only about 30, due to death, and family problems and getting into trouble homies stopped banging. In those days, everybody was just going everywhere yelling Westside Lynch Mob, cruising the avenue starting fights and shooting—trying to let everybody know that we were coming up. It was all good for a while.

As friends, they joined the gang which provided the opportunity to stay together and gave them something to do. Smurf said, "Because of my environment ... I mean that's what you do. If I didn't, what else did I have if I was to stop? I could've said, yeah, I am not in a gang. What was I gonna do? I couldn't get no job at this time ... I'm not going to school full time, you know, what was I going to do? You know what I'm saying? What was I gonna do? I'd still want to party and drink beer. I still would've been ... I'd been with the same people. I'd ran into the same people, the same shit would've happened. I'd go ... there's nothing I could've done."

Lil Garfield, one of the youngest members of the gang when I first met him, claimed, "I've been gang banging since I was ten." I asked Lil Garfield how the gang got started.

"A bunch of *fools* (people in general) that's got each other's back," stated Lil Garfield.

"How did you get involved with the gang?"

"I started *claiming* (participating in gang activities), started kicking back with the *peewees* (young members of the gang), started being down for Manzanita. Started hanging around with everybody."

Hanging around with friends is something we all have experienced. According to Smurf, Juice, and Lil Garfield there was nothing else available. City recreational sports for adolescents were reaching the level of competition found on high school teams. They were too young to get jobs. For Lil Boy Blue, Smurf, Juice, and Lil Garfield joining a gang—being with their friends—was as natural as joining little league, or meeting at each other's homes to break dance.

Some of the concepts affiliated with the gang, such as representing and fighting for one's turf, were part of Smurf's early elementary experiences. In a class writing assignment (see Fig. 3.1), he shared his memories of elementary school. He wrote, "Elementary was all about what class you were in." He was in fifth grade, so "that's what I was claiming." The concept of *representing*, or as Smurf writes, "puttin in work" was developed in elementary school on the playground. Often the "representing" was done through sports as classes competed against one another to see who was the best.

In the gang, to *represent* involved participation in any activity that built the reputation of the gang, such as gang fights, *tagging* (graffiti), and drive-bys. For Lil Boy Blue, Smurf, Juice, and Garfield, being part of the gang and taking on the characteristics associated with a gang was part of growing up.

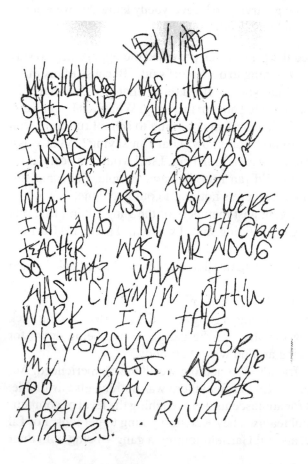

FIG. 3.1.   Smurf's memories of elementary school.

Yet as I listened to the boys, I kept hearing about the hurt associated with the gang community. They often said, "It was good for a while." Sometimes their voices changed and hinted at a second set of emotions and reality. The heartaches that came as a result of being a gangbanger were not part of the natural, almost light-hearted picture of the gang that the preceding descriptions paint.

HEARTACHES

When Lil Boy Blue thought about the homies he had lost he said, "We were young. We didn't know what we were getting into. How much trouble, you know what I mean, you don't realize how much danger." The "trouble" and "danger" that Lil Boy Blue referred to were such things as getting kicked out of school, being arrested with a gun, being shot at, and fighting for the respect of the hood. The greatest heartache came at the deaths of friends to drive-by shootings, gang fights, and other means.

During the 4 years of the study, many of the boys' homies died from various causes. Oso was the first, killed in a drive-by in October 1994. Not quite a year later, in October 1995, Plucy was also killed in a drive-by. In August 1997, Murder died. The police reported Murder's death as a suicide. In the same year, about a month later, Guero was killed in a car accident.

Stories of Oso filled the room when I first started teaching in the alternative program. Lil Boy Blue and Oso grew up together and were more like brothers than friends. Lil Boy Blue said Oso's death "was real hard. Everyone went crazy. He was the first homie to die. Ever since that time it was never the same. That's when it started happening. Not to be fun, you know what I mean? Before we never realized that this gang [meant] killing. We were just out having a lot of fun. After Oso got killed, you know, we realized that it's not really worth it. You know, he could still be alive." I noticed that Smurf sat quietly and never took part in storytelling when the students told stories about Oso. In fact, he often became upset and defensive.

I tried to reconstruct the story of Oso's death. I realized that Smurf was 14 and Lil Boy Blue was 17 at the time. Reconstructing the incident involved the memories of two boys who were still mourning and struggling to make sense of the death of a friend.

Lil Boy Blue, Smurf, Oso, and two other homies were in the car driving around a barrio on the westside of town. A car full of boys who claimed to be Bloods drove up. I'm not sure how the trouble got started, but Lil Boy Blue felt they were literally caught in the middle of the barrio homies and the Bloods. Guns were aimed and fired. Oso was shot between the eyes. The boys drove to the nearest hospital where Oso was pronounced dead. The police came to the hospital and arrested Lil Boy Blue, Smurf, and the other homies in the car.

During the time Lil Boy Blue and Smurf were being detained at the police station, Kristina and Felipé had no idea where their sons were. Lil Boy Blue and Smurf were in the habit of letting their parents know where they were at all times. Kristina and Felipé were scared and worried. After about 24 hours, the police finally called and informed Kristina and Felipé that their sons were at the police station and they needed to come and get them. Kristina and Felipé arrived at the police station believing they would be taking their sons home. Lil Boy Blue was allowed to go home, but not Smurf. He was locked up in juvenile hall and charged for Oso's death. Kristina and Felipé were not allowed to see their son or talk to him until Tuesday, the official visiting day.

On the first anniversary of Oso's death, I heard Smurf talk about Oso for the first time at school. I mean really talk. His whole face was racked with emotions. But he talked! It had been a year since the shooting and Smurf was still hurting and struggling to make sense of Oso's death. I wondered what kind of support Smurf had as he grieved and how I could help him.

Oso's death prompted many changes. The gang members were no longer innocent. More homies died, and hurt seemed to run rampant. Smurf struggled to make sense of their loss by saying, "They died for the hood." Dying for the hood meant the homie died for a reason; it gave meaning to the loss of friends that had no meaning.

Juice's writing told the same story: "The gang was for good times. Homies started getting locked up or moving out of [town] with their families due to gang violence uprising in the city. Some got jumped out because things got too crazy for them." Plucy was Juice's closest homie. Things changed for him the night his friend died.

Late one night, Juice and Plucy were driving home. Another car pulled up beside them and *flashed signs* (showed gang hand signals) representing who they were. The boys in both cars disrespected each other and tried to gain respect. At one time Plucy leaned out of the car and said, "I will die for my hood." The driver in the other car pulled a gun and shot. Plucy fell on to Juice's lap, bleeding to death. Juice didn't know what to do. He pulled the car into a store parking lot and the police and an ambulance were called. As Juice and I talked, Juice still struggled as he remembered crying until he "could cry no more."

Guero was the last homie to die. Even though his death wasn't gang related, his death had a great influence on the boys. Guero had just graduated from high school and had decided to move away to go to college. All the homies were proud of him. Guero had survived gang life, finished school, and was going to college to become an English teacher. They knew he had to move away to reach his goals. One weekend Guero came home to visit his great grandma. He drove back to college with a friend late at night. They hit a black cow that was on the road and Guero was instantly killed. As my students and I came together to mourn, many of them wondered, "How can I make it if Guero couldn't?"

Thinking about the deaths of his homies, Smurf conveyed his thoughts: " I think of all the deaths, Plucy and Guero's hit everybody the hardest. Before Guero died, Plucy's hit everybody the hardest. I guess Plucy hit everybody the hardest, because he was only 15 years old and … Plucy suffered a lot, you know. What I'm saying is he didn't just die. He suffered about half an hour or 45 minutes … at least a half hour. You know, that's a long time to suffer, you know. Everybody knew that he fought for his life."

Trying to understand what Smurf was saying, I asked, "Why do you think Plucy's death had such an influence on everybody?"

"There was just something about Plucy that just bothered everybody a lot. It was like all this time praying. The thing that bothered me a lot about it … because when he first tried to get in the gang and everything. We tried to get him in, you know. We were the ones that influenced him and everything, you know. I was always trying to bring things up. Then he wanted to get out and everybody started talking shit. You don't want to get out. Why, you want to be a pussy? You know. We were all like that with him, and right when he started to come back in, he got to his crazy style. That's when he was really down and everything, and that's when he died. I guess that's why. Plucy was a peewee, because we kind of feel like it was our fault. Cause, you know, he was trying to go away, and we drove him back to us."

Lil Garfield felt the gang was "not really" worth the heartache. Lil Garfield claimed that the gang hurt him more than helped him. Dead homies, fights between family members, and getting arrested were the things that hurt him.

I asked, "Do you believe the gang has helped you in any way?"

"Can't really say it helped me," stated Lil Garfield, "It's like a false kind of help, loyalties. You say loyalties, yeah, when we're on the street, loyalty but … alright, say that me and Lil Boy Blue did a drive-by. Lil Boy Blue is the only one who gets caught. [The police] say, 'If you snitch on this fool, we'll give you a lesser thing. You got a daughter, you know.' You think he's going to … You think he's going to snitch me out, so he can see his daughter? I think he would. I think anybody would."

Lil Garfield sparked my interest as he talked about loyalty. He insinuated that on the street, members in the gang were loyal to each other but off the street this wasn't always true. He called this a "false loyalty," so I asked him if gang banging was worth losing friends and accepting the false sense of loyalty.

He stated without hesitation, "No, but some people just get caught up so bad they don't know what to do. When you are in the gang and it is in your heart and your brain, you can't stop. Can't stop. Won't stop. *BK* (blood killer) till you crash." He actually started rapping the last part.

I asked, "Is it possible to be Crip in your heart but not openly on the street?"

"Fuck, no."

"Why?"

"Cause I no bitch."

"What's that mean?"

"It means, I ain't fuckin be a hen house banger. Gang bangin is like a job. It's what you … It's what you represent. It's who you … are … What you represent, you and your gang colors. I could wear a hat right now—*LA* (little apple)—everybody would know it stands for little apple."

Part of being in the gang is "putting in work" or representing. This concept was hard for me to understand. I decided to ask what was meant by gang bangin' or puttin' in work. Juice said, "You go and put in work and stuff mob around … raps. It doesn't matter, do anything that you can whatever it takes to bring up your name to bring up your hood."

Lil Garfield replied, "Being active, puttin' in work, puttin' in, kickin' back with your homies drinkin' brew not being afraid to pull the trigger."

Lil Garfield's remark opened a door that I hesitated to go through, but I asked, "Have you used a gun or participated in drive-by?"

I was a little surprised by Lil Garfield's answer. He said, "I don't really like guns. I think people who use guns are bitches … can't use their fist so they use guns. I mean you can go out and shoot anybody, go out and kill anybody, but it takes a real man to lose a fight. It doesn't take a man to pull a trigger."

Lil Garfield's answer left me with more questions. If he saw guns as a weakness, why did he carry a gun? The boys' actions in the gang and what they personally believed were in conflict in their everyday lives. Because I was aware of the tension between their actions and their beliefs, I asked Lil Garfield, "Have you hurt anyone and how did you feel?"

Lil Garfield didn't directly answer the question. He responded, "Proud in a way. I'd feel proud around my homies, but I felt bad that I did it. Kind of lost."

Lil Garfield's sense of belonging to something that was important to him outweighed the pain. Even though Lil Garfield didn't see Lil Boy Blue and Smurf that much, when they got together they could still identify each other. They belonged to something that tied them together.

The need to belong and be together was evident in Lil Garfield's response to my question of why he joined the gang. "I wanted a place to go. I wanted to feel like I was loved maybe and the thugs, the money, saw the bitches. Damn, I get jumped in to Manzanita that stuff would all be mine. I didn't have shit," exclaimed Lil Garfield, "My mom was locked up. She was gettin' kicked out of the family by family members." At a time when everything seemed so mixed up, the gang was a place to hang out, feel love, and have friends. In a 10-year-old's eyes that was more than what he had.

Even with the heartache, the gang seemed to give Lil Garfield something he didn't have at home. Nudging more, I asked, "When you think about some of the things you went through as a kid growing up, do you think the gang was kind of a place to go which made it a little bit easier for you?"

"Yeah, get wasted, get faded."

"Did it help you forget?"

"Yeah, some ways it did."

The death of homies wasn't the only hurt Lil Boy Blue, Smurf, Juice, and Lil Garfield experienced as a result of the gang. In class I heard many stories that involved the police or sheriff harassing the kids. Lil Boy Blue, Smurf, Juice, and Lil Garfield claimed the police or sheriff stopped and searched them when they walked home or to the park. During searches the officers took Lil Boy Blue, Smurf, Juice, and Lil Garfield's belts, shoe strings, shirts, or anything else that represented the gang.

Kristina told me of a specific time when Lil Boy Blue and Smurf were walking home from the park with their homies. The sheriff stopped them all. They were *padded down* (their bodies and pockets checked for anything hidden). Felipé came on to the scene and he introduced himself to the officers as the father of two of the boys. He wasn't allowed to talk to the boys, and the officer wouldn't tell him what was going on. Eventually the boys were allowed to walk home.

The police maintain files on kids they believe are gang members. When a crime is committed the police go to the homes of kids on this list. Kristina told about an incident when the police came to their home. She was in the house and Smurf came in and told her the police wanted to take him downtown. She went outside to discover that there were two police officers in her front yard searching the boys. The police informed her they were going to take Smurf downtown for questioning, but he wasn't going to be arrested.

Kristina told me she was scared because the last time they took Smurf she didn't see him for 4 days. She wasn't going to allow that to happen again. She stood her ground and told the officers she would take Smurf down to the police station. The police said never mind and that they would check with their supervisor. They never returned.

I often wondered why anybody would stay with something that resulted in such hurt. I asked Lil Garfield, "You wanted to represent the gang, yet, you seem like you are not quite sure it's really worth it. Is that true?"

"I'm saying it cost me a lot of pain," insisted Lil Garfield.

"Does the good outweigh the pain, or does the pain out weigh the good?"

"Pain outweighs the good."

"If the pain outweighs the good, why do you stay with it?"

Lil Garfield clarified, "Like I said once, it's in your heart. You can't stop, won't stop. Lil Boy Blue and Smurf got their whole life going on and they're still bangin'. Lil Boy Blue still Crippin' it. Every time I see Lil Boy Blue he's still wearing his blue."

I also asked Lil Boy Blue, "Do the benefits the gang gives you outweigh the hurt?" Without hesitation or a thought he responded, "Not really, all it did was get you in trouble with your friends."

I asked my class what they thought Oso, the first homie killed in drive-by, would say to them. Unanimously, they said, "Get out of the gang." Yet for Lil Boy Blue, Smurf, Juice, and Lil Garfield, getting out of the gang wasn't an option. The boys always said, "Once a Crip always a Crip," or "Crip 4 Life." Even with the heartache and trouble, being a Crip is what they were. I asked Juice if he saw himself as a Crip forever. He responded with no hesitation. "Yeah, it don't matter even if I say I don't tag no more. I mean yeah, I still got that in my heart. Forever, I'll always be down for Crip no matter what, nobody disrespect me."

BROTHERS TO BROTHERS

The newspapers report death and criminal activity associated with the world of gangs on a daily basis, but they don't report the strong sense of support and protection the fellow gang members have for one another. This support seemed to be one benefit that kept the adolescents in the gang. I asked Lil Boy Blue to talk more about the friendship found in the Gang Community. He stated, "It's not like we wanted it to happen the way everything happened. We just always wanted to stick together. You know what I mean. Look after each other."

"So being a Crip is more the friendship aspect of it."

"Yeah, like you know friends forever I guess."

"Did you see Juice and everybody Saturday? Were you excited because they're just part of who you were growing up?"

"Yeah, it brings up a lot of memories. Juice and I were talking a lot, like, how before in the neighborhood, at the rock house, or something and now everybody works and they have kids and it's hard to get all the homies together."

During a free write at school, Lil Boy Blue described a true homie as "true friends" (see Fig. 3.2). One of the characteristics of a homie, according to Lil Boy Blue, is that homies are "down for each other. Homies willing to die for us," and "who give much love." Lil Boy Blue puts it powerfully—"brothers to brothers." The love Lil Boy Blue had for his homies then continues today.

When the kids told stories during class, they referred to the older members of the gang as *OGs* (old gangsters) and described how "the older ones

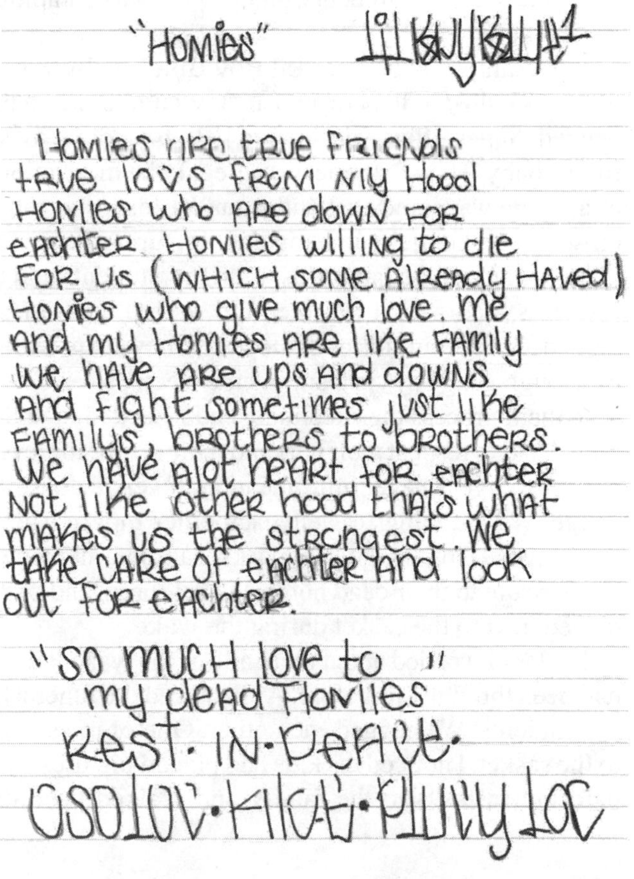
"Homies" Lil Boy Blue #1

Homies like true friends
true lovs from my Hood
Homies who are down for
eachter Homies willing to die
for us (which some already haved)
Homies who give much love. me
And my Homies are like Family
we have are ups and downs
And fight sometimes just like
Familys, brothers to brothers.
We have alot heart for eachter
Not like other hood thats what
makes us the strongest. We
take care of eachter and look
out for eachter.

"So much love to my dead Homies"
Rest · In · Peace ·
Osoloc · Kilo · Pluty Loc

FIG. 3.2. Lil Boy Blue's writing about his homies.

take care of [peewees]." With a deep respect and honor for Kilo, Smurf shared, "When they had a party and a barbeque, and I couldn't go because of probation, Kilo brought me food and talked with me instead of staying at the party the whole time. He watched out after us."

Lil Garfield wrote a letter to a homie in jail, telling him how much he missed him. He wrote, "I wish you could cee [be] here in person cuz, but always in thought. Wen-u-get out I hope you change a lil it's time for-u-man. Don't worry about what people will think or say. Your real homies will understand and be glad and happy to cee [see] a homie turn to a brighter note."

During one of our many talk sessions in class, Lil Boy Blue bragged, "In the hood everyone knows everyone." This loyalty—love—motivated behavior and actions that were often illegal. However, as I came to understand my students and their Gang Community, I started to see why they participated in such activities, and although I didn't support this behavior, their actions began to make sense to me in the gang world. My knowledge enabled me to see the students' gang identity as complex, more than illegal or violent activity.

For example, soon after Lil Boy Blue's baby was born, Plucy did what the boys called a diaper run. Lil Boy Blue didn't have a job and the baby needed diapers. Plucy decided to help his homie by stealing some diapers for his baby. Though the act was illegal, the motivation to help and take care of a homie was somewhat understandable. I especially saw this loyalty and closeness as homies came together to support each other when Plucy was killed. Many of the gang kids, both my students and their friends, came to my class, and we sat together and shared memories. The kids drew and tagged as they told stories of the times they spent with Plucy. That day I saw big, tough gang boys in tears. As the week proceeded, I had to find a way to help them process their feelings, and I needed to understand my own feelings. I had to respect their hurt and their desire for revenge. We talked about how "revenge is never full," meaning revenge doesn't stop with getting revenge. We did things to help each other mourn, such as building a shrine that consisted of three death masks, candles, and letters of farewell the students wrote to their dead homies. They drew and painted a mural that was placed next to the casket during the wake.

In class I worried about them and at the wake, I depended on them. They had been through this before. As I entered the funeral home, I saw several of my students. We hugged each other. One of my students accompanied me to the casket. I noticed the kids had placed pictures and notes in the casket. I paid my respects to the family and walked back down the aisle. I saw

Smurf's mom. I stopped to pay my respects. Kristina and I hugged. I broke into tears. While sitting with Lil Boy Blue and Smurf's family, many of my students and non-students came and sat near me. We hugged each other and shared memories. I watched my students walk to the casket and in their own private way say good-bye to a friend. After this experience, we became more than a teacher and students. They saw me hurting, and I saw them hurting. We supported each other.

My students were aware of the fact that Plucy's family would not have the money to bury their son. Lil Boy Blue, Smurf, Juice, Lil Garfield, and many other homies came together and organized a car wash to raise money. I watched the kids wash cars and share stories. I thought, these are the boys who society looks at as bad—gang members. Young boys who must say good-bye to a friend. They are boys—young boys who laughed and played with Plucy, who worry about Plucy's family. These boys came together early Saturday morning when they would rather have been in bed, stayed all day, and washed cars. No one griped or complained. They raised over $800.00 and gave the complete sum to Plucy's family.

I witnessed similar support when Guero was killed in the car accident. At this point in the story, we were no longer a class in school, so the logistics of coming together as a group were more difficult. We checked to see if the family needed any help with the funeral. They had insurance, but the kids decided to have a car wash anyway. The car wash became a place where the homies could gather and share memories. They spent all day, 8:00 in the morning to late into the evening, washing cars; friends came, left, and came back. They talked and cried. The money was used to buy everyone a shirt that had, "Guero rest in peace" on the back. Blue carnations were bought to cover the casket in the grave. Their concern and respect for each other brought them together.

The tensions involved in the gang scene seem to be inevitable: needing to belong while knowing the consequences, and demonstrating fierce and sincere loyalty while not wanting to be in the gang. Smurf acknowledged this tension. "What I did for the neighborhood, it was good, but it turned out to be bad. Like, when I was young, everybody told me that's the way it was going to be, but I never believed them. Sure enough to this day that's how it is and some of these fools don't realize it. And like, look at Bad Boy. He's 20 years old and he's still out there gangbangin' and doing his little thing. You know trying to be a *G* (a gangster). I want to tell him, like, grow up and shit ... I don't know, he has ... I have a kid, he has a kid, but I think it changes you a lot, but you know his kid is in Colorado .... I don't know, I think he should be doing something to get to Colorado … I don't know. I think it's time for everybody to grow. I mean I've seen a lot of other homeboys grow out of it."

I found a page in Lil Boy Blue's writing notebook that contained the following sentence: "My advice to someone who's thinking about joining a gang is don't do it." Lil Boy Blue knew the gang was not a place to be.

THE GANG COMMUNITY COLLIDES
WITH THE FAMILY COMMUNITY

Kristina and Felipé were the type of parents who wanted to know their sons' friends as they were growing up. They often allowed the kids to have a barbeque with their homies in the backyard. Many times, homies stayed overnight. Lil Boy Blue and Smurf's homies respected Kristina and Felipé, and they regularly went to their house to talk and share their feelings. Inevitably, the heartaches and fears associated with the gang leaked into the family. The Gang and Family Communities merged most painfully at funerals, when families cried and comforted each other.

On a day Lil Boy Blue and Smurf were late for school, I received a phone call from their mom. "I kept the kids home," Kristina said. "Smurf's life has been threatened. I'm going to keep them for the whole week." Later in the week, another student shared with me that Smurf was scared and wanted a gun. The threat was real. The fear was real.

As a result of the threats, Kristina had the phone number changed and unlisted. The boys were not allowed to give the new number to any of their friends. Kristina gave Smurf a pager. The homies could page him and he would return the call. Not long after this experience, Lil Boy Blue's and Smurf's house was shot at several times. Fortunately, no one was hurt.

At another point in time, a headline read, "… teen slain last night; The shooting death of a 15 year old boy the city's 55th homicide." This headline was about Plucy. The picture next to the article was of Juice covered with Plucy's blood. Juice had to move in with an uncle, because his family was afraid the shooter would come looking for Juice.

I was made more aware of how the two worlds of gang and family met head on when on a visit to Juice's home I was puzzled to notice he had rearranged his house. The living room was now in the middle of the building and the front room now held storage. Juice informed me that someone had shot at his house. He showed me where the bullet entered the outside wall of the bedroom, traveled through the bedroom wall, a second bedroom wall and into the outside wall of the kitchen.

During the time I have known Juice and Lil Garfield, a window in their little house was shot out, rocks were thrown through the rear window of Diane's car, Diane's car was tagged, and their home was tagged by rival gangs. The layers of tags in Fig. 3.3 illustrate the history of rival gangs disrespecting the boys and the MLMC responding with their own writing.

One year, Juice informed me he wanted to attend summer school. I talked with Diane. She didn't want him to go to Brighton, which was his home school, because she felt like every time Juice went to that school the gang activity around the home increased. She was worried for Juice's baby.

Many home and school decisions like this one were made by keeping the gang and the gang's activities in mind. Many arguments between parent and child resulted from the boys putting in work for the gang. The parents wanted the boys home and safe. Lil Boy Blue, Smurf, Juice, and Lil Garfield wanted to hang with their *homies*.

LITERACY IN THE GANG COMMUNITY

Humans constantly struggle to make sense of the world. The symbol systems we use to help us understand and express meaning are part of the communities in which we have membership. In the Gang Community, the boys adopted and invented new ways to express their identities and communi

FIG. 3.3.   Juice, Lil Garfield, and Diane's home, tagged by rivals.

cate. Although the literacy tool most recognized as gang literacy is graffiti, or what my students called a tag, I discovered that the Gang Community engages in several meaning-making systems, including tagging, oral language, rap, and other forms of representation. (For an additional discussion of tagging in my classroom, see D. Smith, 1997.)

Tagging

Tags can be found wherever there are gangs. My students taught me that the most important criteria for placing a tag is visibility. Tags can be found on any surface: notebooks, book covers, paper, and furniture, as well as buildings, walls, bridges, and other public sites.

For Lil Boy Blue, Smurf, Juice, and Lil Garfield tagging was just part of the Gang Community. They couldn't remember specifically how they learned to tag. Lil Boy Blue said, "I was still young—twelve, thirteen. I remember when I first started tagging. I didn't know how to tag. You learn later on from other people about tagging and stuff, how to tag better."

"How do you think you picked it up?"

Not knowing how to verbalize how he learned he repeated, "You pick it up. Everybody picks it up from each other."

Smurf started tagging in third grade. He said, "I got in trouble a lot in school for tagging even though it wasn't gang shit. I never wrote Crip or nothing like that. It was just gangster style."

Juice claimed he started tagging when he was 13, and Lil Garfield couldn't remember when he started. For him, tagging was part of being a *peewee*, but he admitted that "not everybody is good at it" and that "it takes time to learn." Lil Garfield confessed, "I got a sorry tag. My tag has always been sorry."

Like all literacy conventions in a community, tags have certain features that help readers construct meaning. I asked Lil Boy Blue what information can be found in a tag.

He replied, "The name of the neighborhood—that's more important than putting Crip or something like that."

"Let's say you are driving down the road with somebody and you see some tags, how would you explain to that person what the tags are?"

"I'd just tell him they are gang tags. Tell him they are territory marks."

"How would I know this (pointing to a tag I had) is a Crip tag or a Blood tag?"

"The color, the B's crossed out, you cross out the B's to disrespect the bloods and vice versa."

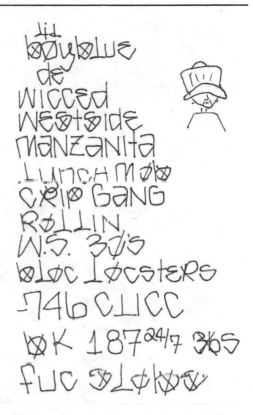

FIG. 3.4.   A typical tag
by Lil Boy Blue.

Figure 3.4 is a tag written by Lil Boy Blue in the classroom. Notice he included the name Manzanita and the street (3100) he lived on. He placed an
X over the letter B as a sign of disrespect. At the bottom of the tag, he again
disrespected the rival gang by writing "bk" which means "Blood killer,"
and he drove the disrespect home by ending the tag with "fuc *slobs* (a name
Crips use to refer to Bloods)."

Tagging was a big part of Smurf's world. I asked him what he put into his
tags. His answer was short and to the point: "Crip, westside Manzanita,
3100 blocc, BK Smurf."

"Those are the important things to tag?"

"Yeah, or an X on what ever I'm crossing out."

Figure 3.5 is one of many tags Smurf wrote in my classroom. His tag
contains all the needed information. The tag reveals where he was from and
who he represented. In the right corner he disrespected the enemy. Smurf
also paid tribute to Oso, who was shot in a drive-by. In the left corner, Smurf
did what is known as a *roll call* (a list of other gang members). Notice that
Smurf wrote "CRIP" with an inverted "i" in this tag. This element of

FIG. 3.5.   Smurf's tag with an upside down "i."

Smurf's style changed over time, as you will see in an example later in the chapter.

Next I asked Lil Garfield, "What elements do you include in a tag?"

"I tag the set WS MLMC CRIP BKERS LIL GARFIELD. It matters how much time you got if you got a lot of time you can put almost anything. You got no time you put, like, CRIP WS WESTSIDE."

When Lil Garfield shared some of his tags (like in Fig. 3.6) he told me that he was still learning to tag. Notice the different elements he includes in his tag and the different style.

As I drove around town, I categorized the numerous tags into two main groups. I wanted to know if I was right. I asked Juice, "There's a lot of different forms of tagging. For me there are tagger's tags and gangster's tags. Do you think there's a difference between the two?"

"A tagger's tag you can't read. Tagger's tag got their own languages. Gangster's tag they just put their hood, their barrio, whatever. You can tell the difference between a tagger's tag and a gangster's tag. It depends on how a person tags. Everybody's got their own style. Nobody tags the same. I don't

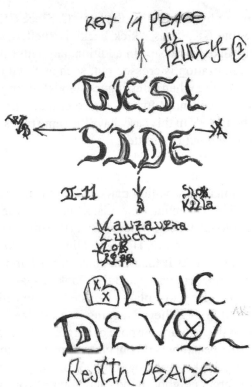

FIG. 3.6.   Lil Garfield's typical tag.

know, tagger's tags it's more connected most of the time, words, letters are
connected, sometimes it starts smaller and goes bigger (he motioned with his
hand to illustrate what he meant). They put like SNR or something. You see a
tag that says 'le sleepy pro vista' or something that's a gangster tag 'cause
Vista is a gang. Taggers got their own language. Spelling and stuff you know
what I mean. I mean certain taggers have their own spelling. They can spell
cane K-A-N-E they can spell whatever they want. Gangsters, they just have
their one, like they quote C's. Crips don't use CK."

"What type of letters do gangsters use?"

"If it's a slob then he'll probably use 'CK' a lot, probably quotation
around B, probably use a lot of B's. He probably won't put C's in his words.
He'll probably use K or c-rap. Then a Crip he'll use probably all C's. He
probably won't use K probably, and will cross out all his B's probably, will
quotation around his C's."

I learned that there are certain conventions that are followed when tagging. Spelling decisions are made based on gang membership. Since the
letter B represents Bloods, a rival gang, B's are eliminated by crossing them

out or by substituting the letter C. Since CK means Crip killer, Crips never wrote CK. Thus, "kick back" is spelled, "Kicc Cacc" and "because" is spelled, "c-cause." In addition, any letter that represents the rival gang or organization is crossed out, such as S, which represents *slob* (a name the Crips use when referring to Bloods), P for *posse* (a gang name for Bloods) or police, and R for red, the color that represents Bloods. Rival gangs, like the Bloods in this case, have the same types of rules, but different letters are crossed out or omitted.

Punctuation marks are also found in the tags in this chapter and add meaning to writing. Periods or dots are placed between the letters for separation and quotation marks around C indicate importance.

The placement of words, letters, drawings, and other symbols is quite intentional. Once I watched Smurf writing a tag in class. He wrote, read, and wrote some more. He moved the paper around as if he was looking for the right spot, as if the right placement of an image or mark would add to the meaning. He wrote and then looked again. The words weren't placed randomly. He had a plan—a place for everything.

At first I believed tagging was a style of doodling, but I quickly learned that the primary purpose of tagging was to gain respect for the gang and to disrespect others. In our classroom there seemed to be other reasons for tagging. I asked Lil Boy Blue, "What do you communicate when you go into different neighborhoods and you put your tag up?"

"Like we're telling them we were there, kind of disrespecting them and everything, having Crip tagged up in a Blood area."

At first Smurf said that tags had no purpose or meaning. "It's just something to do." But as he talked, his answers revealed that there is meaning in a tag and he acknowledged the difference in a tagger's tag and a gangster's tag. "I don't like the way taggers do it. Gangster I love'em because they're never going to change. Taggers got all this new shit. Can't even read. I think it's pretty ugly. I think they ruin our city."

"So what would you say is the difference between a tagger's and a gangster's tag?"

"Gangster is to like represent your neighborhood. Taggers just bring down the property." He also claimed, "If I see a Slob shit or something, I'll cross it out, of course, and put some of mine up." Even though Smurf first stated there was no purpose for tagging and insinuated that tagging destroys property and his city, when he saw an enemy's tag, he crossed the enemy's tag out and put up his own.

Over the 3 years I worked with Smurf, his tag changed. In the tag shown earlier in Fig. 3.5 Smurf drew the letter "i" inverted. The tag in Fig. 3.7,

FIG. 3.7.   Smurf's tag
using the #1 for "i."

which Smurf wrote a year later, shows Smurf's decision to replace the upside down "i" with a numeral "1." I asked Smurf if he was aware that his tag
went through a change.

   "Oh, yeah, I knew it changed the whole time, it was changing every day."
   "Yeah, but when I first met you, you tagged with an upside down 'i'."
   "Upside down with the dot on the bottom," clarified Smurf.
   "By the next year you were doing number one."
   "You know why I was stopping doing that?"
   "No."
   "Guero talking shit, he told me it looked stupid. He made fun of my tag.
He told me to find a new way so alright I'll find a new way. I started writing
CRIP trying to figure how to do … you know with CRIP. I put a one. I
thought CRIP with a one. Next thing I thought, CRIP's number 1, you know
CRIP's number 1, so I just started putting number one in everything. Spe-
cially with CRIP. I liked the way it looked like '4 life.' Life is number one, I
guess I'm saying. Yeah, I don't know. Everything has a meaning to it, kind
of, but lot of it doesn't."

Smurf changed his tag because Guero claimed his tags were weak. He was influenced by meaning and symbolism as he searched for a stronger graphic representation for the message in his tag. He chose the number one because being Crip is important.

Another incident conveyed the meaning in Smurf's tags. His girlfriend, Dea, read the tag found in Fig. 3.5 with no problem until she read the lower right corner. She read, "Crip Oso." Smurf interrupted her, "See right there, it doesn't say Crip Oso. The C is little. It's RIP Oso but I put the C to keep it Crip. That's why the C is small."

Smurf, as the author of this tag, had a specific meaning in mind when he wrote. When Dea wasn't constructing that meaning, he interrupted her to make sure his intention was understood. Smurf wrote what was on his mind in his tags. I asked Smurf, "If it was just something to do, just doing it to mess around, why was it always important that you put Oso on it?"

"I don't know, it's like the hardest time of my life when Oso died. I just can never forget that."

I proposed, "Tagging is like keeping him alive. His memories at least."

"I always have his memories. I don't know, I just wrote it," replied Smurf.

I also asked Juice what function or role tagging played for him as a member in the Gang Community. Juice answered, "People cruise down the street, see your name on the wall. It's a new name in a gang—THAT'S JUICE FROM MLMC. You are just trying to bring up your name. You want people to know who you are, and where you are from, and that there's a Juice from Manzanita, or there are whatever from Manzanita. You know what I mean, that you just want everybody to know you. And you are from Manzanita."

"The function tagging plays is to get people to know who you are?"

"And then if somebody crosses out your name, and he's from a different hood, and he puts his tag, you guys got shit. Because he crossed you out. That's how you start out."

"Another function tagging plays for you is it helps give you respect?"

"Yeah, if you hit up everywhere you get some sort of respect." Juice stressed over and over that tagging brings recognition to you and your gang. The more tags, the more respect.

Lil Garfield also discussed the function for tagging as, "Disrespect. If a Blood was walking down the street and he sees MLMC Bkers and it was in his hood, 'what the fuck disrespect me' or if someone crosses you out it's disrespect ... 'fuck you'."

"Why do you tag on your notebooks at school? Is that important?"

"Yes, so if anyone looks at my notebook they know that I'm a Crip."

Tagging also helped the boys deal with the deaths they experienced on what seemed like a regular basis. I could always tell when something was bothering Lil Boy Blue because he spent more time tagging. Figure 3.8 is a tag created by Lil Boy Blue after Plucy died. The left hand corner of the tag expresses his wish that Plucy was still here. He wrote the motto many of my students lived by, "We live to die and die to live," across the top of the paper. Along the right side of the drawn character is a list of the homies who died.

Oral Language

In oral language, since crossing out letters is impossible, a gangster uses substitutions. For example, one morning Smurf told us he and his family went to "Dead Lobster" for dinner the night before. At first I was startled. Then I quickly remembered that "red" was the color of the opposing gang so the kids eliminated that word from their oral language by using substitutions. Smurf substituted the word "dead" for "red." There was no hesitation—no second thought. Smurf said "dead" as naturally as if "Dead Lobster" truly was the name of the restaurant. Another time Smurf asked me if they were going to get an assignment cacc [back]. I thought I was misunderstanding, but the light bulb went on and I knew what he meant.

FIG. 3.8.   Lil Boy Blue's tag about Plucy's death.

During class, when the answer to multiple choice questions was "b," my students said "fe" or "fle." I have never heard them use the word "blood." Instead they said the word "flood" or "slob." Once, while reading a poem in class, Smurf substituted the word "flood" for the word "blood," again without hesitation or loss of meaning. When my students hurt themselves and bled, they never said "bleeding"—instead they talked about "slobbing."

My students generated a list of the words they used, including definitions and examples of the words in sentences, to help me understand their vocabulary (see Fig. 3.9). Some of these words are associated with the broader adolescent culture. This language was the language of my classroom.

<u>**GANGSTER TALK**</u>

mark: pussy, weak, death victim
slob: flood, snoop, blood, rival gang
gank: steal
strapped: caring a gun
banging: claiming crip
slang: selling drugs
chronic: herb, weed
cuzz: crip
rag: blue bandana
wacced: out, crazy
shank: stab a slob
blunt: big fat joint
book: got to go
faded: drunk or high

capps: bullets
G-ride: stolen car
joy ride: driving stolen car
jacc: take everything the person has
down with: baccing up a hood
west up: whats up, wes up
hood: crip gang Manzanita
talking smak: talking shit
punk: checc
lagging: taking to long
throw down: fight a slob

<u>**EXAMPLES**</u>

Go kicc that pussy marks ass.
Look at that punk ass slob.
lets go gank some shit.
Go strapped fool there might be some snoop's
tripping.
That fool aint banbing cuzz.
That fools slanging lets jacc 'em.
We jacced him for a lot of chronic.
Sup cuzz, Manzanita lynch mob crip.
Sport that blue rag.
That fools wacced our on that shit.
Boy Blue shanked his ass.
Smurf put four capps in his ass.
Sad Boy was cruising that g-ride.
Sad Boy got charged with joy riding.
Icey Blue just jacced him for all his shit.
That slob said he was down with pussy so

Plucy killed him.
West up cuzz.
Saturday we just kicced it in the hood.
That slob was talking a gang of smak.
Smurf checced that slob's ass.
That bitch at the store was fuccin laggin.
The cops were hasseling our ass at the store.
We booked to the hood after the party.
All those slobs wern"t shit. They weren't
even fading.
Guero shanked his ass in the necc.

FIG. 3.9.   Language used by gang members, to avoid certain letters.

Gangster Rap

Language conventions in the Gang Community are also manifested in music known as rap, or more specifically, gangster rap. Listening carefully to rap reveals who the rapper represents. Smurf and Lil Garfield shared a dream to become famous rappers. During the time Smurf was at Nuestra Casa, he wrote over 50 raps. His mom said he sat in his room and wrote raps for hours. Figure 3.10 is one of the raps Smurf wrote in the style of gangster rap. I wanted to know more about Smurf's process in writing raps. I asked him what he thought and did when he wrote a rap.

Smurf shared, " I sit down to write a rap. I write about, like, what I feel, you know, like what I feel about, what's going on, like some of them are, like kind of … Like some of my raps are like there's that hidden message, but you can't really tell like what I'm trying to say cause I don't really want you to know. But I'm just saying it because that's what I feel. I don't know."

"It makes you feel better?"

"Yeah kind of, not really … makes me feel better, but I don't know feel, yeah, I guess I feel good rappin' about it."

```
this is the pee wee clicc this the one they
call smurf l-o-c we kill all c-lobs and
were com-n from that lynch mob got my
homies juice, shag and plucy LOC we go on a
ride and we smoke all snoops that try to
trip on us cripz mothafucc that slob shit
cuzz this strait crip fucc gangin on wax
cuzz we band on the streets slob
mothafuccers cry to slip they get beat fucc
the b-side we crip everywhere when we to in
public rich folks just stare we take one
look at them and they get all scared im a
strait up crip cuzz its all about that C-R-
I-P MR OSO one of the downest homies but he
is still with us com-n bacc from the dead
to haunt all you slob muthafuccers wearing
red thats what you get for being s-l-o-b
muthafucc that shit cuzz you shuda been L-
O-C.....................
```

FIG. 3.10.   Smurf's gangster style rap.

Smurf's response reminded me of my own reasons for writing in a journal. I thought out loud, "I wonder if a writing rap is like why I write in my journal."

Smurf said, "I think a rap is a lot like a poem. I mean it's like almost the exact same thing as a poem, but as it's written except, mostly, well … see like a lot of raps these days don't have meaning to them, but every rap, every single rap I ever made had meaning to 'em. You know and the killin' and the other stuff that I add to it, you know, that's just so people want to hear it, so let them hear it." Smurf laughed. Smurf's comments indicated his awareness of audience and audience needs. On another occasion he rapped after the death of a homie. The gangster language was not as obvious. He had a sad story to tell and chose the style appropriate for his message.

On one occasion, when Lil Garfield was at my home, he asked if he could write a rap on the computer. Of course I said yes. He pulled a little notebook (see Fig. 3.11) out of his back pocket. I was amazed as I watched. A list of words, organized into what looked liked rhyming groups, was written in his notebook. Beside each word was a number. Lil Garfield referred to the list of words while he was writing. He wrote a while and then rapped out loud. Then he went back and revised until the rap was just right.

I asked Lil Garfield how the list of words helped him. He said he grouped words together that rhyme. He first wrote the rap following the groups. If he didn't like the way the rap sounded he revised following the numbers. The

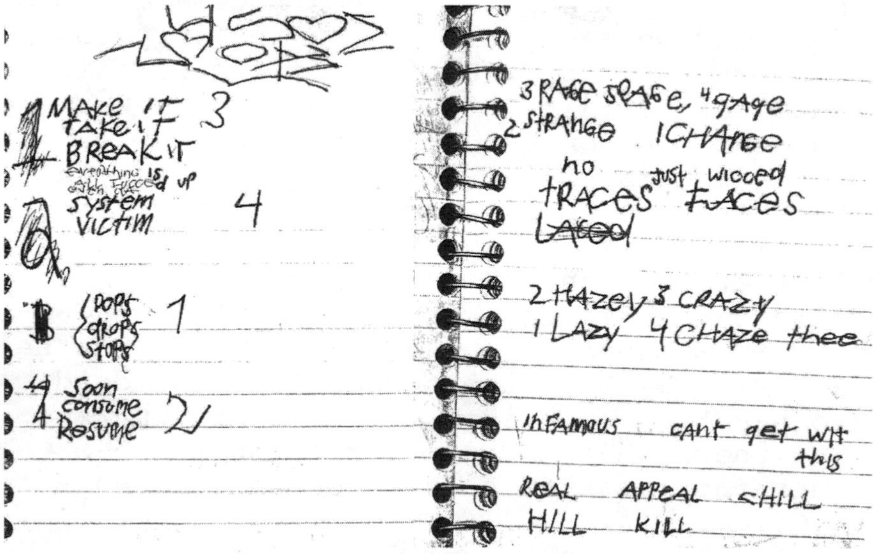

FIG. 3.11. Lil Garfield's pocket notebook.

numbers gave a different order to the rhyming. When Lil Garfield finished writing he uploaded the rap on the Internet (Fig. 3.12).

Lil Garfield did what is referred to as a freestyle rap. That is, he created raps spontaneously. When we were driving home from school one day, he demonstrated how he practiced freestyle. "I pick words off of street signs like [a Shell gas station sign caught his eye] 'Shell.' I start rapping. I add to it by picking other words I see." As we drove, he selected several words from signs and built a rap that had a story. He was so comfortable. He moved smoothly from one word to the next. He claimed he practiced rapping like that all the time.

Hand Signs and Other Forms of Representation

All gang members *throw up* (show) hand signs to each other that carry specific meaning. Hand signs are used to communicate to rival gangs as well as friendly gangs. I often sent a camera home with students to take pictures of their world. Many times these pictures were full of their homies throwing hand signs as if the homies were telling the world who they were.

News from around...   Page 1 of

NIOUZ!!! : add yours...!

Whassup all around the place!!!...

It's up to you. Fill in the blanks and tell 'em whassup in here, out there, and else where...!

CANT FADE IT PREMEDITATED MURDA IN MY EYES WESTSIDE WEN WE RIDE
CUMIN QUICC WIT GAME NOT FO DA FAME BUT FO DA FUN SMOKIN SLOBS LIKE A
BLUNT.
                                                                    /EVEN
DOE I HAD NO POPS I GUESS NOW I KNOW HOW MY LIFE DROPS WONDERING WEN
ALL DIS SHITS GONNA STOP I KNOW NOT SOON SO I PHIZ CONSUME AND RESUME
IF I DONT MAKE IT I'LL TAKE IT OR BREAK IT I MEAN EVERYTHING IS ALL FUCCED
UP EVEN DA SYSTEM... OFF DAT 40, O.E SCOPING FOE DA NEXT VICTIM I MEAN MY
BRAIN IS GETTIN LAZY KINDA HAZEY I THINK IM GOIN CRAZY THE DEVIL IS TRYIN TO
GET THEE., KILL'EM. LEAVE NO TRACES JUST WICCED FACES STILL INFAMOUS AND
STILL CANT GET WIT THIS IM THA REAL DEAL ,MASS APPEAL, SO KICC ON KACC AND
CHILL CUZZ IM DA KING OF DA HILL LIL   GARFIELD W/S MLMC.TUCSON
AZ.746

Email: [   ]

[ADD   ]   [RESET   ]

Click here to go back!

FIG. 3.12.   Lil Garfield's rap sent out on the Internet.

Figure 3.13 shows a special handshake used by the Manzanita gang. They made a "W" to stand for Westside. Then by moving the hands downward, they formed an "M" to stand for Manzanita.

Figure 3.14 shows how the gang members formed the letters B and K with their fingers.

Members of the Gang Community always look for ways to represent their hood and their gang. My students always wore blue clothes. Blue represented Crips. People who are insiders to this knowledge—the Crips and their rivals—knew they were Crip. Often their shirts, hats, and belts had the letters C (Crip), W, (westside), or LA (Little Apple, which is the English translation of manzanita). The boys, like other Crip members, also carried a blue rag or flag.

I will never forget my first visit to the neighborhood. We stopped at the park and the first thing the boys told me was to look up at the mountains—they form the shape of a W. The boys' mountains stand above their hood. This image said to them, it is safe, you are home.

FIG. 3.13.   The handshake used by MLMC members.

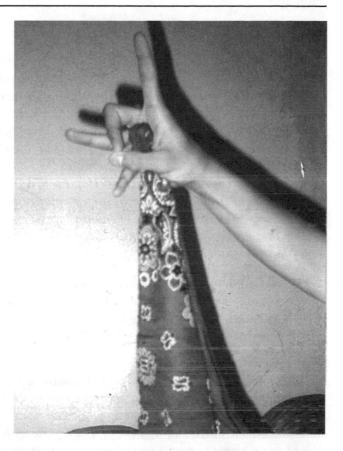

FIG. 3.14. The BK hand sign for "Blood Killer" with a blue rag to disrespect the rival gang.

Lil Boy Blue, Smurf, Juice, and Lil Garfield knew when it was appropriate and when it was not appropriate to use gang symbol systems. During a class assignment, I asked them to write letters to the mayor regarding the need for a new building for the Nuestra program. The kids reminded each other not to put their "gang shit" in the letter because no one would take them seriously. Each time they prepared a presentation for the university, they discussed the language they would use and how they would dress. As a class, they determined the message they wanted the audience to receive. The last year at Nuestra Casa the kids created a yearbook. Again they discussed the appropriate style of writing and the gang symbols they would include in the book. The audience was their criteria for when to use gang literacy. They understood that gang literacy belonged with the gang world and with people who understood their language. If gang language would detract from the intended message, the students decided not to use it.

THE GANG COMMUNITY

Lil Boy Blue, Smurf, Juice, and Lil Garfield are "gangstas." They joined the Gang Community as young teenagers and "gang member" became their primary identity. One time, Debbie found Smurf's answer to a question about the gang revealing. Smurf couldn't understand why Debbie didn't know the answer; the gang culture was so much a part of him that he figured everyone else understood it like he did. This is because gang membership was such a central part of the boys' identities.

According to Lave and Wenger (1991), participating in a community of practice and constructing an identity are essentially the same process. The boys' participation in the Gang Community moved them toward full membership in it in the theoretical sense just as much as having been literally jumped in. Wenger (1998) says:

> *Engagement in practice gives us certain experiences of participation, and what our communities pay attention to reifies us as participants. ... An identity, then, is a layering of events of participation and reification by which our experience and its social interpretation inform each other. (pp. 150–151)*

Language was one of the ways the boys marked their identity as gang members. They read, understood, and wrote tags that had particular and sophisticated orthographic conventions, served particular functions, and communicated to particular audiences. They spoke with an equally sophisticated and systematic syntax and vocabulary. They invented forms of symbol systems like hand signs within the social conventions of their community. In each of these language and literacy events, the boys publicly identified themselves as members of a particular community. They simultaneously expressed and created identity through language. F. Smith (1998) says that, "as we identify with other members of all the clubs to which we belong, so we learn to be like those other members" and "the identification creates the possibility of learning" (p. 11).

A compelling example of this process is the approximations of peewees and gang members who didn't tag as well as others. These gang members were fully accepted—as Lil Garfield's experience shows, even "sorry" tags served the purpose of representing individual members and the gang as a collective and disrespecting other groups. Thus, such gangsters were newcomers who were "legitimate peripheral members" of the community of practice (Lave & Wenger, 1991). They had secured and empowered posi-

tions because they were on a trajectory toward full membership. Debbie also had a "legitimate" empowered position. She never became a full member, nor did she want to, but her increasing knowledge base and access to participants and resources meant she was "located in the social world" (p. 36) of the Gang Community.

As Lil Boy Blue, Smurf, Juice, and Lil Garfield moved outside of the gang world into other worlds, their "gangsta" personification and identity went with them. Not surprisingly, their dedication to being CRIP4LIFE was one of many complications in the boys' paths as they tried to participate in the community known as formal education. In chapter 4, we share Lil Boy Blue, Smurf, Juice, and Lil Garfield's stories as they struggled to participate and succeed in their neighborhood schools as children and adolescents. We refer to this part of the School Community as Part One (I).

4

School Community, Part One (I): "They don't want us here."

> Today is something else. I try to get into school and I did. They said that
> I still got a chance in school to graduate with my class. I don't want to
> mess up in school so I'm going to try to stay up and do well.
> —Juice's Journal, 12/20/96

*Juice wrote this journal entry after he registered for high school. He was ex-
cited about the possibilities of graduating with his class, but he was also
nervous and scared. He didn't want to "mess up." He wanted to stay caught
up in his work and to "do well." His journal entry represents the voices of
many students who are labeled dropouts, trouble makers, at risk, and delinquents, who want to be in school and graduate but can't navigate the system successfully and believe themselves to be the reason for their failure.
The boys in this study all wanted the high school diploma because for them
it carried a hidden power. For Lil Boy Blue the dream was real. After many
false starts and hard work, he graduated in May 1996. Smurf toyed with the
idea of going back to school to finish his requirements and receive his diploma, but he didn't believe graduating was possible. Juice and Lil Garfield carefully calculated their graduation dates. Juice graduated in May
2001. Lil Garfield graduated in May 2002.*

*In this chapter, Debbie shares early experiences Lil Boy Blue, Smurf,
Juice, and Lil Garfield had while participating in the School Community
(I), which refers to their school lives in the regular public school system
before they entered Nuestra Casa, an alternative program where Debbie
was their teacher for four semesters. This chapter also recounts some*

events that occurred when Debbie became the boys' full-time advocate in order to support their return to high school. She begins their stories in the elementary and junior high years, pulling from the boys' and their parents' memories. All four boys dropped out of their neighborhood high school at different times. We set the argument in this chapter that literacy in the School Community (I) is one explanation for the boys' unfulfilled dreams and their school realities. In contrast, stories from Nuestra Casa, where Debbie was the boys' teacher, are told in chapter 5, "The School Community (II)." Strongly related, details about the boys' graduations are told within Debbie's reflection on her experience as an advocate in chapter 8.

THE EARLY SCHOOL YEARS

The stories the boys told me indicated that elementary school was a time of good memories. Their parents told me that the boys were average elementary students. Lil Boy Blue wanted to go to college. Juice came home and did homework before he did anything else. The parents couldn't figure out what went wrong as their sons moved into high school.

Kristina claimed that "Lil Boy Blue always wanted to go to college. Lil Boy Blue just went along with school. Smurf didn't like his fourth grade teacher. He wasn't going to give in to her, and she wasn't going to give in to him. I swear to God, I was in the principal's office every other day. I used to dread answering the phone." Kristina often told me that Smurf lived up to the expectations of his teachers.

"What type of grades did the boys get in school?"

"They all had average grades."

Kristina felt that when Lil Boy Blue and Smurf got into middle school, they started to "spread their wings, but they were still controllable." In middle school, she had to "let them start taking on their own personality and do their own thing. I figured they had to be street smart."

Diane told me about Juice and Lil Garfield when they were in elementary school. "They attended many different schools. They were just typical grade school kids. They didn't start to change until they went to middle school, and that's when I went to prison."

"When they were in grade school do you remember what type of grades they got?"

"Average, like average kids."

"Do you remember if they liked school?"

"Yeah, they did like school. Lil Garfield always had a little problem with school, but Juice, he always liked school. Juice didn't have any problem," Diane bragged.

For Lil Boy Blue, elementary school was fun because his friends were there, and he thought "school was a lot easier." He recounted one of his memories of a sixth grade teacher. "I had a good teacher in sixth grade. He was a Mexican, if I remember right. He was a cool teacher, man."

Curious, I asked, "Why was he cool?"

"He liked … he made it fun to work. You know what I mean? Because I had … pretty good teachers, but there was another teacher that was supposed to be all mean and stuff. I never had her or anything. All my other teachers were pretty … they weren't all mean or anything. But he made it more interesting the work. I liked his class."

Lil Boy Blue's third grade report card (Fig. 4.1) shows he achieved satisfactory scores and excellent grades. He also brought home awards and certificates.

According to Lil Boy Blue, things changed in middle school. He never got into big trouble although he had to stay after school a couple of times. He earned C's.

"What was middle school like?" I asked.

"I don't remember …. Lots of things started changing. Like friends … started hanging out with different people. Everybody started like, kind of like, to separate to different crowds and stuff. That's how I remember junior high."

Lil Boy Blue graduated from eighth grade, was promoted to ninth grade, and attended Brighton High School.

Smurf had a different experience with school. He brought home awards that he earned at school, but he didn't really remember them.

Smurf claimed he never really liked school. "No," he told me. "I didn't like it, but it was school. I liked it cause I liked to see my friends, cause when you are young you don't really get to do a lot of things."

I wasn't shocked by his answer, but I was puzzled. I had heard Smurf talk about elementary school memories with his homies. His stories were of good times. Confused, I asked Smurf how he saw himself as a student.

Smurf bragged, "I got in a lot of trouble. I was like the only person in elementary to get suspended."

He didn't answer the question, but this was a story I hadn't heard, so I asked, "What were you suspended for?"

"I don't remember. It was in fifth grade, but my dad went and complained, told them, you know, I was too young to get suspended. So what

LANGUAGE ARTS				
Listening	P.L.	S		
Listens with understanding N	S.L.			
Speaking	P.L.	S		
Expresses ideas effectively	S.L.			
Speaks clearly/audibly N				
Reading	P.L.	S		
Reads with understanding#	S.L.			
Learns new words appropriate to level of instruction				
Uses phonics and other word-attack skills N				
Grade Level of Instruction	2^2 _ _ _			
Writing	P.L.	S		
Expresses ideas effectively	S.L.			
Uses correct grammar				
Penmanship.............		S		
Writes legibly and neatly				
Spelling	P.L.	N		
Uses correct spelling in written work N	S.L.			
Learns new words appropriate to level of instruction N				
MATHEMATICS	P.L.	E		
Understands the meaning of numbers	S.L.			
Reads and writes numbers correctly				
Solves problems by reasoning				
Grade Level of Instruction	3 _ _ _			

SCIENCE, SOCIAL STUDIES AND HEALTH/SAFETY
Gathers information from multiple sources
Organizes information logically
Communicates information
Understands concepts

SCIENCE	P.L.	S		
	S.L.			
SOCIAL STUDIES........	P.L.	S		
	S.L.			
HEALTH/SAFETY.........	P.L.	S		
	S.L.			
PHYSICAL EDUCATION......		S		
Takes part in organized activities				
Displays development of physical education skills				
FINE ARTS...............		S		
Demonstrates interest and appreciation in music, art and drama				
INSTRUMENTAL MUSIC......		X		

Student's Name ▓▓▓▓▓▓
School ▓▓▓▓ Grade 3
Teacher ▓▓▓▓
Language Other Than English _____
P.L.-Primary Language of Instruction _English_
S.L.-Second Language of Instruction _____

SUPPORT PROGRAMS

PERSONAL/SOCIAL GROWTH

Shows positive attitude toward school	S		
Practices self-discipline........	S		
Gets along well with others.....	E		
Respects rights and property of others	E		
Observes safety rules..........	E		
Practices good sportsmanship...	E		

WORK/STUDY HABITS

Attends to tasks.............	S		
Follows directions............	S		
Completes work.............	S		
Works well independently......	S		

Conference Date 11/5/85
Parent Signature ▓▓▓▓
Teacher Signature/Student Signature ▓▓▓▓

COMMENTS

Period 1

Period 2

Period 3

19 - **ATTENDANCE**

Days Present..............	
Days Absent..............	
Times Tardy..............	
Assignment Next Year _____	

FIG. 4.1. Lil Boy Blue's third grade report card.

they did, they took me out of my class for the last two months of school."
Smurf continued, "I had school in the principal's office. That was my
school. I still got my lunch and recesses and everything, but my class was in
the principal's office. It was me and these other two guys. Three guys at the
end of the year. The principal took us, he wanted us to see his house, so we
can know what an education can get you—nice things. He took us to his
house. He had a nice house. They had dirt bikes, and a Jacuzzi in his house

and everything. He showed us all that and he took us to eat pizza. We were the worst kids in school, and we got all this. He took us to Dairy Queen. He was a pretty cool principal."

Now, I wanted to know more. "Did you do the work when you were in his office?"

Smurf explained, "Yeah, he helped me more. I guess maybe I had more attention because in the class, other teachers, they would just worry about me being quiet and not making any remarks. They always had my desk in the corner or right next to their desk."

I quickly thought back to our classroom and remembered Smurf did in fact have a lot of remarks to make. He liked to stir things up at times, but he also was a hard worker and very much aware that the teacher should be respected. In one incident, I had to ask one of the students to leave the classroom. Smurf asked me to let him stay and then told the student to treat me with respect, "like one of the homies."

I wondered if Smurf's expression of dislike for school was more of a learned behavior. At Nuestra Casa, Smurf shared stories of fun times in elementary school, of good teachers, and of good friends. Although Smurf stated that he hated school and his memories were of being in trouble, he also spoke of a principal who seemed to care.

In a telephone conversation, Kristina shared that a counselor told her Smurf would end up in jail. Smurf's answers about school reflected the type of student the counselor described him to be rather than who he really was. If they saw him as a trouble maker, he became that trouble maker, but if a teacher saw him as a good student, he would do well in that teacher's classroom. He was successful with the principal.

Smurf knew how to act in school, but he chose not to at times. He didn't like middle school. Kristina felt she was always in the office. Both Kristina and Felipé attended parent conference meetings where all they heard were negative comments. Kristina and Felipé believed that if Smurf could hang in until he graduated from eighth grade, things would be better for him in high school. The teachers wouldn't know him in high school, and he could start new.

Juice called himself a "school boy." Through the seventh grade he completed his homework and played the violin. He claimed he ran home, and before doing anything else, sat down and did his homework. I asked Juice to describe the type of student he was in elementary school.

"I was a very good student. I was a quiet, listening student. I was quiet, and I would listen all the time, do my work and hand it in on time, do everything right. After school, I would walk home. I turned on my light. I wouldn't do nothing. I would wave 'hi' to my mom and do my homework. When my homework was done, I would eat. Then I would go outside. I was more responsible when I was a kid."

Juice had the opportunity to participate in the Young Author's Festival and earned recognition while in elementary school. "I got like one D, two C's, the rest I hardly get B's. I mostly got A's." Figure 4.2 is a copy of a letter Juice received from the vice mayor.

In seventh grade, when Juice's mom went to prison things changed for Juice at school. His grades dropped and he was frequently in trouble.

Lil Garfield also enjoyed grade school, but what type of student was he? With his head held high, he confidently stated, "I was a B average, maybe an A. I was on honor roll a couple of times, a pretty good student. [School] wasn't that easy to fuck up. It was more fun back in those days. I got away with more shit in elementary."

CITY OF TUCSON
OFFICE OF THE CITY COUNCIL
TUCSON, ARIZONA 85745

RODOLFO C. BEJARANO
VICE MAYOR

WESTSIDE COUNCIL OFFICE
940 WEST ALAMEDA
(602) 791-4040

March 27, 1986

Congratulations on your recent selection of "Citizen of the Quarter" from your class.

It is indeed a special honor to receive such recognition of outstanding behavior. I know that your parents must be proud of you for your accomplishments.

You are to be commended for your exemplary conduct. Best wishes for a bright future.

Respectfully,

Rodolfo C. Bejarano

FIG. 4.2. A good citizen letter Juice received in elementary school.

Once again my curiosity was piqued: "What do you mean by 'it wasn't that easy to mess up?'"

"Well, you could mess up, but it's not like they were going to suspend you and shit. You mess up, you get detention. Cool well, you learn the next time," explained Lil Garfield.

"Do you remember getting into a lot of trouble or a little bit of trouble in elementary?"

"I used to get in little trouble but a lot of times. Like cussing, class clown, that was the biggest one on my report card, class clown, different stuff."

Lil Garfield's mom found some of Lil Garfield's work from grade school to share with me. In one assignment he answered three questions about the book *Stone Fox* (1980) by John Reynolds Gardiner.

Lil Garfield, like Lil Boy Blue and Juice, enjoyed his elementary years and was successful. Smurf never willingly said he had a good time in elementary school, but I heard him talk about good memories on occasion. Experiences with caring teachers and principals and rewarding events led to predominately positive memories. Nothing in the memories could have predicted the events in high school when things changed dramatically for all four of the boys.

HIGH SCHOOL EXPERIENCE:
THE TROUBLE BEGINS

Lil Boy Blue, Smurf, Juice, and Lil Garfield entered high school as ninth graders, freshmen. Like most students, they were excited and nervous. Unlike many students, high school became an obstacle to conquer. Lil Boy Blue completed his ninth grade year with no trouble. Tenth grade changed his view of school and college. Smurf's high school experience was short and filled with trouble. Juice and Lil Garfield were in and out of school, with very little success.

According to Kristina, Lil Boy Blue never really got into trouble until high school. She realized that Lil Boy Blue wasn't perfect, but he wasn't suspended until his sophomore year. I asked Lil Boy Blue what his thoughts were about high school.

He said, "It was fun … high school … freshman. We messed around a lot, so we didn't really, I mean, we ditched a lot of classes."

"Did you get in trouble your ninth grade year besides ditching?"

"Naaah, I never got suspended or anything at all."

Lil Boy Blue's sophomore year was the turning point in his educational experiences because that was the year he was found in possession of a gun on the high school campus and forced out of school. I attempted to obtain his school records, but when I contacted the schools in order to reconstruct the time line of the experience, no one could locate the file. I heard the story several times from members of Lil Boy Blue's family, but I wanted to hear Lil Boy Blue's reaction to what happened during this period of time, so I asked him.

At first, Lil Boy Blue's remarks caught me off guard. He said, "Sophomore year was nothing. But because, you know, other people, they got more into gang stuff that year. Before my freshman year, it was bad. But everybody just kind of kept to themselves, you know what I mean? And sophomore year, the first day of school, everybody started going at it, dogging and talking shit. I remember Bad Boy, like the first ten minutes, he had already had a fight."

"Your mom told me about when you got in trouble and going to different schools. I want your version of it."

Lil Boy Blue shared, "I remember after I got caught with the gun, my dad was trying to get me back into school. I was trying to get back into school, and they were giving us a hard time. I got caught with the gun the second month of school, early in the year. They kind of like, bullshit with us. It ended up I could get back to school by the semester, and that came by, as you know. That came by at the end of the school year …, too late, so I didn't start school until next year. They finally let me in at [another high school across town]. They lied to my dad, too. My dad didn't want me going to a school that didn't have transportation and stuff. They told my dad that they would let me back to the high school downtown or something, 'cause they have a bus that goes by, if I did good at the other high school. I had a semester to do good. I just had to pass all my classes, I think, and I went to a new high school. I passed it, and they still didn't let me back into Brighton."

His version of the story was similar to the version given by his parents. Kristina and Felipé's account of this incident shows just how hard they worked to keep their son in school and how they tried to gain access to the system.

Kristina recalled the day the trouble began: "They pulled in both Lil Boy Blue and his friend, but Lil Boy Blue had the bag [with a gun]. Even though the bag didn't belong to him, they got Lil Boy Blue."

Felipé added, "Arrested him."

I wanted to make sure I got all the details, so I asked, "When did they call you into the office?"

Kristina answered, "When this happened, they called me and told me that Lil Boy Blue was being arrested. I said why, and they said possession of a gun. Everything fell apart, you know." Knowing Kristina, she fell apart. This was her son.

Felipé said, "I didn't believe them."

Kristina continued, "I called Felipé up at work. He dropped everything. I rushed over there, and he met me [at the school] shortly after. The police helped us and everything. When we were talking, they said, you know, Lil Boy Blue seems like a really nice guy. It doesn't seem like it's going to be that bad."

At that point, Kristina believed everything was going to be all right because the police officer stated that Lil Boy Blue seemed like a good kid, and she started to relax. She wasn't prepared for what the school would put them through. During our conversation, Kristina and Felipé used the word "expelled," but from what they were saying, it sounded more like Lil Boy Blue had been suspended.

The student handbook defined expulsion as "the permanent withdrawal of the privilege of attending a school unless the governing board reinstates the privilege." Expulsion usually refers to all schools in the district. Yet, Lil Boy Blue was allowed to attend a high school within the district along with several alternative programs. I asked, "Originally they told you he was expelled for 30 days?"

Kristina replied, "I didn't worry too much because I knew he could make that time up. Summer school or whatever. Then when we went back, they prolonged [the suspension] another 30 more days."

"What was their reason for prolonging the expulsion?"

Felipé answered, "The reason was for me, [gang activity] was happening more and more." Felipé believed there was no policy, because this was the first time a gun was on campus and the gang concern wasn't prevalent at the time.

"So you really understood that after the 30 days Lil Boy Blue would be back in school?" I asked.

"I took him back to school. When we went back to school, [the officials] said, 'No another 30 days'," explained Kristina.

Felipé then explained that after the second 30 days, "I took him to school. When we got there to enroll again, the principal came out and said 'Oh no, no, you're not allowed here. You have to leave,' and I said, 'Why?' 'Well because ... because you are going in for a hearing now for expelling him.' I said, 'How long is that?' The principal said, 'Probably 60 days.'"

By this time, Lil Boy Blue had been out of school for 60 days. According to the district handbook, as the result of a hearing, a student can be suspended for no less than 10 days and no more than 60 days. There had been no hearing or notice of a hearing. At this point the story became even more confusing. I could tell that Felipé was also frustrated. I asked him if the hearing was in 60 days, and he said they gave them a date which was about a month ahead. The whole time Lil Boy Blue was out of school, Kristina collected his work from his teachers. The teachers and parents seemed to think Lil Boy Blue was coming back to school.

Felipé shared how he remembered the hearing. "We went up against the board, five members, two teachers, and the principal. I presented that I felt that I should have Lil Boy Blue go back to school to get back into getting on with his education. They looked at me and said, 'We'll let you know'." I could hear Felipé's frustration as he continued to tell me what happened. "I had to leave the room. I came back in. They said no."

I asked, "Did they give a reason?"

"Yeah, they said they were following guidelines for this kind of behavior. They couldn't tolerate this kind of behavior," said Felipé.

Felipé once asked me why he had to go down there and tell them why his son should be in school if they were not going to listen and simply follow the policy. This was a question I could not answer. Lil Boy Blue was suspended/expelled for one semester. At this point I wondered if Kristina and Felipé were aware of the difference between suspension and expulsion. It was obvious that school officials did not help them to understand their rights in this situation.

Felipé and Kristina were also told that if Lil Boy Blue attended another high school for a semester and passed all his classes, he could return to Brighton High School the following semester. Felipé contacted a former teacher of his, who was now the vice principal of a high school within the same school district. Arrangements were made for Lil Boy Blue to attend the school.

He attended and passed all his classes. The next semester, Felipé took Lil Boy Blue back to Brighton High School as intended. Remember, Kristina and Felipé were told that if Lil Boy Blue attended another school for one semester, stayed out of trouble, and passed all his classes, he would be allowed to attend Brighton. To Kristina's and Felipé's surprise, however, Lil Boy Blue was denied access to the school. They were finally told that the school officials never planned to let Lil Boy Blue return. Felipé decided to take the matter up with the district superintendent.

Felipé continued telling the story, "So, I said I'm going right to the top. I don't want to talk to the teachers. I don't want to talk to principals. I wanted to talk to the superintendent. I went down to [the district offices]. I would go on my lunch hour and [the secretaries] would tell me he would be back about 11:30. They would ask, 'Could someone else help you?' 'No. I want to see the superintendent.' 'He's not back, but he will be back.' 'I will wait.' He never showed up."

"How many times did you go?"

"Oh, I went 15 to 20 times. Every time I went in there, they tell me he's coming. He'll be back."

Felipé told me that he talked to four different assistants, but he never saw the superintendent. He sat in the receptionist's area waiting and the superintendent never showed up. He figured there must have been a back door because the superintendent never came through the receptionist's area.

At one time, Felipé and Kristina decided to talk to the school board. They went to a board meeting but were never given permission to speak. I believe that part of the problem was that Felipé and Kristina didn't understand how the school board meetings were run, and school district officials did not help them. During the retelling of this story, I could hear the sincere belief that Lil Boy Blue would be allowed back into Brighton High School in Kristina and Felipé's voices, but this was never to be. Kristina told me that during this time, Lil Boy Blue became discouraged and gave up on school.

Lil Boy Blue attended an alternative program and an alternative high school while this series of events occurred. I asked Lil Boy Blue what the alternative schools were like. He said, "[The schools were] all right. It was like regular school. They let you get away with a lot of stuff, but they didn't care how you dress, like a regular school. They were pretty good, but I don't know."

"What about ALP [the first alternative program Lil Boy Blue attended]?"

"No, because ALP was kind of sorry. All they did was put you on a computer, and you worked on the computer the whole time. They let the computer do all the explaining. If you had a question you would ask [the instructors], but they wouldn't really tell ya. This kind of sucked."

"Why did you leave Kino Alternative High School?

"At Kino, you had to have a good grade point average in order to stay. My first quarter, I think, I didn't pass one of my classes so they didn't let me stay. If I didn't stay in school, Mom and Dad would be pissed off. So this other dude at Kino … he was talking about Nuestra Casa so we went over there. And I went and I started talking to them. I brought everybody else."

Lil Boy Blue decided to attend Nuestra Casa. He was aware of Smurf's problems at Brighton, so he talked his parents into allowing Smurf to attend Nuestra Casa, too.

Smurf originally failed eighth grade, but Kristina was told that if he passed summer school he would be allowed to move on to the ninth grade.

He passed summer school and registered for ninth grade as planned. That fall Smurf entered Brighton High School as an excited freshman, but trouble seemed to follow him like his best friend. One morning the middle school called Smurf's home and reported him absent. Kristina couldn't understand what was going on. After all, Smurf was registered for and attending high school, not middle school. She later came to understand that the middle school continued to list Smurf in the eighth grade and did not consider him to have been promoted. During that first month of the fall semester, Brighton High School and the middle school debated where Smurf should attend. Brighton High School "won." As a result of this set of circumstances, Smurf didn't have a good start.

Once Brighton High School officials decided Smurf could stay at the high school, a new set of problems surfaced. Smurf informed me that the office called him in almost every day to be padded down. He asked me, "How I'm a supposed to stay caught up if I'm in the office all the time?" A good question. One for which I had no answer.

Smurf spent a little more than 1 month at the traditional high school before he started his career in an alternative program. About 3 months later, I started teaching at Nuestra Casa. I was Smurf's teacher for the next four semesters.

Toward the end of the second year that I was the boys' teacher at Nuestra Casa, we were informed that a district policy stated that students could only attend 2 years in a community alternative high school program. The policy meant that Smurf and six of my other students had to return to traditional high school. Smurf wasn't excited about having to go back to Brighton. He was nervous and scared. He knew he would mess up. "Messing up" was a fear all my students shared. I wanted to spend more time on my graduate studies, so I decided to stop teaching at Nuestra Casa and become their advocate. In the words of my students, I had their back. I would be there to support them. My students seemed to relax knowing I would not abandon them. Advocating was not new to me. As a teacher I believed part of my responsibility was to advocate for my students. However, I wasn't sure what my role would be as a full-time advocate. I reflect on my experiences in chapter 8.

At Nuestra Casa, Smurf was in class for 4 hours in the morning. All assignments were completed as a group, there were no bells, and breaks were taken as needed. I worried about Smurf's return to Brighton because he wasn't accustomed to a strict structure of bells and moving from class to class for an entire day. While registering the other students at Brighton, I heard about an alternative program on campus. The program convened for

4 hours in the morning and met on campus. I believed the program could help Smurf make the transition back into a traditional school.

With hope and enthusiasm, Smurf, Kristina, and I met with the director of the alternative program. The director explained the program requirements. She reviewed Smurf's transcript and agreed that this program was a good transitional step for Smurf's return to traditional high school. We all left the meeting feeling like the alternative program was best for Smurf. He was particularly pleased and excited.

The week Brighton High began classes, and 1 week before the alternative program was to begin, Murder, one of my students who had just graduated, committed suicide. When we reported to school, the kids were understandably still upset and mourning the loss of a homie. As I reflect back on that first day, I realize the events that occurred were a foreshadowing of what was to come. The day was also a classic example of how road blocks continuously materialized to keep the students out of the School Community.

My students and I arrived at Brighton early on the first day of school and waited for someone to tell us where the students' classrooms were located. Every time I think of the experience now, I want to laugh. I wanted so badly for everything to go perfectly for the kids. I wanted them to start off on a good foot and experience success. I probably should have known we were destined for trouble. As the kids waited, they shared memories of Murder, their lost homie. They laughed and talked. I told them to wait and I would find someone to help us get situated. When I returned a few moments later I heard the director of the program yelling at my students and I saw them clearly panicking. Loca turned to me. She looked like a deer caught in the headlights of a car. The director of the program informed me in no uncertain terms that I needed to tell my students that I was no longer their teacher. I wasn't going to confirm such an idea; there was no way I would abandon them when they needed me most. In my students' eyes, I was their teacher for life. I got the kids to settle down and eventually we headed for class.

Next I learned that Smurf wasn't completely registered, and they were going to drop him from the program he was so much looking forward to—with no exception. I had to think fast. I called Felipé to come and finish the registration process. Smurf did get registered and was in class later that morning. I walked to my car breathing more easily. I just knew things were going to work out, and the kids would be successful. I laugh today at my own naiveté.

I went to Brighton once a week to check on all the kids' progress. Smurf's teacher kept telling me, "Things are going well—no problems."

Every Friday, I picked the kids up and we went to lunch to celebrate the completion of the week. Smurf seemed to be adjusting well to school. One morning, I visited the boys before school. The bell rang, and Smurf told the rest of the students to head for class. I watched them head off. I believed Smurf and the other students were on the right track. In actuality, we were experiencing the calm before the storm.

During this time, I worked at a yo-yo factory with Smurf and his family. One day at work, Smurf came in notably upset. He was told that he had until Monday to get the "required points," or he would be dropped from the program. Smurf explained that in the new program, the students started out with F's or zero points, and it took 500 points to get a D. He didn't know how many points he needed to be at the D, or passing, level, but since he didn't have enough, Smurf was ready to quit. I told him there wasn't a problem. He could get everyone together this weekend, and I would help them get caught up to save his enrollment. As I talked with Smurf, I thought, Why would you want to start students who have not been successful in school with zero points?

The grading system had never been shared with me or the parents, and we had assumed it was like common procedures. I had checked Smurf's progress every week and his teacher had reassured me he was doing fine.

Thursday, Smurf came to work feeling better because he and the other students had planned to get together with me that weekend. I was excited! Smurf made a good decision in relation to his education. I knew things were going to work out, and I felt good—my naiveté talking once again. Smurf went to school Friday.

Kristina greeted me at work that day with, "I need to talk to you. Smurf was dropped from the program." She continued, "Smurf said he sat the complete morning being told everything that was wrong with him. He was also told he didn't earn his credits [at Nuestra Casa]. They were just given to him, and that you are not a real teacher." I had to calm Kristina down. I got on the phone to figure out what was going on, but my hands were tied. Smurf was too upset to talk, and he didn't want me to try to get him back in school. Felipé stated that he wouldn't put another son through what Lil Boy Blue had experienced. He remembered the frustration of fighting for Lil Boy Blue and wasn't going to let the school hurt his son.

Kristina and I decided we needed to let things settle down. Smurf didn't even want to talk about the incident. Smurf never returned to school. I believe this last school trauma was too much for Smurf. He was out of school for more than 1 year before I learned just how much going back to Brighton meant to him. We were driving to a music studio when Smurf shared his feelings. He said he had been excited about going back to campus, seeing old friends and going to school. He wanted school to be different, but school was the same old thing.

There seemed to be a common thread running through Lil Boy Blue's and Smurf's experiences. Education officials had the power and the final say. Juice's and Lil Garfield's stories were similar and intertwine so closely there came a time when their stories became one.

Within the first 9 weeks Juice was at Brighton High as a freshman, he was suspended for fighting and was failing all of his classes. According to Juice, he was tired of failing. He had heard about Nuestra Casa, and he decided to go there.

Juice was only with my class for about 2 or 3 months, however, before he transferred back to Brighton. His mother was released from prison. I remember having long talks to try to convince him to stay at Nuestra Casa because he could build credit. Brighton didn't take ¼ credits so he would lose his already earned credits if he transferred. But Juice's girlfriend was at Brighton so he made the transfer. I saw him only when he returned to visit the class. During those times, I asked him why he wasn't in school. He always responded, "I'm suspended." He did not complete that semester.

At the beginning of the fall semester, 1995, Juice registered for a second time, but he lasted only 1 week. He ended up at a third alternative school. During this year I was always aware of Juice and his activities even though he was not part of my classroom. He was part of the gang and he visited frequently.

During the fall semester of the 1996 school year, Juice asked me to help him with his credits. He was back at Nuestra Casa and having a hard time. I met with him a couple of times, trying to get his credits in order and helping him with the packets that were the "curriculum." Eventually, Juice was dropped from Nuestra. He spent the rest of that semester at home. The goal was to get him back into Brighton in January 1997, for the second semester of the school year.

Meanwhile, about 2 weeks into the 1996-97 school year, my students asked me if I would help Lil Garfield get back into school. I was aware that Lil Garfield was a member of the gang, and he was also an unofficial member of the class, having visited several times. I was happy to help Lil Garfield.

I stopped by the Alvarez house to set up a time to meet with him and his mother to review the papers that were sent from the school. Lil Garfield was serving a 10-day suspension. At the end of the 10 days, I took him to meet a counselor at the high school who had been helping me with my other students. She arranged a new schedule for him with new teachers who she felt would be willing to work with Lil Garfield.

Within a month, Lil Garfield was in trouble.

He explained, "I had to prove something tō somebody ... that I was something, that I wanted people to know that I'm gangsta'. I wanted a lot of people to know that I'm a loc, ain't no bitch ..." Lil Garfield had wanted his fellow students to know that he was "down" for his homies. He was suspended for another 10 days for what was labeled as sexual harassment and participating in an illegal group, a gang. A hearing was scheduled to determine whether or not he would be suspended for up to 60 days. Diane invited me to attend the hearing.

Lil Garfield, Diane, and I were ushered into a vice principal's office where we sat around a small table. Lil Garfield sat with his back against the wall. Two vice principals were present: the vice principal who suspended him and recommended long-term suspension, and a vice principal who was the hearing officer. The vice principals immediately took command. The hearing officer informed us that he had a checklist he must follow. I took the opportunity to record the hearing. The following is a partial transcription:

> Oct. 25th, 10:00 a.m. We are convening a hearing for Lil Garfield. Lil Garfield was suspended Oct. 14th for violation of codes 11, 10, 4, 3. Present Diane (Lil Garfield's mother); Lil Garfield; Debra Smith, advocate; Mr. P. representing Brighton High School, Assistant Principal; and Mr. B., Assistant Principal at Brighton and hearing officer. We have a checklist of things we have to go through here as a part of the papers we have to file. The purpose of the hearing is to do just that. Mr. P. will explain why he suspended your son. After he's through, then Lil Garfield will be given the opportunity to respond. All right, so at that point you have the opportunity to ask any question, to add any additional information ... present any witnesses or whatever you need to. My [assistant principal Mr. B's] responsibility is to listen and to make a decision as to what can and what will happen. (tape transcription of hearing, 10/96)

The meeting ended and we walked out to the car. I thought, the goal of the meeting was to complete due process, not to hear what Lil Garfield's mother said or I said. Why did we go? During the meeting, following the checklist seemed more important than Lil Garfield's education. The meeting ended when they had finished the checklist. We were informed that the outcome of the hearing would be mailed. Lil Garfield was given a long-term suspension. The suspension would end before the end of the semester. Lil Garfield would be allowed to return to classes, but would not receive credit. It was suggested that he withdraw for the time of the suspension and re-register when the suspension was over. This would also solve a related problem of 10 absences. Diane and I decided to keep Lil Garfield out of school until the spring semester.

I felt getting the boys registered before the start of the second semester was important, so we arrived at the school on the last day before winter break. I was told that Juice and Lil Garfield would have to meet with a vice principal—another surprise, because this requirement hadn't been shared with Juice's mother. I pushed to meet that day so Juice and Lil Garfield would be able to start class on the first day of the new semester. The secretary gave in and notified one of the vice principals.

The vice principal, Juice, Lil Garfield, and I sat at a round table. The vice principal asked the boys for their names. I thought it was strange that he didn't remember Lil Garfield. This was the vice principal who had suspended Lil Garfield only a month before. He addressed both boys together, and he also addressed them individually. He told them such things as, "If a problem comes up, you have to find a way to solve the problem so it doesn't interfere in school. Make the system work for you. I will assure you, if you don't, the system will grind you up. It makes no difference to me. I can write you off. Brighton is a bureaucracy. The main problem is to process paper." I wasn't sure what message he was trying to convey to the boys, or how it would help them be successful. They had been "ground up" by the system already.

The vice principal told Lil Garfield he needed to go to the library every day. He wanted Lil Garfield to promise he would go to the library. I thought, "Is this the answer to all the problems Lil Garfield deals with daily?" I mentioned that his mother worked and there was no transportation. The vice principal said Lil Garfield could ride the bus. I talked about money. He felt Lil Garfield could figure out a way and wanted a commitment from him. The vice principal wasn't volunteering to help. Lil Garfield gave the commitment and the vice principal was happy. Lil Garfield and I both knew that he would not go to the library every day.

The vice principal then talked with Juice. He pointed to Juice's teardrop tattoo and suggested he remove it. There was no talk of why he had the teardrop. I watched Juice manipulate the vice principal. He gave all the appropriate responses. I thought he was a smooth and bright operator. Juice knew the system. He knew how to answer the questions in such a way that the vice principal believed he was helping Juice.

The meeting lasted 30 to 45 minutes. We were then allowed to register, but our problems were not over. Juice did register and met with a counselor with whom I worked closely. Lil Garfield was told he could not register because his grandmother was his legal guardian, not his mother. This presented an interesting obstacle. Juice and Lil Garfield were half-brothers. Last semester, Lil Garfield registered and attended classes. All of the school's official letters and suspension notices were sent to his mother, not to his grandmother.

I told the registrar that his grandmother had passed away a year ago and that Lil Garfield had been living with his mother. I reminded the school personnel that he had registered last semester and that Juice was his brother. My explanations made no difference. I called Diane. She told me they had sent in papers over a year ago. We couldn't figure out why Juice could register and Lil Garfield could not. Eventually, the vice principal gave permission for Lil Garfield to register, but his mom was threatened that she had to take care of the paperwork right away, or he would be dropped. Several hours later, the boys were registered. It gave them a good feeling.

Juice and Lil Garfield completed the semester successfully. Juice completed the first semester of his high school career at the age of 16. He passed four classes. Lil Garfield didn't pass any classes, but he was never suspended. By summer, he wanted to turn things around. He reasoned, "If I'm trying to get an education, why get suspended for fucking somebody up when I could just [fight] after school." Both boys went to summer school and were able to make up some lost credits.

LITERACY IN THE SCHOOL COMMUNITY (I)

Families immediately encounter literacy events when they enter schools. The first literacy event is registration. Parents or guardians must complete several forms. One form requires accompanying print documents, such as utility bills, with the parents' names, or letters from landlords that have the parents' names and address, to prove the family resides within the attendance boundaries. I sat with several parents and completed these forms. It was a mechanical activity. Meaning was not constructed by the parents. They were simply trying to provide the information needed so their child could go to school. If the forms were not filled out correctly, as in Smurf's case, or if the participants couldn't prove they live within the boundaries, as happened to one of my other students, the students were denied entrance.

Literacy events and print were tied to every disciplinary action in this community. Once registered, the family was given a student handbook that detailed policies and rules. If a student was given a detention and must spend time after school, notes were sent home and documentation was filed. If a student was suspended, a letter was sent home explaining what the student did and their punishment (see Fig. 4.3). If a student was going to be suspended for more than 3 days a discipline hearing was scheduled. A letter sent home stated the rule that the student was accused of breaking, the section from the student handbook dealing with the rules and consequences, and the date of the hearing. At first, it appeared that the power in these events clearly belonged to the school administration, as was evidenced

Date:
RE:
Matri
Grade

Dear

This letter is to confirm the action taken concerning your son   He has been placed on a short-term suspension from 3/11/97 through 3/13/97, a period of three(3) days. The circumstances which require this suspension are:

> **Violation of Guidelines For Student Rights & Responsibilities: #11**
> **Date of Violation:** 3/11/97
> ILLEGAL ORGANIZATIONS: was observed by monitor throwing the "Westside" gang sign with his hands.

We regret that   actions made this suspension necessary, and I invite you to confer with me prior to his return to school.

            is to remain away from all classes and   School District school campuses and activities. He may return to school on 3/17/97.

Homework has been requested from his teachers and you may pick it up in the Counselors' Office. Calls regarding homework are made to the Counselors' Office, telephone number

We sincerely regret the necessity of taking this action, but this problem had to be dealt with firmly. If you desire any additional information, please contact me at

Sincerely,

Assistant Principal

c: Governing Board
      Superintendent
      Assistant Superintendent/Region IV
      Violence Prevention/Security
      PHS Administration

FIG. 4.3.   A letter notifying family of suspension.

when parents were told when to report; parents were never contacted to see what would be a good time for them. Likewise, parents and guardians came into a hearing with no previous knowledge about what procedures to expect and were therefore powerless to actively participate or disagree.

When Diane and I attended Lil Garfield's suspension hearing, we believed that if we explained Lil Garfield's situation, the school would offer support to help him succeed in school rather than kicking him out. The group sat down at the table together and I began to speak. I was immediately silenced. "Ms. Smith, excuse me, we have a checklist we must follow in order to maintain due process." Due process, we came to understand, required that Diane and Lil Garfield had opportunities to speak, but said the administrator's decisions were based solely on policy and their determination of the student's guilt. I saw that the real authority/power lay in the policy. Why were family members, students, and advocates allowed to speak when their words had no value or affect?

Lil Boy Blue's parents had had no power or recourse when they addressed the school board to try to get Lil Boy Blue back into school. Felipé, Lil Boy Blue's father, was told "they" (administrators, governing school board) had to follow procedures—decisions were determined by policies. Felipé asked me, "Why do I go if what I say makes no difference?"

School literacy in the classroom took the forms of worksheets, teachers' handouts, textbooks, work packets, notes on chalkboards, tests, research papers, book reports, and answering questions about chapters read. In the classroom, literacy was designed to show one's knowledge and to have it evaluated. An assignment Lil Garfield was given in summer school included alphabetizing words and adding suffixes to words (Fig. 4.4). In his English class, Lil Boy Blue was given a worksheet to learn when to use "a" or "an." Notice there were 72 words to which he was to attach "a" or "an" (see Fig. 4.5).

Far less visible and clearly unofficial, was literacy created by students in the School Community (I). As students met before and after classes and migrated from one class to another, they had time to converse with friends using literacy associated with their peers. Students passed notes to one another. They wrote messages on their notebooks and had pictures of friends and family in their binders.

THE SCHOOL COMMUNITY (I)

In this chapter, Debbie shared Lil Boy Blue, Smurf, Juice, and Lil Garfield's experiences in what is often referred to as "traditional school." Like many

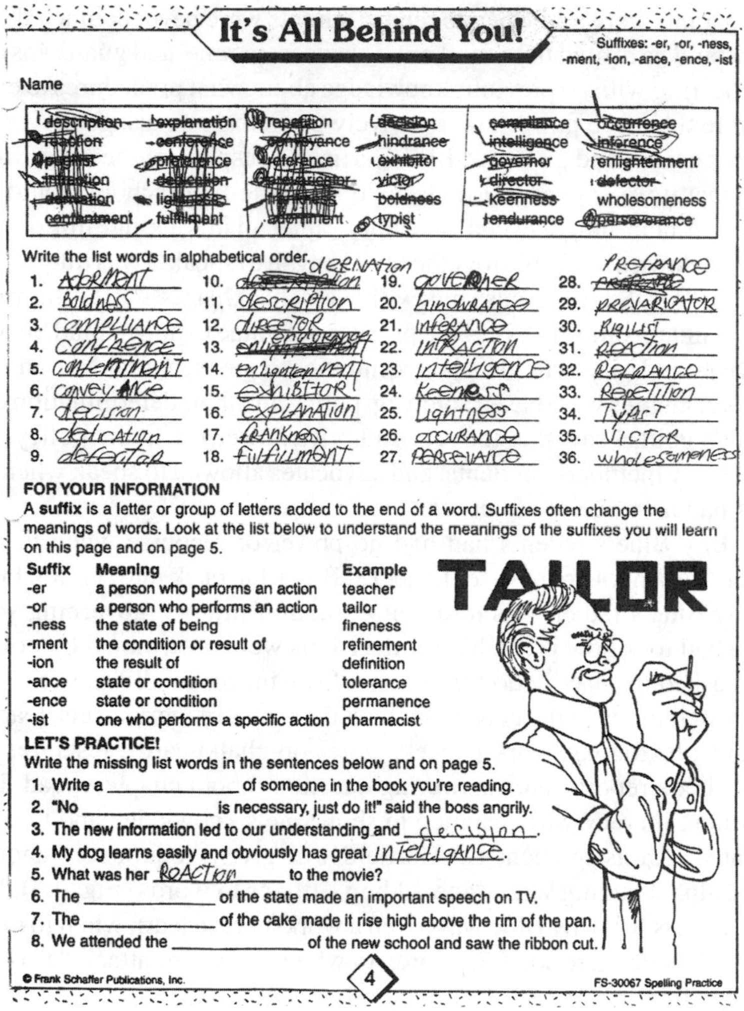

FIG. 4.4. Alphabetizing worksheet.

students, they had good times and bad times in elementary school, but overall they were successful. During their junior and senior high school years
they struggled to find a place in school and moved back and forth between
traditional and alternative high school settings.

Education is commonly, but mistakenly, held as the mechanism by which
the "American dream" can be reached by everyone. Schools are assumed
to be safe places to send children. For Lil Boy Blue, Smurf, Juice, and Lil
Garfield, school was the opposite. Every time Debbie's boys attempted to

Adjectives

Exercise 60

An adjective is a word that modifies a noun or a pronoun. EXAMPLES: He likes *oatmeal* cookies.
I need *two* more nails.
Some adjectives describe: *pretty, bright, smooth*.
Some adjectives show how many: *two, seven*.
A few adjectives point out: *this, that, these, those*.
An adjective derived from a proper noun is a proper adjective: *American, English*.
The articles *a, an,* and *the* are adjectives.

REMEMBER:

Use *a* before a word beginning with a consonant sound: *a* peach, *a* book.
Use *an* before a word beginning with a vowel sound: *an* elm, *an* apple.

A. Write *a* or *an* in each blank.

1. An ant	19. An author	37. An apricot	55. A library
2. A book	20. A egg	38. A elevator	56. An error
3. A chair	21. A tower	39. A newspaper	57. An automobile
4. A palace	22. A soldier	40. A highway	58. An envelope
5. An orange	23. A journey	41. A radio	59. A dollar
6. An American	24. An hour	42. A peninsula	60. A minister
7. A clock	25. A carpet	43. A college	61. A object
8. An evergreen	26. A island	44. An eye	61. A needle
9. A bank	27. An office	45. A merchant	63. A garden
10. An atom	28. A astronaut	46. A invitation	64. A compass
11. A school	29. A country	47. A class	65. A hospital
12. A patriot	30. An alligator	48. A bridge	66. An athlete
13. An Indian	31. A year	49. A ocean	67. An icicle
14. A ear	32. A shrub	50. A attic	68. A farm
15. A friend	33. An engineer	51. A melon	69. A allen
16. A letter	34. An honor	52. A oyster	70. An answer
17. A insect	35. An auditorium	53. A sentence	71. A window
18. A holiday	36. An adventure	54. A citizen	72. An accident

Subtract 1 point for each error.   Score: ....

FIG. 4.5. "A" or "an" worksheet.

break into the School Community (I) they were pushed out again, often literally pushed out the door through official acts of suspension and expulsion. They were frequently refused admittance by administrators who
shielded themselves with school policy. During their brief times in the
neighborhood public high school, they were pushed to the very margins of
the community when they were padded down, humiliated, and deemed failures on a regular basis. Regardless of their intentions, their parents' efforts,

or their sincere hopes to complete high school, they remained in the disempowered position of being "kept from participating more fully or legitimately" (Lave & Wenger, 1991, p. 36). Thus, they existed without access to resources or benefits. Their lack of membership, or as Lave and Wenger refer to it, legitimate *peripheral participation, was a source of powerlessness. Although Lave and Wenger (1991) suggest that "illegitimate" participation may not exist in their conceptualization of a community of practice, if illegitimate participation can exist, this must be a prime example. And while we accept and agree with Lave and Wenger's assertion that "peripherality" can be a positive and dynamic term and concept, especially for newcomers, we also call attention to their acknowledgment that peripheral participation must be "connected to issues of legitimacy, of the social organization of and control over resources" (p. 36), none of which were experienced by these students. The boys' "illegal" identity in one community of practice (the gang) denied them legitimate peripherality, much less membership, in another.*

The literacy found in the School Community (I) was cold and voiceless and actively marginalized these boys. The so-called "academic" literacy events of the classroom (such as the "a/an" papers) were, in essence, nonsense. They involved filling in blanks without thinking or voice. The boys were coerced into completing numerous worksheets because compliance meant they might "graduate." Focused on skills and drills in isolation from any purpose or meaning, the boys became "raw material, supposed, at the price of 'failure,' to comply and conform" (F. Smith, 1998, p. 56).

Much of the literacy events Debbie observed and the boys experienced at school was bureaucratic, rather than academic, and controlled the students and their families. Accountability and authority rested literally in the texts of school policies; administrators used print to validate their decisions and to abdicate responsibility for listening to students or attending to students' schooling histories. These texts defined Lil Boy Blue, Smurf, and Lil Garfield's identities at school as illegal and unsuccessful. They were "all forms of literacy used by those in authority to exercise power over those who are denied such liberty" (Taylor, 1996, p. 10). Taylor labels these forms of literacy toxic.

Lil Boy Blue, Smurf, Juice, and Lil Garfield, who were literate in the Family and Gang Communities, came to be viewed as having limited literacy at best in the School Community. The literacies they brought with them from their identities outside of school were not recognized. In short, they were not members of the club (F. Smith, 1998). Even more critical, literacy events in the School Community were structured in ways that sup-

ported and reified the school's definitions of who the boys were and the boys' beliefs about themselves. Juice articulated this position in the quote that opened this chapter. He wrote, "I still got a chance ... I don't want to mess up ... I'm going to try to stay up ...." Inevitably, Lil Boy Blue, Smurf, Juice, and Lil Garfield accepted the identity of failure constructed for them by school.

In chapter 5, the School Community story continues in Part Two (II) as Lil Boy Blue, Smurf, and Juice entered Debbie's classroom in the alternative school called Nuestra Casa.

5

School Community, Part Two (II): "This is our school."

Lil Boy Blue, Smurf, and Juice, along with Plucy and three other students, were attending Nuestra Casa, an alternative high school program, when Debbie was hired to be their teacher. In the district where the boys attended school, students who were suspended for longer than 10 days lost the credits they'd earned in the term. Students may have been given the opportunity to return to school in the same term, but the time they invested would not be equivalent to the credits they needed to graduate. As a result, suspended students often looked for alternative schools or programs where the credits they earned were transferred back to their home school. Lil Boy Blue, Smurf, Juice, and Lil Garfield attended both alternative schools and alternative programs.

In this chapter, Debbie tells the story of how she and her students learned from each other in the Nuestra Casa classroom and describes the boys' perceptions about themselves as good students. Lil Boy Blue, Smurf, Juice, Lil Garfield, and the other students taught Debbie about the gang and what their world was like. In turn, Debbie incorporated the boys' world into a new classroom curriculum. This curriculum consisted of literacy experiences that valued the boys and encouraged their input. This chapter describes how the boys and Debbie, as well as the other students in the class, became a different kind of School Community—one that evolved into a community of practice where all the students were full members.

94

JOINING NUESTRA CASA

When I became the Nuestra Casa teacher, about 12 names were on the role, but only six students showed up regularly. Smurf and Juice, along with several other students, greeted me the first day. A couple of days later, Lil Boy Blue came back to class. The official curriculum consisted of packets of worksheets, originally designed for migrant workers in California (see Fig. 5.1). As the students completed a packet, they took a test, which was 50% true and false, 50% multiple choice. They needed to score 75% to pass. If the students didn't pass, they could take the test over until they scored high enough to pass. Some of the students took the test without having completed the packet and failed, knowing they could retake the test as many times as needed. All they had to do was remember the right answer from their previous attempt.

US HISTORY A   UNIT V   31

1. Lincoln runs against Douglas in 1858.

2. Lincoln and Douglas differ most sharply over one topic in their debates.

3. On December 20, 1860, one of seven Southern states secede from the Union.

4. When Lincoln is sworn in as President, he makes a last effort to keep peace.

C. Answer the following.

1. Name the four candidates running for president in 1860.

a. _LiNCOLN_

BRECiYNiNg

c. _DOUGLASS_

d. _____

2. How did the South feel about Lincoln's election?

THE SOUTH WAS diSPleASed

3. List the seven states that seceded from the Union when Lincoln was elected.

a. _FloRidA_   e. _TEXAS_

b. _AlAMBA_   f. _MISSISSIPPI_

FIG. 5.1.   Worksheet from curriculum package.

I spent about 1 week observing this process. I quickly realized the kids came and went and did schoolwork when they wanted. I decided my first step was to develop continuity and structure—a learning environment—on which the students could depend. I anticipated that building a community (Peterson, 1992; Gillis, 1992; Whitmore & Crowell, 1994) would encourage the students to attend the program regularly and create the opportunity for them to learn and succeed academically. I knew I would need to work toward the students revaluing themselves as literate and able to accomplish school.

I decided to construct a reading course that would allow all students, no matter where they were in school, to receive credit for participation. The rest of the schedule could then be built around the reading course. My first step was to bring in books.

One day, I scattered about 12 adolescent novels on a table. I selected novels that had been read and enjoyed by my previous students in other contexts—books like *Running Loose* by Chris Crutcher (1983), *Too Young to Die* by Lurlene McDaniel (1989), and *Starting Over*, by Jesse Maguire (1991). I knew these books had worked well in my classrooms before, so I set them out on the table and watched what would happen. The students handled every book, looking at the front and the back, but they acted like books were strange objects. They never refused to read, they just simply didn't select any books to read. They walked around the table, looked at the books and then sat down. Smurf's, Juice's, and the other students' reactions to the books startled me. Their reactions expressed curiosity—turning the books over, thumbing through the pages, and placing them back on the table, but no one read. I thought maybe they had no experience with books.

Not wanting to believe that, however, I optimistically decided the problem was the types of books I brought to class, so for the next class meeting I brought books and magazines on topics I had heard the kids talk about. *Brave* by Robert Lipsyte (1993), *Do or Die* by Leon Bing (1992), and *Monster*, by Sanyika Shakur (1998) were some of the book titles. *Low Rider*, *Vibe*, and *Source* offered magazine reading choices. I also brought comic books that resembled characters from video games. This time the kids took the books and or magazines back to their seats. Not everyone read, but they all seemed to be interested. They thumbed through the books and magazines, maybe read part of a page and talked to each other about what they read. As I watched them I sensed they were hunting for something specific, but not finding it. As the weeks went by, some students read during reading class and some students sat quietly writing raps or tagging.

Lil Boy Blue, Smurf, Juice, and the other students struggled and fought doing anything that seemed like schoolwork. They hated the packets I was required to use. I decided to take some risk and design projects. The first project invited them to plan a trip around the world. I brought in lots of travel magazines and brochures I picked up from several travel agencies around town. I told my students to plan a trip around the world. They could go anywhere they wanted. At first they just studied the magazines and all the different countries. They talked to each other and then slowly they went to work. The Wall of China was the kids' first place to go, because they wanted to tag on the wall. Jamaica was also a place everyone wanted to go. My students believed good marijuana comes from Jamaica.

Two and a half hours into the project, Smurf realized they hadn't had a break. He insinuated that I was in trouble because I hadn't told them to take a break. I simply smiled as they left the room. Not every day was as successful as that day. Sometimes we struggled. There were days when everyone worked, days when some students worked, and days when no one worked.

On more than one day when it came time to read, Smurf reminded me, "I don't read, Miss. We don't do this here. Miss, if we wanted to read, I'd have stayed in school." On several occasions, Smurf led the group and reminded me that I was attending their school. They said when and what they were going to do, and they hated reading.

Smurf had strong feelings toward school. He often expressed them in his writing, and one theme of my teacher journal was Smurf's refusal to do work. There were days when he just sat and tagged or wrote raps. He did very little work on his assignments. Yet, the only time I remember Smurf being absent was when his life was threatened.

I wasn't aware of how much the gang dominated my students' lives until I handed out some poems written about gangs from a barrio in California. Smurf volunteered to read aloud. He read with no problem. As he finished he stated, "Miss, we don't like things that tell us gangs are bad. We're in a gang. We know what they are like."

He walked out the door.

I sat in silence, thinking. Gangs were a part of who the students were. They knew better than I how dangerous the Gang Community was. How could I assume it was my job to teach them about gang realities? I needed to respect these students. I realized that I needed to learn about gangs from them.

From then on the kids' gang culture became a part of my classroom. I watched them tag over the stories and worksheets. They tagged as they answered questions. They crossed the "B" out of multiple choice questions.

Posters they made for their projects were written in the tag style of writing and the hip hop style of drawing.

As time passed, I still struggled, and my new students still fought any aspect of the curriculum that looked liked school. I experienced times in my classroom when nothing seemed to work, as well as times when everything clicked. One specific day when everything clicked, I handed out a small collection of writings by other teens. The students read them. Referring to one of the writings, a student said the author was black. I asked how he knew. He said the words and the names that were used. Smurf read a poem out loud. Guero, a visitor, stated he thought the poem was stupid because girls could change easier than boys. The other boys agreed. I asked Smiley if she agreed and she said no, the ability to change depended on the girl and how involved she was with the gang. Smurf moved on to read the article on violence. He read the first page and Lil Boy Blue stated, "Blacks don't have it as bad as before, and they bring it onto themselves." Lil Boy Blue talked about how the blacks were slaves and how they got their freedom.

After some discussion, Smurf continued reading the rest of the article. Smurf read as though he were a robot. He had no emotions. He read about shootings and homies dying. All you could hear was Smurf's voice. Everyone listened. After the reading, they talked about the hood and the homies they had lost. Stories of their homies and of the gang were relived. The room took on a whole new feeling. These short poems led my students to share stories of their own gang and to challenge what the writers were saying. They struggled with their own prejudices and ideas about "others." The day ended; I took a deep breath.

I continued the routine of reading time, and I selected readings that I felt engaged their interests. On one occasion, I decided to read an article out of *Rap Sheet*. This day started as a day we struggled. Smurf and the other students were not ready to read. Lil Boy Blue, however, got a copy of *Rap Sheet* and started reading. He started talking to the other kids about what he read, and they got interested and started to read. He shared some quotes, and the kids asked questions and talked. They were reading and discussing what they read. They even looked through other articles. On that day, I observed my students' resistance to reading. Yet, I also watched Lil Boy Blue bring the group together and take ownership in the assignment. I was learning.

I kept asking myself why the kids refused to complete some assignments on some occasions, yet worked hard on others. I concluded that if an assignment had no relevance to them, they resisted. If an activity fit in their perception or definition of "school," they resisted. Yet, when the kids had ownership in assignments, and when they were exploring, they worked so hard they often forgot to take breaks. I believed the behavior my students exhibited at first—their resistance to reading and school—was related to their negative conceptions of "school" and "school learning." I believed they were resisting school because school had resisted them. Clearly, their refusal to do work wasn't due to a lack of ability.

Lil Boy Blue was always quiet in my classroom, but I noticed that when the students were just talking or telling stories, he participated. As I observed closely, I realized the whole class participated in classroom talk and storytelling activities. They frequently relived memories as they talked. I decided to sit back to listen and watch. Talking, recalling and sharing memories, and storytelling were very important to them.

I became more aware of the value of talk when I handed out copies of *Lowrider*, a magazine the kids liked to read. The day the magazine came, the kids went crazy. They sat and looked through the magazine cover to cover. They talked about cars, ads, girls, and parts of cars. They returned to the magazine, looked through the articles and talked more. This was the moment I decided to include talk in all aspects of the curriculum. From then on, all activities took place in groups where the students worked together, talked, and shared. Assignments took longer to complete with this procedure, but I started to observe small changes. I was required to use some of the packets, which the students (and I) hated. To get the packets out of the way, we sat around the table and worked together on the worksheets. Everyone talked, shared, and asked questions and the worksheets were completed. One particular moment occurred while we were talking about the United States government. As I explained how the President can veto a decision made in Congress, Lil Boy Blue sat with his eyes glued to me. He listened and asked questions.

At another time, to study the solar system, I asked the students to form groups and build models of the solar system. I placed a collection of material on the table and instructed them to go to work. Lil Boy Blue joined a group of two other students while Smurf joined in a different group. They worked nonstop. Each group worked on their own interpretation of the solar system. While working, students gave advice and helped each other. I observed my students enjoying school, taking risks, and learning.

My students had similar feelings toward writing as they did toward reading. They hated to write. Nonetheless, when I interviewed one of the kids long after my time at Nuestra Casa ended, we laughed as he told me the kids knew that no matter what happened, they had to write and talk about the experience in class.

During their storytelling the kids often referred to the Rock House, their place to hang out in the hood. They wanted me to see the Rock House, and I decided that the students might be more willing to write in their own environment. The Rock House was located in a field within the kids' neighborhood. Bushes, weeds and small trees grew up and around it. The Rock House did look like a house built from rocks. It was falling apart. The roof was only partially complete, and some of the walls were only half there. The striking characteristic that made the space feel like home, however, was the tagging on every part of the building.

We decided to take a trip to the Rock House to write. We met at the school and traveled together to the Rock House. There was no place to park by the house, so we had to hike in a couple of hundred feet. Once inside and after some stories were told about the place, I told the students they needed to find a quiet place to write—everyone had to stay within hearing distance and they had 15 minutes to write. After 15 minutes we would come back together to share what we had written. The students went in search of quiet places. Some students stayed in the Rock House, preferring to sit together; some climbed boulders or found fallen logs in the area to sit on. After the 15 minutes we came back together to share, and the kids did share. Smurf shared a rap, and two other students read freshly composed poems. Some kids wrote about Oso and the cross on the mountain.

Soon the group moved out to write for a second 15 minutes. I watched five of them work. Their moving pencils implied that their thoughts were flying. Writing at the Rock House seemed to be easier for all of the kids than writing in the classroom had ever been. After sharing a second time, we drove to a nearby pizza joint to eat. I was raised with six brothers and have watched them munch down food, but this was a different experience. While the group inhaled one pepperoni, sausage, or cheese pizza after another, more stories were told. I listened in. Later, as I wrote in my researcher's journal, I realized I'd learned more about the kids' world to be sure. I had also learned that they were writers.

There were three computers locked up in my classroom. One morning, I got the key and unlocked the cabinets. My students arrived and moved straight to the computers. We spent almost the whole morning learning three different programs: a word processor, Wheel of Fortune, and a banner program. Smurf learned to operate the computer with ease. He taught the other students. One morning, I arrived to find Smurf and Sad Boy at the computer writing a story. They read the story to the class, and the other students got involved by making suggestions. I heard Smurf say, "No, we want it real life." Sad Boy and Smurf talked about writing a book. They gave me the disk to save—protect. They worked several days on the story (see Appendix D). They didn't want to be interrupted during their writing.

As I said earlier, not every day was a "good" day. As a class, we struggled. My students were somewhat successful, but they also still resisted doing schoolwork. We learned together. I learned to celebrate the little successes, such as the students showing up to class and taking risks to work on some of the assignments. As Lil Boy Blue, Smurf, and the other students started to feel success, they worked more and seemed at times to enjoy school.

I later asked Lil Boy Blue, "What do you think about Nuestra Casa?"

He said, "It was bad. It was easy to do the work."

A little concerned with his answer, I asked, "What made it easy?"

"The environment, not worrying about the strict rules."

For Lil Boy Blue, an environment that accepted him and didn't hassle him made being successful in school possible. Ironically, during free write times, Lil Boy Blue often wrote about how much he hated to write, but as he gained trust in the school and in me, he took risks and wrote more. My class wasn't hassle free, because I often had to strongly encourage Lil Boy Blue to do his work, but I knew Lil Boy Blue worked full-time and wanted to graduate. We worked together to make graduation a possibility.

Smurf's response to the question about Nuestra Casa was similar to his brother's. He stated, "There we didn't get treated like we did everywhere else. It's just the way they treated me. I didn't have to ditch there [Nuestra Casa]. I guess, I mean, it's only 4 hours and not even that sometimes. I don't know, it was just … it was nothing you had to ditch. You know what I mean, like you didn't have to be there. Well, you know, we had a special time to be there, but you didn't get sent to lockout if you weren't there." Smurf had a hard time explaining what made Nuestra Casa different from his other school experiences. He didn't want to suggest that Nuestra Casa was an easy school. Smurf felt good in my class so he had no reason to ditch.

As my 2 years at Nuestra Casa came to a close and students were exiting and going back to traditional school, we decided to make our own yearbook. As the yearbook project progressed, it came to represent the School Community (II). My students had complete ownership in the project. They chose the pictures, they included poems they had written, and each student designed their own page. They wrote in their own language about their own topics. As the deadline grew closer and the writing process moved toward revision and editing, we talked about audience. Who were they making the yearbook for? They decided they would be the audience rather than their parents or other outsiders so they included photographs and terminology that would otherwise be inappropriate. This meant conventional high school yearbook features took on community-specific characteristics. A good example is the awards the class gave each other, which included "biggest pants," "smokes the most," and so on.

THE BOYS' VIEWS OF SCHOOL

When I first met Lil Boy Blue, Smurf, Juice, and Lil Garfield, I believed they hated school and saw no value in it, but as I got to know them, I discovered I was wrong. Extensive interviews shifted my beliefs from assumptions and stereotypes to new understanding. The interviews were sometimes planned and formal and sometimes completely spontaneous as I interacted with the boys in and out of school. I took every opportunity I could to see the boys' worlds, particularly related to school and literacy, from their points of view.

I asked Lil Boy Blue why he didn't give up on school after the experiences he had.

In Lil Boy Blue's nonchalant manner he said, "I don't know, I was determined. I always said I was going to graduate. I just wanted to do it."

"Do you think graduating from school made that big a difference?"

"Just knowing that I did graduate, that I didn't give up through all the shit they did give me." Lil Boy Blue reflected angrily on the principal, who in his mind, started the whole problem, "Lot of people stick out like the principal. She got on my nerves cause she didn't give a shit. Just wanted me out of school and that she didn't give a shit about me getting back into school."

"Lil Boy Blue, do your parents feel school is important?" I asked.

He replied, "Yeah. My dad made [graduating] really important. They made it seem when we were little, you're going to graduate it's something you got to do. We always thought they [graduated]. We found out later that neither one of them did, so that made me want to graduate even more."

"Would you describe a successful student?"

"Somebody who stuck with school from day one, passed all their classes all through high school," he said.

"Do you consider yourself a successful student?"

"I don't know, maybe, through all the stuff I went through ... I wish I had done things different and stuck with school. Graduated with my class, with my friends."

I saw changes in Lil Boy Blue during our shared experience at Nuestra Casa. He participated in every topic—history, science, a current article in the newspaper, or a TV show. He listened and asked questions. When he was interested in Al Capone, I checked out several books on Al Capone for him to read. For a period of time he came to class sharing different facts he had read the night before. He wanted to know and understand. Lil Boy Blue told me, "I like to learn. I like to know about [different things]. Sometimes I will turn on the TV to the Explorer channel. I just watch it to learn about different things." Lil Boy Blue valued education. He acknowledged that he made wrong choices and didn't blame the school. I was amazed by the strength and resilience Lil Boy Blue demonstrated by coming back to school when the School Community said, "We don't want you."

When talking about school, Smurf composed a short rap:

Fuck school

never paid attention

tell ya the truth

the only thing I learned was suspension.

Smurf's rap about school expressed a feeling toward school that still exists in him today. Smurf once told me, "School and I don't see eye to eye." I wanted to know if Smurf valued school, so I asked, "Is school important to you? Do you think school is something kids should do?"

He didn't hesitate, "Yeah, if they have the chance, I do."

"What do you mean by chance?"

In a contemplating voice, he answered, "I don't know why, but I guess [going to school] seems like the right thing to do. I would want my daughter to go to school, but just some people—well everybody has a chance. Well, not everybody got treated like how we got treated."

I had to ask, "If things were different, if you were treated differently, would you have stayed in school?"

"Yeah, like if we would have stayed at Nuestra Casa, probably yeah. Because there we didn't get treated like we did everywhere else."

Issues concerning the treatment of kids surfaced in many of my conversations with Smurf. As Smurf shared his feelings, his voice became angry, "How do [school officials] expect somebody to learn if they're pulling you in the office worrying about your clothes more than about worrying about ya getting an education. Worrying about your haircut and your tail, earrings. They were more worried about my appearance than they were about if I was learning or not."

I decided to probe more about his visits to the office, "How often were you pulled into the office?"

"All the time."

"What did they do?"

"Gimme clothes to change my shirt, change my laces, tell me not to wear them again. Most the time just waiting."

"You mean like sitting around?"

Smurf said, "Yeah. Just keep lecturing us. Like this guy, 'Let me tell you about gangs this and that' and I said, 'Hell, what do you know about gangs, you never been in one.' You know what I'm saying? They thought they knew everything, the answer to everything. They weren't in the positions that we were."

In other words, Smurf's visits to the office required listening to someone tell him about the gang culture he lived every day. My students were not allowed to wear more than one article of clothing that was the color blue. The Crip gang color was blue. It was significant that the school color was also blue, meaning other students could wear as much blue as they liked to signify school spirit. Smurf, however, had to change his clothes or go home, and many times he just sat waiting.

I wanted to know if he saw a difference between school and education. He replied, "School is more like they are forcing you to learn and education is like you want to learn."

I asked him if he felt he was a learner. He went so far as to say he was a teacher.

"A learner ... I consider myself a teacher in my music," said Smurf. "Like I told you earlier, my teachers used to tell me I could never do what they did. I could never teach, and like I said, I mean, I could if I wanted to go to school and all that, but I wouldn't want to. But I am a teacher, but in a different way and that's my raps. I can teach people in my raps. Like the rap I made up the other day. I've been there. I've done it and I survived by my skills. I didn't survive by luck. It's like I think I could teach some people some stuff in my rap and my music."

Smurf answered my question about being a learner by talking about being a teacher. I asked again, "Do you see yourself as a learner?"

Smurf repeated the question back to me, "Am I a learner?"

"Yeah; if you take school completely out of the picture, are you a learner?"

"Like I said, I want to go to the music thing to learn about it, to learn how they do it. I mean music is my thing. I can't go straight to what I learn about. I tried that so I am trying to go around to learn everything about music, every kind of music equipment there is to learn."

Again, Smurf could not say he was a learner. He did point out that he wanted to learn about music and that he could easily see himself as a teacher. However, I believe his perception of himself as a learner was tied closely to his idea of being successful in school. I decided to ask him, "How would you describe a successful student?"

"Ahh, somebody that took a dream, made it all the way. They got their dream, they're doing what they always dreamed of."

Smurf's answer had nothing to do with school. "Are you a successful student?"

He responded, "Nah. I'm working on it. I'll be there in the next 3 years … could be 3 or 4 years from now could be 1 month from now." He laughed and picked up his daughter saying, "Going to take time, huh honey?" For Smurf, school was out of the picture. Being a successful student was about reaching one's dreams.

I asked Smurf, "What makes a teacher a good teacher?"

"You're the only … well I liked other teachers, but you're the only teacher … I don't know, that I can say actually made me think about school at all. I still don't like school, truthfully."

"What do you think is the difference between the other teachers and me?"

"Some people probably say that you let us get away with everything, but I don't think it was that. I think it was that you understood us more than anybody. That's all it is, you understood us. You didn't know what we were going through, but you tried to look at it from our point of view, but that's all and you listened to what we had to say."

Smurf emphasized that a good teacher takes the time to understand her students, to listen to them, to see the world through their eyes. While he continued to talk about what made a good teacher, he took a jab at the curriculum: "The teachers were boring. I think they need to do something with, what's it called, curriculum. I think it needs to be renewed or something because it's like too old, man. That's why everything is too boring, because, like, you didn't make us do the old curriculum. You made us do what was going on these days. We learned the same thing that everybody else learned, but we learned it differently. Because we learned it through things these days."

"Do you mean more current?" I asked.

"Yeah, because you ask everybody what is their most boring subject and it's mostly history, and the whole curriculum is based on history. They need to change it. They're trying to get kids ready for the future, but teaching them the history. I mean, in a way, it makes sense, but in a way it doesn't." Smurf struggled with what he believed about teachers and school, but he knew that what we did at Nuestra Casa was "better."

We studied both world history and United States history in our classroom so I believe Smurf wasn't referring so much to the subject of history as he was to the method of teaching and making learning relevant. We told stories from history and used movies and historical fiction to make history come to life. These multiple sources made dialogue about history and the current events exciting. Everything we did tied directly to my students, their gang, and their worlds. After reading from *Night* (Wiesel, 1982), my students wanted to know why Hitler hated the Jewish people. I asked, "Why do you hate the Blood gang?" As we discussed this question, we moved on to identify differences and similarities between what happened in WWII and what is happening today among the gangs.

I discovered I couldn't push Smurf. At first he refused to work, but as we learned to trust each other Smurf did work and completed many assignments. When I first met Smurf his immediate response to an assignment was always no! He had no intention of doing the assignment. So I went about my activities helping and talking with other students and acted as if Smurf was doing the assignment. All of a sudden, there sat Smurf working on his assignment! I never was sure what triggered the change. He just had to have his time to decide to work.

Even though Smurf claimed that he and school "never saw eye to eye," he knew what made the School Community (II) a different and better place than the School Community (I).

Juice's high school experiences were never positive. Yet, he continued to try to get into school and earn his diploma. He didn't want a GED. I asked him, "Do you think school is important?"

Juice answered without hesitation: "Some of it. I think reading and writing and learning your math skills, and I guess if you want to learn your history you should learn it, but how in the hell is that going to help you later in the future, you know what I mean? Like if you want to, you know what I mean, I think you should have a choice: what you want to be educated in high school to what your goals are and to what you want in life. To see where you want to go. Take your classes." Juice's voice got stronger, and he spoke with conviction: "I think they should sit down with you and help you pick your classes. They just give you a sheet and say, 'Pick out your classes.' They don't care, and if you're lucky, you get the classes you want. I think school here doesn't really give us a chance. Back in the days, I thought school was very important. But now that I'm in the community I'm growing up in, you don't really need that. You need to be street smart. You don't really need an education other people are taught, you just need it to fit into their world."

Interested in his phrase "fit into their world." I asked, "Education helps you fit into the white man's world?"

"Yes. This ain't ours. This isn't our country. It's the white man's country, you know what I mean? If they tell us to jump, we ask how high do we jump, you know what I mean? To get to where we want to go, they can humiliate us. They can tell us whatever they want and stuff like that, but if you want to be successful, you're going to have to take it. You have to swallow your pride, that's the way I see, that's the way I was raised, but education doesn't help me survive on the streets. Me, myself and my streets smarts I picked up over the years is what is helping me to survive over the streets."

Juices's statement about "they can humiliate us" came from several experiences he had in school. One particular example of a humiliating experience stands out more than the others. A teacher smelled marijuana on Juice. Now, students cannot get into trouble for smelling like marijuana. They must be smoking or in possession of marijuana. But Juice was sent to the office where he was made to stand in the middle of the room as several school officials and secretaries walked around him, sniffing for a scent of marijuana. He eventually was ordered back to class, but the experience humiliated him. Juice never tolerated this type of experience on the streets.

While we were talking, Juice shared another school experience with me in which he sat quietly feeling humiliated. "When one of us says 'MISS,' the teacher says that's a southside thing. Why is it a southside thing? Because that's where the Mexican's culture is." Juice learned that the southside—the Mexican side—is different. He learned that he was inferior because he grew up on the southside. His teacher had communicated that to him. When I think about Juice, the one thing that stands out the most is his need to be respected. Yet, in his eyes, to be successful in school, he had to give up respect and be "humiliated."

I asked Juice about the way teachers treated him or showed him respect. He responded, "Teachers just say it [harass us] because they know if we talk shit to them they can just send us to the office. Of course they will take the teacher's side over the student's. You know what I mean? They're going to listen to the teacher. No one listens to the student, you know what I mean?"

I asked him what his thoughts were about the school he was attending at the time. He said, "Kino says they care, but they are always calling in the thugs into the office and talking shit all the time. They just be walking down the hall. They look into a classroom and they'll see one of us. They say, 'I need to borrow what's-his-name,' or whatever, so and so, or they may take you to the office to make up some bullshit lie, like some stupid shit."

"Have you been called into the office?"

"I've been called in three or four times."

"You haven't done anything. They just call you because of who you are?"

"That's the way I feel. We look high, they call us in. When we walk out of the school, they're looking at us."

Juice was constantly called into the office or watched. At Brighton, a monitor was stationed to watch the table where Juice and his friends sat at lunch time. Juice believed educators didn't want gangsters in school at all. He told me, "Actually, I feel like if you're a gangster they really don't want you for school, or if you're pregnant they don't want you for school, or if you're a different culture or race sometimes they wouldn't want you in school. Betcha if I went to [name of a different school] or something they probably won't accept me." School never seemed to be a place where Juice received any form of respect.

I asked Juice if anyone in his family ever talked to him about school and college. Juice said, "My tia and tata. They told me I can be anything I want to be, just put my mind to it. Seriously that is the truth, but they just say anything, you can be anything you want to be and you're like 'damn, yes, I could.'"

"How many of your family have gone to college?"

"Actually my tia [aunt] went to college and that's the only person in the whole family that's ever graduated from college except my cousin, she graduated from college."

"What about high school?"

To my surprise (some of my own stereotyping was surfacing), Juice said, "Everybody graduated from high school."

Juice wanted to graduate from high school. He didn't want to be the only one in his family without a diploma, so he kept going back and trying. I asked, "What are the characteristics of a good student?"

"Characteristics of a good student is a person who shows up to class on time, stays in class for the whole period, listens to the teacher. He does his work and hands his work in on time. Doing everything right."

"How do you describe yourself?"

"Me, I'm just the type of student that goes whenever I feel like it. I try my hardest to be on time, but I get distracted really easy. That's one of my main problems. I get distracted really easy then I go into class and just talk to people, and if there's girls, I just chill. Then when I see other people do their work, I just go up to the nerd, and I just talk, say 'Bro, what do we have to do? Can I copy off ya?' Yeah, yeah, they want to fit in, too. You know what I mean, fool you know you're like one popular fool in the school. You know, 'It's cool, copy me' and I just copy off them. I just hand it in, you know what

I mean. That's cool or I just read it and put it in my own words, shit like that you know. What I mean it's easy like that. School's easy like that. That's the lazy way," explained Juice.

"What do you consider good grades?"

"A's and B's and C's. I think C's are kind of low-life, but I think A's and B's are good grades."

"Where would you put a D?"

"Low-life category."

I wanted to challenge him a little and stated, "You're still passing with D's."

"I know that. I think it's just like averaging D. Not average. I think average and below are low-life."

"Really. What about your grades?" I challenged.

Juice answered honestly, "Yeah, cause I can do way better than that. I used to get straight A's and B's and stuff like that, so I know I can do it, but I'm just too lazy."

"Considering everything you have been through, describe yourself as a student."

"I'd describe myself as a good student, a smart student, a nice student, a cool student. I like to joke around and stuff like that, but I also listen. I can talk and listen at the same time or I just talk and not listen. I do whatever I can do to survive." He discovered something about himself as he continued, "I went from DAMN ... I went from good to shitty and picked myself slowly and slowly trying to pick myself up, but I can't forget about the past. That's what's keeping me down." Not too happy, Juice realized what had taken place. He went from good grades to "shitty" grades.

Our discussion continued, and I asked Juice who his favorite teacher was and why. Juice said, "You." We laughed. "Since kindergarten, you. You are my teacher. You are my favorite teacher."

"OK, how did I become your favorite teacher?"

"Because you try to help us. You're like the only teacher that I ever knew that ever cared about anybody."

"What about your other teachers?"

"I had a lot of nice teachers, but not teachers that ever cared about how we ended up, or who we're going to be. You know what I mean? You made sure we don't get cheated out of our dreams and hopes. You know what I mean? You won't let the government get our dreams and hopes and just crush them. Everybody has their goals." As I listened I discovered that being a nice teacher wasn't enough. Teachers need to "care" according to Juice.

"If you were in charge of teacher education, what would you teach teachers?"

"I would teach them to, if they didn't want to be a teacher and they didn't really want to help the kids, then don't be a teacher," said Juice, "I would tell them to just walk out the door. Because that's what teaching is all about. I think it is when you really try to help somebody. When you take the time to sit down in the classroom to just work with a person, I think that's a teacher. You know what I mean? A teacher cares. You know what I mean? That gets on you to hand in your homework. You know what I mean? You don't do it, you're going to do it right now. I am going to see you, and I want you to read it, and everything. You know what I mean? That's, I think that's a person that cares, that's a good teacher not a teacher that just says, 'This is your assignment, this is how you do it, blah blah and so this and that,' and you turn it in. 'Who cares if you even turn it in? It's less papers for me to grade anyway,' you know what I mean? Because they're lazy, all of them. I would tell them that."

Juice believed in school. He believed that an education could make a difference. He believed teachers—good teachers—cared. Teaching and caring belong together. Being street smart was important to Juice, but he had dreams that took him out of the street. I decided to ask him, "Do you think a high school diploma will get you out of your situation?"

"It could, but I'll still be in Tucson. What I really think is if I join the military, I'd be out of that situation. If I join the military, that's like my ticket out of Tucson, out of everything." A high school diploma is necessary to join the military. Juice needed the diploma, but the military offered a way out of Tucson and the gang for Juice.

I only had Juice as a student for a short time at Nuestra Casa, and he, like Lil Boy Blue and Smurf, resisted at first. I did have the opportunity to observe Juice taking risks and reading on several occasions before he transferred back to traditional high school. What was most interesting was that when he came to the class as a visitor he joined in and participated in all activities as if he was enrolled and receiving credit. Something about the School Community (II) compelled him to engage.

Lil Garfield had his ups and downs in school. Like his brother, he kept coming back. He wanted to be successful and get his diploma. I once asked him why he skipped school if he wanted to be successful. We sort of laughed; he couldn't really answer the question, except to say, "I just keep fuckin' up."

While driving around town, I asked Lil Garfield, "When you think of school, what pops into your mind?"

Quickly, Lil Garfield said, "Stereotyping, a lot of [teachers] do."

"Do you feel that is something they have done to you?"

"Yeah, I feel like you're wearing your blue shoes and blue shirt. They all, you know what, try to kick me out or whatever." He continued, "Oh, your brother is Juice. Oh, so, well, you're a Crip. Just cause he's Crippin. Not even giving you a chance."

"What good teachers do you remember—what good memories do you have?"

"My fifth grade teacher, she like paved the way for me to do good, you know what I mean?"

"What's the difference between her and your other teachers?"

"There's a big difference. A lot of teachers, they don't give a fuck about you. They don't give a fuck about your education. All they give a fuck about is the check. There's only some that are left that take time, really take time, not just go over basic shit."

Lil Garfield believed caring and taking time made a teacher a good teacher. We continued to talk. I asked, "What is your overall impression of school?"

"School's pretty dope. Well, it matters how you kind of make it for yourself, but you know. You can go over there and fuck around, get fucked up grades, get suspended you know. Or you go and try and do good, get good grades. It matters how you make it."

"If you made it and you got good grades and all that stuff, what do you think school will provide for you after you get through?"

"Well it should, high school should provide ... a good education, job opening. But like you know, for like a high school diploma, college, sometimes it is how you make it, but sometimes, you know, people stereotype you. How you dress? How you walk? What color you wear? How you look? The color of your skin, so there's lot of that." He added, "It is very important, 'cause I want my tata to see that I'm doing good, and that I'm what he wanted me to be. Second of all, I need an education if I want to do good."

"Is there a difference between school and education?"

"Yeah, school is a building with rooms. Education is something that stays with you. Ain't always going to be in that same building, but if you keep on, you know, you want to learn and you put your mind to it that's education that's going to be with you later on."

"Can you get an education without going to school?"

"Yeah, there's lots of education. There's street edu ... you know, you can grow up on the street education. It just ain't by the books. There's different things. Well, life situations."

I asked, "Describe yourself as a student."

"Pretty good, depending on how I feel that day."

"What are the characteristics of a successful student?"

"Someone that's focused, someone that's on task, does what they gotta do, does homework. They got a question and are not afraid to ask."

With that in mind I asked, "What do you consider are good grades?"

"A's and B's and C's."

"Where would you put a D?"

"It's passing, but ain't way up there. Got to get at least a C average."

"Do you consider yourself a successful student today?"

The answer did not come as easily as the others. He said, "Well ... with all the setbacks that I had, I'm just barely trying and starting learning."

Not satisfied with his answer, I asked, "If you just look at today, do you consider yourself a successful student?"

Again, not sure how to answer, he said, "Mmm ... hell yeah, but I fuck up, too, just as much as anybody else, but I am doing way better."

I asked Lil Garfield why he failed in ninth grade. Replying honestly, he said, "It was more like, I didn't give a fuck. I was sidetracked by people and gangs."

"It wasn't the fact that you may not have had the ability to do the work?"

"No. I could do it. I'm lazy. I didn't like doing it. I'd rather smoke a joint than do homework."

Lil Garfield wanted to believe that school could make a difference or, at least, that school should prepare you for a better job. However, he still came back to the problem of stereotyping he saw in school. We then talked about the school system and "playing the game." "I don't think it's the matter of playing the system," he insisted. "It's the matter of doing what you got to do."

For Lil Boy Blue, Smurf, Juice, and Lil Garfield, school was more complicated than just liking or hating it. When school was considered the enemy, I watched them refuse to do work or to be a part of it. At Nuestra Casa, school felt different. I watched my students work hard to complete the assignments they needed to get a high school diploma. I saw tension in their multiple identities and watched them wrestle "success vs. failure" as they defined it and as it was defined for them.

LITERACY IN THE SCHOOL COMMUNITY (II)

Some of the literacy found at Nuestra Casa was similar to Brighton High School. Most obviously, although there was no handbook, there were numerous bureaucratic texts such as registration forms, withdrawal slips, and signed contracts between students and the school. Literacy in my class-room was quite different, however. The students were encouraged to write on topics they chose and to fuel their writing with their lived experiences. Smurf often wrote raps, but he also took risks and wrote poems and multiple journal entries on his feelings about school, the gang, and the loss of homies. Lil Boy Blue was a resident expert on Al Capone. Multiple texts—books, movies, newspapers, short stories, and magazines, often associated with the hip hop world—were considered legitimate academic texts. Students' work was valued and placed on the walls. Student-generated literacy had a legitimate place in the classroom for academic as well as interpersonal purposes. The students tagged on their personal property, such as their own notebooks. I kept a big piece of butcher paper on the wall for the students to write/tag/draw on whenever they chose; at one point the class used the paper to list and define gang terminology (see Fig. 3.9). They created this list to help me keep track of their vocabulary. I accepted and encouraged all types of reading and writing. The students wrote on topics of their choice, and their written products ranged from poems to stories to plays to rewriting fairy tales. Figures 5.2 and 5.3 are two pages of Lil Boy Blue's renditions of "Little Red Riding Hood." Opportunities to legitimately control classroom writing and to talk and share meant there was no need for subversive note passing. Reading and writing, in whatever form, were ways the group made meaning around events that were important to their personal and social lives.

I was required to use some of the Nuestra Casa curriculum worksheets, but they were secondary to the extensive work the class completed to do real content-based learning. To make the mandated worksheets more tolerable, the class gathered around a table to work together. I read the questions and the students debated the information and shared answers. All our assignments were about discovering knowledge together in problem-solving activities, and I altered anything I could about "school" to invite students to engage in literacy.

THE SCHOOL COMMUNITY (II)

Lil Boy Blue, Smurf, Juice, and Lil Garfield regularly agreed that they were made to feel they didn't belong and weren't wanted in the neighborhood schools they were supposed to attend—what we refer to as the School Community (I). They all found their way to Nuestra Casa, an alternative high school program, where Debbie was their official teacher for four semesters and their advocate as they continued their educations in and out of various

"Lil boyblue'z hood"

once upon A time
there WAS CRIP name Lilboyblue.
One day Lil boy blues mother had just
got done drying out some home grown herbs

mother: LiL boyblue can you take some herbs to
grampA O.G. milkweeds house Across the hood.

Lilboyblue: Cool, well mom jus hook me up with A joint
for the WAlk

narrator: So Lilboyblue was on his way threw the
hood when he dicided to take A short
cut threw the Aleg. when he met up
with Iceyblue.

Iceblue: Whats up cuzz whats in the bag?

Lilboyblue: Some weed for my grampA.

Iceblue: Hook me up with some.

Lilblu: nAH. my grampA will get piss!

narrator: So Lilboyblue walk off. And Iceyblue
was piss And decided to cut threw the
hood And beat him to his grampAs house
so he could jacc him.

FIG. 5.2. Lil Boy Blue's rendition of Little Red Riding Hood, page 1.

schools and programs. *The School Community (II), with similar features to the Family and Gang Communities, was a community of practice in which the boys had all the knowledge and access they needed to achieve full membership. The boys' membership began the moment they stepped over the threshold of Debbie's classroom door as themselves. They wore the clothes they were comfortable in, they used the language they knew, they had no need to hide or shed the identities they owned in their Family and Gang Communities. With their multiple identities intact, they could learn.*

Lave and Wenger's (1991) view of membership in a community of practice "suggests a very explicit focus on the person, but as person-in-the-world, as member of a sociocultural community" (p. 52). As such, "participation is always based on situated negotiation and renegotiation of mean-

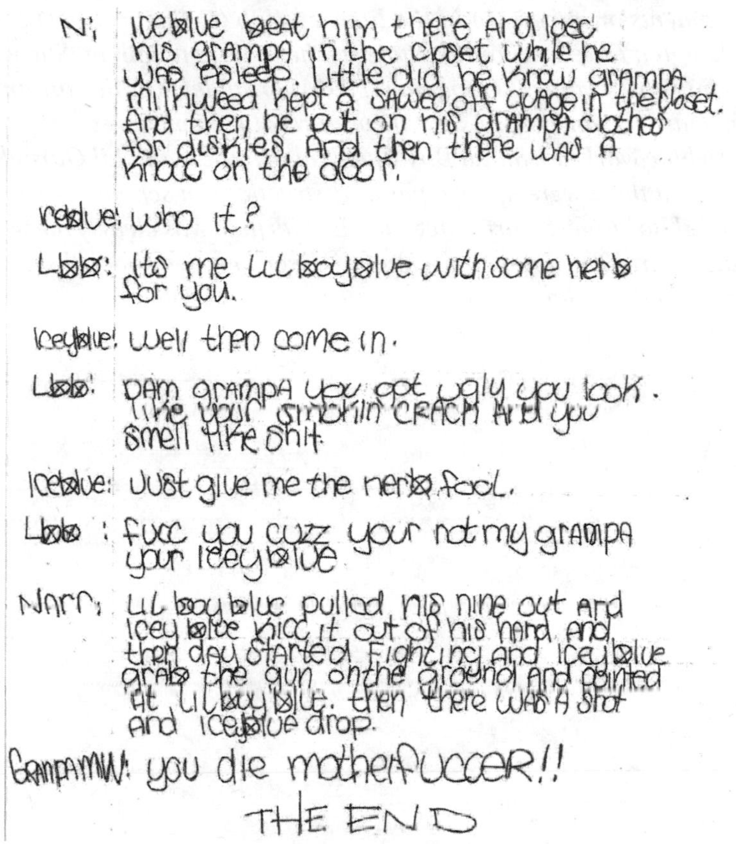

N'. Iceblue beat him there and loce his grampa in the closet while he was asleep. Little did he know grampa milkweed kept a sawed off guage in the closet. And then he put on his grampa clothes for diskies. And then there was a knocc on the door.

Iceblue: who it?

Lbob: Its me ul boyblue with some herb for you.

Iceblue: well then come in.

Lbob: Dam grampa you got ugly you look. like your smokin CRACH And you smell like shit.

Iceblue: Just give me the herb fool.

Lbob: fucc you cuzz your not my grampa your Iceyblue

Narr. ul boyblue pulled his nine out and Icey blue knoc it out of his hand and then day started fighting and iceyblue grabe the gun on the ground And pointed it at ul boy blue. then there was a shot and iceyblue drop.

Grampamilk: you die motherfuccer!!

THE END

FIG. 5.3. Lil Boy Blue's rendition of Little Red Riding Hood, page 2.

ing in the world" (p. 51). Debbie accepted the boys as legitimate members whether they were newcomers or visitors, sanctioned students or observers, readers or taggers. Whether they rapped or sat silent. These actions meant all her students experienced legitimate peripheral participation that signified membership in the community. It meant that the boys developed an identity *as members of the group; "learning and a sense of identity are inseparable: They are aspects of the same phenomenon"* (Lave & Wenger, 1991, p. 115).

Membership in the School Community (II) was enabled as Lil Boy Blue, Smurf, Juice, and Lil Garfield's literacy from the Family and Gang Communities was incorporated into legitimate schoolwork. In this community, students and teacher had equal opportunity to teach and learn. Debbie *made students' membership in the literacy club (F. Smith, 1998) a given, even though it took time for the students themselves to join in. She worked incessantly to "revalue" (Goodman, 1996) her students as literate and successful learners, and she pushed them to revalue themselves.*

As Debbie worked with Lil Boy Blue, Smurf, Juice, and Lil Garfield, she learned that there were many types of distractions in school. One distraction for Lil Boy Blue, Smurf, Juice, and Lil Garfield was clearly the world of juvenile court. The following chapter describes the effect the Juvenile Court Community had on these students, and the role the courts played within their formal education.

6

Juvenile Court Community:
"In and out of juvie."

Lil Boy Blue, Smurf, Juice, and Lil Garfield became participants in the Juvenile Court Community when they allegedly broke the law. Lil Boy Blue became a participant when he brought a gun to school. Smurf's participation was a result of the drive-by incident that caused Oso's death. Juice and Lil Garfield became participants as a result of domestic violence and alcohol abuse. During the period of time surrounding the study, Smurf served time in the juvenile correctional facility, commonly referred to as juvie *by the boys, Lil Garfield spent time in a residential rehabilitation center, and all four boys were on probation.*

When minors are placed on probation their lives are changed, and the effects are felt in the Family and School Communities. Probation marked an overlap of the School Community and the Juvenile Court Community and necessitated Debbie's entry into the boys' relationships with the courts and her learning about legal procedures. For example, although probation reports, which contain a section on school expectations, include the order: "Shall attend school every day, every class, on time, with good behavior, and demonstrate academic progress," there was no support for the boys or their parents to find a school that would accept them as students. Debbie was an advocate (not always successfully) for the boys during these times.

In this chapter, Debbie shares distinct occasions when court-ordered probation kept Smurf, Juice, and Lil Garfield from attending school or directly interfered with their attempts to be successful at school. The stories from these occasions are structured by telling Debbie's personal experiences and perceptions as she attended court sessions and by retelling discussions she had with the boys' parents. They reveal the boys' restricted "participation" in the Juvenile Court Community and highlight how liter-

117

acy events in the court system kept the boys and their families from becoming members of the community of practice.

ENTERING THE JUVENILE COURT COMMUNITY

Smurf entered the *juvie* world when he was arrested after the drive-by shooting that caused Oso's death (see chapter 3 for a complete description). This incident took place before I met Smurf, so I put the story together through stories I heard from Smurf and his parents. The drive-by took place at 11:00 pm. At 10:00 the next morning when Kristina and Felipé Espinoza arrived at the police station, they learned that Smurf was being sent to the juvenile correction center, charged with one count of a drive-by shooting and one count of aggravated assault.

Smurf served 3 months in juvenile detention, followed by strict probation known as *JIP* (juvenile intense probation). Smurf never talked much about going to court or being detained in the juvenile detention center, but he occasionally described what the towels were like, the fact that they didn't have shoes (only slippers), and that they had to check out tennis shoes to play basketball, which he never did because they were "crusty and you don't know who wore them." In *juvie* Smurf attended classes for school, but the work was computerized worksheets. The guards or staff handed out pencils which, according to Smurf, were about 2 inches long. The inmates could check out books, but they were books like the Babysitter Club series.

Smurf didn't talk much about the trial, either. He didn't understand what took place. All he remembered was going before the judge about once a month where he was told he hadn't learned his lesson. Kristina and Felipé corroborated that Smurf went to court at least once a month to be told he hadn't learned his lesson and ordered back to the juvenile correction center. Minutes from such an event are in Fig. 6.1.

I was confused as I listened to them recount this incident. No one was clear about the charges against Smurf. Felipé stated over and over that Smurf never fired a gun. Kristina talked about going every month to the courts not knowing if Smurf would be able to come home. The judge continued to state that he wanted to make sure Smurf understood that a young man's life was lost. Oso was like a brother to Smurf. Smurf wasn't allowed to attend the funeral service or to mourn with his friends and family. Smurf understood a lot more than the judge.

Smurf was allowed to come home a little before Christmas after 3 months in juvie. The condition of his release was to be on JIP which is dif-

⎦E TWO   DATE: ████████   CASE NUMBER: ████████

████████, previously sworn, is examined and cross-examined.

State's Exhibit 11, being an 8" x 10" color photograph, is identified.

State's Exhibits 7, 10, 3 and 8, previously identified, are admitted.

████████ previously sworn, is examined and cross-examined.

State's Exhibit 12, being a diagram, is identified.

State rests.

████████ makes a Rule 20 motion and argues same to the Court.

████████ argues the motion to the Court.

IT IS ORDERED that Minor's Rule 20 Motion is denied.

Defense rests. Both sides rest.

Counsel make closing arguments to the Court.

████████ argues the Motion to Suppress to the Court.

IT IS FURTHER ORDERED that Minor's Motion to Suppress is denied.

THE COURT FINDS, beyond a reasonable doubt, the minor guilty of the
offense of DRIVE BY SHOOTING (Count One).

THE COURT FINDS that the State has not proven beyond a reasonable
doubt the offenses of AGGRAVATED ASSAULT (Count Two and Count Three).

IT IS FURTHER ORDERED that the minor is adjudicated delinquent as to
Count One, DRIVE BY SHOOTING, a class two felony.

IT IS FURTHER ORDERED that Count Two and Count Three are dismissed
with prejudice.

████████ moves for minor's release from detention.

████████ recommends release.

████████ objects to the minor's release from detention.

* * *

* * *

████████ Deputy Clerk

FIG. 6.1.   Minutes from Smurf's appearance in court.

ferent than regular probation. He was assigned a surveillance officer
(*SO*)—a police officer whose responsibility was to watch Smurf, and a
probation officer (*PO*)—an officer of the court designated to make sure
the conditions of his release were met. The SO and the PO had the authority to enter the family home at any time, day or night. Smurf was ordered
to actively participate in either school or community service for 32 hours
every week. Once a week he turned in a plan outlining his weekly activity
to his SO. Smurf was not allowed to participate in activities that weren't

written on his "weekly planner." No spontaneous family drives to a restaurant or to visit relatives. No walking down to the park with friends. The SO had to be able to locate Smurf at any time during the day or week. If Smurf was not where his weekly planner said he would be, he could be arrested and locked up.

When I started teaching at Nuestra Casa, Smurf had been out of the juvenile correction facility for about a month and a half. I was about to learn what having a SO and PO was like for Smurf as a student and for me as a teacher. Like the family home, the PO and SO had full access to Smurf at school. My classroom had to be open to the students' probation officers, and they entered and/or pulled Smurf out several times without even acknowledging me, much less asking my permission. Smurf lived in fear that his PO would show up unannounced. Every time he took a break, he reminded me not to tell his PO. I was never sure what I wasn't supposed to tell, because Smurf always did what I asked him to do. One day Smurf was leaving the room for a break and turned to look at me. I said, before he could, "You don't need to remind me about your PO." He smiled as he went out the door. Smurf never left the Nuestra Casa grounds when he took a break or did anything to break his probation. Yet he was always afraid that he was going to get in trouble. The fear of doing wrong often carried over into our assignments and sometimes meant that assignments weren't completed.

I discovered just how real Smurf's fear of getting in trouble was when I re-entered the classroom after a break. Smurf confronted me with, "Miss, my probation officer was just here and he saw me tagging." Smurf explained that part of his probation was the "gang condition." He wasn't allowed to associate with students who were in a gang, dress in gang apparel, or do anything that is associated with gangs. Tagging was considered a gang activity. I was a little confused because the probation officer had approved Smurf going to Nuestra Casa, a high school program that many gang kids attended. It was inevitable that he would work alongside other gang members. I calmed Smurf down, and spoke to his probation officer to explain why I allowed my students to tag in class. The PO informed me that the tagging in my class was inappropriate. I was startled—really taken aback. I thought, "How do you know what is appropriate in my classroom?" I took a deep breath and explained to the PO why I allowed the kids to tag.

As a Nuestra Casa teacher, my goal was to establish a learning environment where all students had equal access to knowledge and all students were supported to take risks. As a professional educator, I made a decision to bring my students' lives into the classroom. Tagging was their writing, so tagging became part of my classroom. I also wanted to learn and gain a better understanding of tagging. I placed a big piece of butcher paper on the walls. My students had permission to tag on this paper and not on school property.

I informed the PO that the students were preparing a presentation about tagging for a graduate class at the university. I'm not sure what the PO thought, but he moved on and Smurf was not in trouble. Even after the shock of this interaction wore off, I was amazed that the PO felt he could tell me what was appropriate for my classroom. Meeting Smurf's PO was the beginning of my relationships with many probation officers.

There was another specific time when Smurf's probation officer came into my class, which not only upset Smurf but disrupted the whole class. The PO poked his head into the classroom and summoned Smurf to follow him. The PO didn't feel obligated to talk with me or to inform me he was removing Smurf. A little concerned, I quickly walked up to him and introduced myself. Without being asked, I informed the PO about our current classroom activity and emphasized that Smurf was being successful in class. I thought knowing what was going on in class and how Smurf was performing was the information a PO would like to hear. I was brushed aside. The probation officer took Smurf into the hall.

My students at Nuestra Casa were a ready-made community—the gang. When Smurf was removed from the class, all work came to a standstill. "Will Smurf be OK?" was the big question and concern. I noticed many of the students took time to go to the restroom so they could conveniently walk down the hall. They were making sure he was okay. I'm not sure what they thought they could do, but not knowing what to do didn't stop them from caring. I felt uneasy myself. Why did this visit cause so much concern in my classroom? I decided to take the time to talk with the probation officer. My goal was to reinforce the fact that Smurf was being successful at school and completing what I asked of him. I joined Smurf and his PO again in the hall. As I talked about the different activities Smurf was participating in, I noticed a change in Smurf and realized the PO had no interest in what I was sharing.

Instead, the PO informed Smurf that he was wearing too much blue. I started to question the PO because Smurf was dressed in a grayish bluish shirt, grey pants, and blue tennis shoes. I asked, "What do you mean too much blue? What is too much blue?" The PO pulled at Smurf's necklace, which was macrame blue with religious pictures, gesturing that this was too much blue. I knew Smurf's mother bought the necklace to help him deal with Oso's death and the confinement of the probation when he was released from *juvie*. I started to challenge the PO until I observed a very submissive Smurf. His stance changed dramatically. His head went down, his eyes looked at the floor. He asked no questions and gave no information other than to respond to all the PO's questions. He addressed the PO with "sir." Not knowing what was really happening, I followed Smurf's lead and decided not to ask questions or to challenge.

After Smurf was dismissed, I took the opportunity to ask the PO about his job. He informed me that he was an advocate of the court, not the adolescent. His job was to make sure the adolescent followed the court order. This visit resulted in Smurf being placed on 30 days house arrest for wearing too much blue. I began to understand Smurf's fear.

After the PO left, we had to put "school" aside. Smurf and the kids talked about the experience. They became the teacher and I was the learner. I asked Smurf why he didn't question the PO or tell him about the necklace. Unanimously, the students informed me that they don't question or share too much information for fear they will get in trouble.

Learning takes a back seat when students continuously worry about someone coming without warning to remove them from class and chastise them. I learned I could provide Smurf with a safer environment if I became more proactive. I started calling and informing the PO about our activities and how Smurf was doing. I also took the opportunity to meet his SO. My advocacy strategies before events, rather than after the fact, facilitated the SO's decision to allow Smurf to participate in all our class activities, including field trips, as long as I took responsibility as the teacher and made sure the PO and SO knew what was taking place.

My work with Juice introduced me to a new fear associated with probation—the fear of getting locked up. Juice was on probation when I first met him. In an argument with his brother, Lil Garfield, Juice picked up a knife and threatened to use it. He never served time in the juvenile correctional facility for his actions, but he was found guilty of one count of domestic violence. Although I wasn't sure if I understood the stories accurately, because I was aware of the tension that often existed in Juice and Lil Garfield's home, I decided that asking questions about the incident was unimportant. There was no need to stir up old feelings.

Like Smurf, Juice's probation stated he had to be in school. The problem for his family, however, was locating a school that would accept him as a student. Juice and I checked out several schools. The alternative programs had long waiting lists. At Brighton, which was his home school, he would not earn any credits. Juice's mom, Diane, and I believed that attending school for no credit would only lead Juice to trouble. Even though not being in school was a violation of his probation, his mother and I decided to keep him out. I called his PO and informed her of our decision and plan. She said as long as we were trying to get him admitted, Juice would not be in violation of his probation. There was no school, but as long as we pretended we were looking he would not be locked up.

The second semester of the school year 1996-97, Juice was admitted to Brighton High School for credit. He attended classes and stayed out of trouble. One day Juice announced to me he wanted to play on the school baseball team. I saw this as a big step, because it indicated that Juice was seeking ways to join the School Community. I was bursting with pride. As an advocate and a friend, however, I also felt a need to protect Juice. I was a sports coach in my earlier teaching years, so I knew that getting cut from a team is a hard blow and realistically making the competitive team would be hard for him. Juice played baseball as a young kid and shared stories of how good he was when he played in little leagues, but that was a long time ago. Juice and I discussed these issues and he still wanted to try out for the team.

Juice picked up the permission slip and found out when everything needed to be turned in and when tryouts began. I let him borrow my baseball glove and I bought him a batting glove. He was ready. I picked him up at his home the morning of tryouts and took him to school. He was nervous, but he was ready. The counselor allowed Juice to keep his equipment in her office. There were still some road blocks, such as fees, but we were systematically removing obstacles when they emerged. I left school excited. I wasn't convinced that he would try out, but he was in the position to make his own decision.

Halfway home my pager went off. My students and their families were the only ones who knew my pager number. I thought, "What could be wrong?" I called the number on my pager. It was one of the *homies*, who said Juice had been arrested. I called Diane. She didn't know what was going on. Juice had been doing so well staying out of trouble and attending school. I rushed back to school. Lil Garfield was sitting in the counselor's office. The counselor was trying to find out what had happened. No one seemed to know what was going on. The two vice principals and three secretaries who were located in the office where Juice was handcuffed claimed they didn't know. All anyone would tell us was that Juice's PO and a couple of police officers were waiting for him. I could hardly believe that a student could be handcuffed and hauled off the school campus without anyone knowing why. Eventually, Diane's calling, my calling, and the counselor's calling uncovered that Juice was arrested for violating the condition of his probation that stated, "The adolescent shall contact the probation officer by phone once a week." As Juice had turned his papers in to the secretary so he could practice baseball, he was arrested, handcuffed, taken out to the police car, and driven to the juvenile detention center because he hadn't made his weekly phone call. Through it all, students and school officials watched.

The school counselor and I attempted to convince Juice's PO that he was doing excellent work in school and that this was an important day for him. The PO said there was nothing she could do, that he was going to have to stay locked up for the night and have a court hearing the next day. No one heard how important this day was for Juice and his success in school.

I believe Juice hadn't called his PO because he was doing well, and calling reminded him that he was in trouble. The PO never called Juice or checked with the school about his progress. Juice violated his probation by not calling his PO and had to be held accountable. The fact that he was doing well in school made no difference. Police officers handcuffed him and hauled him off in front of several students. He was going to be locked up for the 2 days set aside for trying out for the team.

In all fairness, the PO did call the school later and made arrangements for Juice to try out when he was released from lock up. Trying out on tryout days was hard enough for Juice; trying out on a special day proved to be impossible.

As a result of the arrest, the PO informed us that she was going to have Juice switched to the PO on campus. Juice was petrified. I met with the PO and explained to her how important feeling safe in a learning environment was for Juice to be successful at school. He would not be able to learn if he was always worried about someone looking over his shoulder, worried that for the least little thing he could be hauled back to court and locked up.

A few days after the hearing that occurred as a result of the missed phone call, things were getting back to normal, or so I thought. Then I got a call early in the morning, before school. "Miss, I want to go to an alternative school," Juice said. I was shocked. "What is the problem?"

"I won't let them lock me up again. I will run first." In Juice's eyes, school was where you got caught. Juice missed school that day. He said he was sick. I believe he was afraid.

I took Juice to breakfast and learned that he had missed 2 days of school. Juice was afraid the teachers would be mad. I'm not sure why he felt the teachers would be mad. He felt like he had "messed up."

Before Juice was arrested, he was learning to take risks at school. He wanted to be a part of school sports. He no longer saw himself just going to school; he was willing to take the risk to become part of the School Community.

"Let's go talk to the counselor and arrange a time to meet with your teachers," I suggested. I hoped that by meeting with his teachers, Juice could see he was doing okay. During the meeting, the counselor changed Juice's first-hour class to "office aide." As the counselor's aide, Juice handed out passes and delivered messages. Having class with the counselor helped Juice relax, because he trusted her. I took a breath of relief, because I believed we were back on track.

As the semester progressed, Juice started to have success again, but the fear of getting locked up stayed with him. On several occasions he stressed his fear of going to school. "They can get you easier at school," he said.

Lil Garfield's experience was different than Smurf's or Juice's, but just like in the previous stories, going to school for Lil Garfield meant education took a back seat to the desires of the courts. Lil Garfield was placed on probation after I got to know him. He was charged and found guilty of domestic abuse. During a mother–son fight, Lil Garfield's mother, not knowing what else to do, called the police and charges were pressed. Again, because I was aware of the tense and emotional family situation, I decided not to ask questions concerning the fight. I did however, have several opportunities to meet with Lil Garfield and his lawyer and to attend court with Lil Garfield and Diane.

My observations of Lil Garfield's interactions with his lawyer caused me to question how many resources and what kinds of knowledge were available to help him. A typical meeting took place a couple of minutes before we entered the courtroom. Lil Garfield had to make some decisions, and he didn't know what to do. He asked me and I didn't know what to tell him. Lawyer confidentiality—the security that conversations between lawyers and their clients stay between them—meant that the lawyer only met privately with Lil Garfield and that I wasn't privileged to the content of their talk. How does a 15-year-old boy make a decision when he doesn't understand the law? Several comparable sessions that focused on decisions about future courses of action occurred, and Lil Garfield never knew what to do. Dissatisfied with the way things were going, we discussed obtaining a new lawyer. I learned we needed to write a letter to Lil Garfield's court-appointed lawyer and ask him to step down so a new lawyer could be appointed. I also learned that the lawyer first assigned to a case stays with the defendant until he or she leaves the juvenile court system. We never received any response to the letter we submitted. Lil Garfield's lawyer was never changed. Lil Garfield was placed on probation.

While Lil Garfield was on probation he was picked up several times for being drunk, which was obviously a violation of his probation. His PO tried to get him into a residential rehabilitation center for teenager drug and alcohol abuse. Needless to say, we were in and out of court several times, but I was not always sure what the various court sessions were about. Sometimes the reason to return to court sounded like the lawyer wasn't ready. Sometimes the court session was to set an appointment for the next court date. This went on for about 4 months.

During this time, Lil Garfield attended an alternative high school in the district. He had some success in his classes, passing enough to continue the next quarter. He was no longer ditching classes and wanted to go to school. Just about this time, the court ordered him to attend a 30-day, live-in residency rehabilitation center for teenager drug and alcohol abuse. An opening in the center came in December. Lil Garfield got permission to stay home for Christmas, but he had to enter the center December 27 during a break between the second and third quarters at school. The quarters lasted 9 weeks. Lil Garfield would be in the center for 4 weeks.

Neither court officials nor his PO were worried about the educational ramifications of these orders. The courts never contacted the school to make arrangements. Diane and I contacted the school, but the school would not give us a guarantee he would be able to attend the following quarter. All the alternative schools had waiting lists, so we would need to start the whole registration process over again if Lil Garfield was to continue school. Lil Garfield had been experiencing success at school; maintaining that success was important. Now his education was placed on hold.

I am not suggesting that the court order for rehabilitation was wrong. It is notable, however, that education in the abstract, and school registration in the literal, were not considered in the decision. No arrangements were made to assure his continuation in school.

Over the time that I worked with him, Lil Garfield had shifted from not going to school and being in trouble all the time in school to attending every day and being successful. His progress was not recognized as important by the courts. The single goal of the court was to punish him. Getting him back into school following punishment was left up to the parent.

LITERACY IN THE JUVENILE COURT COMMUNITY

Several literacy events automatically occur upon entry to the Juvenile Court Community. Before entering a court session, when a family can't afford a lawyer, they must complete a financial statement (see Fig. 6.2). Families are assessed according to income and how much they can pay a month for a lawyer.

IN THE SUPERIOR COURT OF THE STATE OF ARIZONA
IN AND FOR THE COUNTY OF ████

J U V E N I L E   C O U R T

In the matter of: Juvenile No.

A Person(s) under the age   AFFIDAVIT OF FINANCIAL STATUS
of eighteen years

I ,_____, being first duly sworn, upon oath,
deposes and says:

    That the following information is being furnished for the
purpose of assisting the Court to determine whether or not the above
named minor(s) and/or his/her parents are entitled to Court appointed
counsel, and to determine the amount of Court Costs, Support Fees,
etc., which may be assessed at a later date.

Full Name_____Date of Birth_____

Dr Lic#_____SS#_____Tele#_____

Address_____City_____St AZ Zip_____

Mailing Address_____ '' ____City____ '' ____St_Zip_ '' _

           Age__39_____   Marital Status__Single__

Other than yourself, how many people do you support in your
household?_2_

Children_2_ Ages 15-17 _Adults_____Ages_____
                 7hrs Daily
(X)Employed ()Full-Time (X)Part-Time ()Unemployed ()Student () Other

Employer Disabeled AmeRICAN VeteRANs Tele#_____

Address_____Contact_____

Spouse's Name_____Dr Lic#_____SS#_____

Spouse's Employer_____Tele#_____

Address_____Contact_____

Contact: (Supply Two References: Name, Address, Telephone Number)

TOTAL MONTHLY INCOME   (Must Report All Household Income)

Your Monthly Gross Income_580 00____Net Income 500 00__
Spouse's Monthly Gross Income_____Net Income_____
Other Monthly Income_____
Public Assistance _Food Stamps_301 00_
              _____
              (List Programs)
*TOTAL MONTHLY GROSS INCOME _____ TOTAL MONTHLY NET INCOME 801 00
CAO (04/94-2)   880 00

FIG. 6.2. Financial statement form from the court.

After a hearing and when a juvenile is placed on probation, the juvenile
and parent sign a probation order. The order is a generic form that reads like
a contract to repay the community (see Figs. 6.3 and 6.4). The court official
checks the conditions that dictate what the defendant is allowed to do and
not do in four areas (community, accountability, competency, and other).
The orders are directed to the parent or guardian of the minor and state the

IN THE SUPERIOR COURT OF THE STATE OF ARIZONA
IN AND FOR THE COUNTY OF ⬛⬛⬛⬛
JUVENILE COURT

In the Matter of)
)
DOB:) JUVENILE NO:
person(s) under the age) ORDER OF PROBATION
of eighteen (18) years.)

IT IS HEREBY ORDERED that the above-named juvenile be placed on Probation
for _one year _____ or until further order of the Court, under the
care, custody and control of _____ subject to the
supervision of the Probation Department under the following terms and
Conditions:

CONDITIONS OF PROBATION ORDER

COMMUNITY PROTECTION
_X_ 1. Shall obey all laws.
_X_ 2. Shall not leave the State of Arizona without permission of the Court.
_X_ 3. Shall obey the reasonable rules of your parent(s), guardian(s) or
custodian(s).
_X_ 4. Shall not possess, use, or carry a gun, firearm, knife, or any
other deadly weapon.
_X_ 5. Shall abide by a _6:00 p.m. to _6:00 a.m. curfew unless in counseling,
at work, on house arrest, or modified by Probation Officer.
_X_ 6. Shall not associate with anyone on Probation, Parole or gang
affiliated_____ : _____.
___ 7. Shall not go on the premises of _____.
___ 8. Shall be placed on the Post Adjudication Monitor (electronic monitor)
for a period of _____.
_X_ 9. Shall submit to fingerprinting and identification photography as
required by Probation Officer.
_X_10. Shall not possess/ use any illegal substances.
_X_11. Shall abide by [X] Gang Conditions; [] RISE Conditions.
_X_12. Shall not change residence without prior notice to Probation Officer.
___13.

ACCOUNTABILITY
___ 1. Shall make (earn/ pay) restitution in the amount of $_____.
Shall compensate victim(s) as follows:
$_____ to victim _____.
$_____ to victim _____.
$_____ to victim _____.
Payments are to be received by the Clerk of the Superior Court and shall be in
the amount of $_____ at the scheduled rate of _____.
___ 2. Shall participate with the Restitution Accountability Program (RAP)
and comply with all program conditions.
___ 3. Shall repay the community through _____ hours of community service
work to be completed by _____; provide written proof to
Probation Officer.
_X_ 4. Shall confirm drug and alcohol free lifestyle by providing specimens
for analysis or breathalyzer as directed by Probation Officer.
___ 5. Shall develop understanding of victim's perspective by participating
in a victim offender mediation session or a crime impact panel as
arranged by Probation Officer.

FIG. 6.3. Official form for probation, page 1.

conditions they must agree to follow. My students and their parents signed
the probation form, followed directions, and did what they were told.

A second constraint, known as the "Gang Condition of Probation" may
also be ordered by the courts. This was a common probation order for my
students. Smurf was placed on juvenile intensive probation which required

___ 6. Shall provide a written apology for their actions to the victim, _____ to be submitted to Probation Officer by _____.

_X_ 7. Shall contact Probation Officer by telephone or in person [X] once a week [X] every _Monday_____ or [] as directed by Probation Officer; and follow all reasonable directions of your Probation Officer.

___ 8. Shall pay a monetary assessment of $_____to the Clerk of the Superior Court by _____.

___ 9.

COMPETENCY

_X_ 1. Shall attend school every day, every class, on time, with good behavior, and demonstrate academic progress at

_X_ 2. Shall participate and complete the following skills group and/or counseling program to the satisfaction of your counselor and/or Probation Officer; _

___ 3. Shall attend and complete a General Equivalency Diploma (GED) program by _____; provide copy of certificate to Probation Officer.

___ 4. Shall actively seek and maintain employment. Until employed, shall participate in the Community Renewal and Enrichment Through Work (CREW) Program for _____ hours, _____ times per week.

___ 5. Shall participate in a community activity as directed by the Probation Department _____ [state activity].

___ 6. Shall attend _____ [] Alcoholics Anonymous (AA) or [] Narcotics Anonymous (NA) meetings per week; provide proof of attendance to Probation Officer.

___ 7. Shall abide by all the rules and regulations of the following placement or day support program; _____.

___ 8.

OTHER

Per Arizona Revised Statutes (A.R.S.) 8-235, the Court may make an order directing, restraining or otherwise controlling the conduct of a parent or legal guardian and may invoke its Contempt Powers for Failure to Comply.

_X_ 1. _____ parent(s)/ guardian(s), or custodian(s) shall comply with the following orders:

_X_   a. attend and cooperate with counseling and parent training classes as arranged, or if deemed appropriate by Probation Officer, counselor, or day support program by _____.

_X_   b. report any violations of Conditions of Probation by the minor;

_X_   c. provide or take responsibility for transportation of the minor for purposes of compliance with Conditions of Probation;

___   d. complete _____ hours of community service work with [] son/ [] daughter; and,

_X_   e. not change residence without prior notice to Probation Officer.

___ 2. Shall per ARS 8-241G pay $_____ Probation Fee and ARS 8-290.28 $_____ Victims'Rights Fee.

I understand the Conditions of my Probation. I also understand that if I violate any of these Conditions, it could result in the revocation of my Probation and placement with the Arizona Department of Juvenile Corrections (ADJC), until I reach the age of eighteen (18).

JUVENILE:_____   _____   DATE:_____

PARENT OR GUARDIAN:_____   DATE:_____

APPROVED AND SO ORDERED THIS ____   ____ day of __   _____, 19

_____
JUDGE OF SUPERIOR COURT

FIG. 6.4.   Official form for probation, page 2.

yet another form. This generic form can be adjusted according to what the judge orders by "filling in the blanks."

As I sat in the sterile court room on more than one occasion with the boys and their families. The waiting area was filled with chairs situated in clusters of twelve. The courtroom itself was relatively small and uninviting. The judge was symbolically positioned up front, as well as actually elevated above all other participants. On one side of the judge was the court clerk. In front of the judge, two tables were located in a curved arrangement. The district attorney sat with the probation officer at one table, and the public defender and the accused sat at the other. There were rows of chairs behind these officials for family members and people who were waiting their turn in front of the judge. The only literacy visible to me was a list of hearings for the day written on a board on one wall. There were stacks of files on the clerk's desk, and I watched the judge rifle through files and sign papers. We sat quietly, whispering, afraid to talk. A court stenographer recorded the procedures. After the hearing, the parents received a copy of the proceedings in the mail. For example, after Juice was arrested for breaking the rules of his probation, his mother received a letter from the court. I had attended this particular court hearing and heard comments by Diane, Juice and the different lawyers firsthand. Their voices were not recorded anywhere in the trial records (see the minutes in Fig. 6.5). I kept asking myself as I read the minutes, "Where are the people's voices?" I also realized, with an eerie feeling, that the official records of the Juvenile Court Community were remarkably like the official texts in the School Community (I).

The texts that participants may encounter in the Juvenile Court Community in the form of official court documents, amount to filling in blanks, checking off boxes, and providing signatures; the print is designed to access and provide limited information for the legal purposes of the court. The outcome of these literacy events is a reduction of real people, events, and identities to whatever is constructed by the ink on the page of the official text.

THE JUVENILE COURT COMMUNITY

Lil Boy Blue, Smurf, Juice, and Lil Garfield were already participants in the Juvenile Court Community when Debbie met and began working with them. The court was an inevitable part of the boys' lives as gang members and overlapped the other communities. The identities constructed by the court for the boys was manifested as fear in all other aspects of their lives, but with the most damage at school.

Our conversation around our analysis of the stories from the Juvenile Court Community prompted much of our theorizing about the nuances and distinctions among concepts like "participant," "member," "periphery," and "boundary," particularly as related to status and power in communities. "Membership," whether in a community of practice (Lave & Wenger, 1991) or in a literacy club (Smith, 1998), denotes a sense of rights and priv-

IN THE SUPERIOR COURT OF THE STATE OF ARIZONA

IN AND FOR THE COUNTY OF ▇▇▇▇

JUVENILE COURT

IN THE MATTER OF

DOB: JUVENILE NO.

                                              PETITION TO REVOKE PROBATION
A Person under the age of
eighteen (18) years.

Personally appeared before me this day of   ,who being duly sworn upon
information and belief,complains and says:
    1. That   is a 15 year old Male, who resides:
    2. That the father of said child is unknown.
    3. That the mother of said child is same as minor.
    4. That the person(s) having guardianship,custody,or control of
said child is/are mother.
    5. That the above-referenced juvenile was placed on probation on the
    day of   ,for an indefinite period of time with the following
conditions:

        Obey all rules, regulations and laws of
        probation, home, school, city, state and
        Federal Government.

    6. That in that   is in violation of his/her probation.

COUNT ONE: (MINOR IN POSSESSION/CONSUMING ALCOHOL, A CLASS ONE
MISDEMEANOR)

On or about the day of   , under the
age of 21 years, bought, received, had in his possession, and/or
consumed spirituous liquor, in violation of:

COUNT TWO: (VIOLATION OF PROBATION,A PETTY OFFENSE)

On   ,the minor was out past his curfew.

SUBSCRIBED AND SWORN to before me this

Commission Expires:

                              Notary Public

FIG. 6.5.   Minutes from the court.

*ileges, increased engagement and relationships over time, and a growing
knowledge base associated with a community. The stark absence of basic
rights and privileges in the Juvenile Court Community illuminated and defined for us the contrasting lack of membership the boys experienced in the
School (I) and Juvenile Court Communities as opposed to full membership*

in the Family, Gang, and School (II) Communities. These relationships are discussed in greater detail in chapter 9.

Recognizing Lil Boy Blue, Smurf, Juice, and Lil Garfield's full membership in the Family, Gang, and School (II) Communities prompted us, in fact, to shift our label for the boys' experience in the Juvenile Court Community to "participant." The boys were forced to participate, albeit passively and unwillingly, in a variety of events, including literacy events, in the Juvenile Court Community. Their lack of insider knowledge, as well as their constant fear of doing something wrong that would get them into more trouble, severely disempowered them, however, and limited what they could accomplish. Members of the community of practice (court officials) had knowledge, but participants (accused individuals and families) were not given access to it. Taylor's (1996) study of literacy in the court system documents that access for individuals accused of crimes varies according to their status, power, and the amount of money they can pay for representation.

Literacy in the Juvenile Court Community was specifically designed to control and to punish. All print in the courts was pre-written by court officials, meaning print was produced by the courts, for the purpose of the courts, with the sterile, official, censored voice of the legal system that recast the boys' lives (Taylor, 1996) in their other communities. Lil Boy Blue, Smurf, Juice, and Lil Garfield were represented in print when their names filled blanks on probation orders and when full community members referred officially to them in minutes as "defendants" or "minors." Individual voices were not relevant or evident. The print thereby eliminated personal identity. The only story heard was what the court allowed to be constructed. This was most evident in the "minutes" of the court session which were written and interpreted by court officials. The boys, their families, and Debbie as an official advocate, had no voices and were rendered invisible. All the paperwork was done by some official who was unknown. As Taylor (1996) found, once events and decisions were in print, any action could be justified because it was in the record. Power was the court, and it was often manifested in literary documents.

In the next chapter, we step away from the stories about Lil Boy Blue, Smurf, Juice, Lil Garfield, and Debbie to review and respond to knowledge that exists about gangs available via the media and research. We consider where and how CRIP 4 LIFE fits within the existing literature. Then, in the remainder of the book we turn to issues about literacy research in communities of marginalized students. In chapter 8, Debbie reflects on the experiences she had as an advocate and we suggest that advocacy is a form of critical ethnography. In chapter 9 we consider theoretical insights as a result of this study.

7

Images of Gangs
in the Media
and Research Literature

After reading Lil Boy Blue, Smurf, Juice, and Lil Garfield's stories you might be asking yourself, is this true? It doesn't match what I have read in the newspaper or seen on the local TV news. Plus, I've grown to care about these boys and yet I strongly disagree with much of their behavior. Every story challenges and readjusts my moral gauge. What should I be believing and feeling about gang members in my community? In my school?

The general public acquires the bulk of information and knowledge about gang members, gang behavior, and gang problems, as well as about youth in general, from the media (Nichols & Good, 2004). Stories of gangs are found in newspapers, on news shows on the radio and TV, in documentaries, on talk shows, in magazines, and in movies. Newspapers across the country print headlines such as:

> *2 Teens Injured in Shooting Rampage: The Victims Innocent Bystanders, Caught in Gunfire that was Prompted by a Gang Related Dispute, Police Say (Catherine Gewertz, Lily Dizon. Los Angeles Nov 20, 1992)*

> *Resurgence of Violence by S.D. Youth Gangs Feared (San Diego County Edition, Los Angeles, Calif. Jan 3, 1997)*

In the first headline, it's difficult to discern who or what is "gang related." In the second, violence in the city is getting worse and gangs are blamed. In both headlines, "gang" is the enemy—the implied evil destroying the local society—but no face exists for who the gang is.

Raul Tovares (1996) examined how Chicano gang members are presented in the newspaper. He focused on two Texas newspapers, the Houston Chronicle *and the* Austin American-Statesman, *and made two important discoveries. First, reports that "print the names of gangs and identify them by the ethnicity of their members, in this case, Hispanic, ... could serve to marginalize minority groups members who become identified with gangs" (p. 149). Second, which is "closely related to the first is that in keeping with the 'problem people' news frame, the gang is overwhelmingly presented as a negative phenomenon that must be stopped by either retributive polices ... or rehabilitative measures" (p. 149).*

The news reports are similar to what is available on television documentaries, such as When Colors Bleed, *a 35-minute documentary on the dangers of gangs, which is designed to teach the public how to recognize and deal with gangs and to show how other communities are addressing this issue. The images in the film are groups of young male juvenile delinquents driving by, firing guns at kids who wear the wrong color, or walking through the wrong neighborhood with spray paint cans, destroying the walls and buildings with graffiti.*

Sharon Nichols and Thomas Good (2004) provide a comprehensive discussion about images of teenagers, the media, and schooling. They say images constructed in the media are usually incomplete, one-dimensional pictures, particularly regarding gangs, violence, substance abuse, and other negative behaviors and "... the media play a large role in fueling citizens' fears of youth" (p. 55). For example, "[r]eports on teen crimes fail to note that juvenile violent crime has been decreasing over the past decade, not increasing" (p. 56).

The problem isn't just that the picture is incomplete or inaccurate, however. It's that the "media exaggerate youth violence" (Nichols & Good, 2004, p. 56) and construct the idea that gang members need to be eliminated or repaired (Jankowski, 1991). "Not only do the numerous stories about youth crime create the illusion that it is out of control, but the content of the stories, especially the headlines, distorts and exaggerates youth violence to the point that it suggests youth should be feared" (Nichols & Good, 2004, pp. 56–57), even though, according to some researchers (Moore, 1978; Vigil, 1993, 2002, 2003), most of the youth associated with gangs are not violent and drug use is no more common with gang members than among adolescents in general.

A primary goal of media representations of gangs and gang life is to teach communities how to remove gangs (Jankowski, 1991). However, when a gang is highlighted in the media both sides actually win: the media has a compelling story the public wants to attend to, and the gang has a new way to promote themselves, thereby gaining respect.

Contradictory images of gangs, gang members, and gang life exist in the research literature. In the rest of this chapter, Debbie provides brief descriptions of these portrayals that are intended to contextualize CRIP4LIFE within other existing representations of gangs. Descriptions of a range of studies are organized according to deficit images, images with more depth and complexity, images that relate specifically to literacy, and images offered by gang members themselves in the research and popular press. Across the descriptions, consider the proximity of the author/researcher to the gang community and the emphasis (or lack thereof) of the gang members' voices.

DEFICIT IMAGES IN THE RESEARCH LITERATURE

Deficit images are as prevalent in the research literature as they are in the media. Some research shares only the violent side of gangs and claims that the violence found in the general society is a direct result of gangs. Some researchers view gangs as a sickness that has grown to epidemic proportion. Just a few examples of this orientation in the research literature are offered here before turning to the more compelling and helpful complex images in other studies.

In the introduction to his book, *Gang Intelligence Manual: Identifying and Understanding Modern-Day Violent Gangs in the United States*, Bill Valentine states, "I believe that the problem of illegal street and prison gangs is a national epidemic ..." (1995, p. 5). Valentine believes that the first step toward eradicating the community of this disease is to learn about gangs. He takes responsibility to inform the reader of the identifiers associated with gangs, such as different types of tattoos, hand signs, style of dress, and the language used by gang members, information he gathered from his experiences working as a prison guard for 18 years.

In keeping with the theme that gangs are a disease is the idea that they may be a mental health problem. Curtis W. Branch, a professor of psychology, sees gang membership as a mental or personality disorder. His book, *Clinical Interventions with Gang Adolescents and Their Families* (1997), was constructed from his own experiences working with gang members and the literature he chose to read. He says the "unconfirmed assumptions that I made in the early days of my work grew out of the folk wisdom about gangs and their families" (p. xiii). Branch continues to say that clinicians must go deeper and "unravel the relationships between many factors in these clients' lives" (1997, p. 3).

Branch seems to be aware that there is more to gang members and membership than what is seen at first glance or in the media. However, he approaches gangs with a medical model that wants to fix the gang members and their families rather than analyze the social factors that lead kids to the gang. He helped develop the Family Intervention Project, which is both educational and therapeutic. The purpose of this project is to "reshape" gangsters into "prosocial beings" (1997, p. 4). The goal is to cure the adolescent and the family. In his conclusion, Branch acknowledges that it is hard to know if the Family Intervention Project worked. However, the Family Intervention Project model did make "a significant difference in the level of understanding that a clinician is able to reach in a short period of time" (p. 214). A question to raise in response is, did any clinicians go to the community where the gang members were from?

An Introduction to Gangs, by George W. Knox (1994) promotes itself (on back of the book) as the "most knowledgeable" and most "thorough analysis of gangs." The book is designed to be used in an introductory course on gangs or as a training book for people who will be or are working with gangs. Knox selectively gathers information from studies already conducted and goes to great lengths to criticize any research that uses qualitative research techniques or provides multiple views of gangs. He claims that participant observation or "hanging out with gangs" can only take place in neutral settings and that "the offenders [gang members] are prone to lie." In other words, researchers get false information which can "fatally flaw one's research" (pp. 154–155). Knox writes several pages pointing out what he sees as weaknesses of qualitative or ethnographic research. He justifies limiting his research to a specific type of research and regards other research (that may be contrary to his own beliefs about gang members) as flawed and invalid. The book provides a specific type of information (negative and blaming the victim) associated with gangs.

Knox also asks the question, "Can gang members be deprogrammed?" (p. 287), suggesting that gang members are brainwashed or programmed to accept the gang lifestyle. He asks, "In what sense do gangs represent a threat to freedom itself?" (p. 617). The information in Knox's book promotes a negative picture of gangs and blames the adolescent who joins the gang for the violence found in today's community.

The findings from these studies and others didn't match my experiences with the MLMC and didn't accurately portray the boys with whom I worked. I knew there was a lot more to my informants' lives and I wondered if there might not also be more to the lives of the subjects in these studies. Lil Boy Blue, Smurf, Juice, and Lil Garfield's stories illustrate that their identities extended far beyond being a gangsta. I wanted and needed to find the literature that also looked at gangsters as real people with layered identities. In the next section I share some of the research that examines more than the superficial aspects of gang members' lives.

COMPLEX IMAGES IN THE RESEARCH LITERATURE

Martin Sanchez Jankowski's book, *Islands in the Street: Gangs and American Urban Society* (1991), is a comprehensive, comparative study on many levels. To construct a complete picture of the gang community, Jankowski gathered data in New York, Boston, and Los Angeles, cities where gangs included different ethnic groups. He spent 10 years and 5 months with gang members as a participant observer. In his words, "I basically did what the gang members did for months at time, traveling between each of the cities and gangs .... I ate where they ate. I slept where they slept. I stayed with their families. I traveled where they went, and in certain situations where I couldn't remain neutral I fought with them" (p. 13).

Jankowski was able to collect data to examine every aspect of the gang culture: from the initiation, to why kids join gangs, to the environment that fosters the gang phenomena, to the power structure within the gang, to the relationship between the gang and the community. This book is a complete picture. Jankowski (1991) points out that there are many types of kids who join gangs. Many of them are quite intelligent and capable of developing and executing creative enterprises. He goes on to say that people who join gangs do so for many reasons. The decision to join a gang is thought out and seems right at the time. If there are no benefits, then there is no reason to join.

The general-consensus assumptions about why kids join gangs are that they come from broken homes, lack a father figure, or have a desire for fun and for intimidating people. Jankowski (1991) documents many more reasons for joining a gang, such as recreation and social events, physical protection, a way to get away from family traditions, a chance for money, the protection of a group identity, and commitment to community. It is important to remember that a young adolescent doesn't wake up one morning and say, "Hey I think I'll join a gang!" Joining a gang is a very complex process (Sheldon, Tracy, & Brown, 2000). To simply stereotype the people in gangs or to generalize the reasons for joining a gang is to fail to acknowledge the individual and his or her story (Jankowski, 1991).

Jankowski (1991) discovered three main organizational structures, or models of leadership, in gangs. In a "vertical hierarchical" model, there is a president, vice president, warlord, and treasurer. Each officer has specific duties and responsibilities. Different officers also exist in a "horizontal commission," but they are not in a hierarchical order. Finally, in the leadership model labeled "influential," there is an unstated and assumed understanding among gang members about who is the leader.

There are many urban myths about the recruitment and initiation of gang members. Jankowski, because he lived with many different gangs in three different cities, discovered that gangs use three systems to recruit new members. Fraternity-type recruitment involves making the organization seem hip or cool to join. Obligation recruitment informs youth that it is their duty to join the gang and if they choose not to join they are accused of turning their backs on their community. Coercive recruitment uses physical and psychological intimidation to bring in new members. In all three recruitment styles, it is important to bring in only new members who have the ability to fight and are courageous and committed to the gang. It is important for all gang members to know their "backs" will be covered by other gang members. The initiation of new members involves beating up the new member by older members. Surviving and handling the initiation indicates that the new member will bring strength to the gang.

James Vigil has been associated with street life and gangs all his life. In Vigil's words, "As a youth I was in moderately close association with street life, having more than casual acquaintanceship with the Thirty-Second and Thirty-Ninth street gangs" (2003, p. 12). His involvement with street kids and gangs didn't end when he grew up. He was involved with kids as a high school teacher and worked with various youth groups. Thus, insider knowledge added to Vigil's formal study of the gang phenomenon. From 1976–1981 Vigil conducted an acculturation and school performance study with Chicano adolescents in which the issue of "marginal cultural placement and gang membership" was central. After building a rapport with some of the gang members and gaining their trust he started "cruising" and "hanging" with them on street corners, at parties, and in their homes. Some of the members became informants for his research. He also collected data from life histories, held formal interviews, and administered surveys.

Eventually Vigil collected 67 completed life histories, 20 from Los Angeles County area, 42 from San Bernardino county, and 5 from Orange County. The ages of his informants ranged from 12 to 40, with half under 19 years. Vigil was aware of his personal involvement. He claimed, "no distance here, for a self-reflexive examination provides liberties to speak to several levels of issues" (2003, p. 14).

James Vigil has conducted several studies to help better understand the complete picture of gangs. In Vigil's terms, his research is "both informal and formal" (2003, p. 12). Informal because as a youth in the barrio where he grew up he was associated with street life and acquaintances. Given his life experiences and the studies he has conducted, he "provides a broader fabric" by which we can better understand why adolescents join gangs.

In *Barrio Gangs: Street Life and Identity in Southern California*, Vigil (2003) took the aforementioned data, integrated it with the findings of earlier studies, and interpreted it in terms of the multiple marginality construct. According to Vigil, multiple marginality "offers an integrative interpretation, a way to build theory rather than a theory itself" (p. 173). Multiple marginality "shows how gang members experience multiple crises and confusions over living, working, associational, developmental and identity situations and considerations" (2003, p. 173). Multiple marginality and conflicting forces have created the opportunity for detached youth to group together into gangs.

Typically, kids live in communities that are segregated. The jobs available are hard labor jobs often paying minimum wages or less. In two-parent families, both parents work to meet the everyday needs to survive. A single parent may work two or more jobs. Good day care costs too much or isn't available. As a result, the kids are left to fend for themselves. The street becomes the day-care center. There is no age when street life becomes the place where kids seek refuge. The street socializes the kids into the street culture. We now have what many people have called "street-wise" kids. Such adolescents have to learn the ways of the street and modes of socialization. Vigil claims, "The gang has taken on the responsibility of doing what the family, school, and other social agencies have failed to do—provide a mechanism for age and sex development, establish norms of behavior, and define and structure outlets for friendship, human support, and the like" (2003, p. 168).

Vigil (2003) writes about the three levels of involvement as a gang member. First are the regulars, who "have a more problematic early life, become street oriented earlier, become gang members sooner, and ... participate in the destructive patterns over a longer period of time." The next level is the peripheral member, who is "just as intense as the regular member once he is a member of the gang, but his level of commitment is mediated less by a problematic early life and more by a life turning event ...." The last group, the temporary member, "is neither as intense nor as committed as the others and primarily associates with the gang during a certain phase of his development" (p. 66).

In his conclusion Vigil writes, "Viewing the gang subculture in a broader, macro to micro way aids interpretation of how and why the subculture arose and outlines when and where youngsters gravitate to it as a solution to urban adaptation. It is a holistic interpretation precisely because social behavior is multilayered and for many Chicanos it is the cumulative functioning of these marginal situations that account for their deep gang membership" (p. 175).

Vigil's book *A Rainbow of Gangs: Street Cultures in the Mega-City* (2002) is the result of research he started in 1989. This study began with "a cross-cultural investigation with a questionnaire-guided survey of 150 out of 820 incarcerated youths in Nelles School, sampling blacks, Chicano, Salvadoran, and Vietnamese in the wards" (p. xvi). Next, he gathered "life histories for 50 of the individuals surveyed, then, through out the 1990s augmented this baseline information with ethnographic research in the various ethnic communities, including a three-year project at a public housing development in East Los Angeles" (p. xvi).

Vigil states, "It is clear from my research that gangs and gang members are indeed primarily generated in low income ethnic minority groups." In fact, he discovered that gang members tend to come from the "poorest of the poor and that poorest poor had many more emotional and personal problems" (2002, p. 173). Substandard housing and inadequate jobs place many families under undo stress. In all four minority groups the youth who are subject to the many "combined effects of economic, social, cultural, and ecologic marginalization continue to fall prey to the streets when disruption in parenting, learning, and sanctioning routines occur" (2002, p. 159). Peers competed with the family, school and other authority figures, and they were winning.

Vigil, in his conclusion, states, "to combat the street gang subculture and subsociety, we must look at the ways separate social control influences—family, school and law enforcement—are integrated and interact with each other" (2002, p. 165). He continues and points out that "the seeds of the solutions to the gang problem are found in the root causes, there is always an opportunity to salvage many of the children who have been marginalized and left to the streets, despite the powerful historical and structures forces that have undermined the social control institutions of the family, school, and law enforcement" (2002, p. 175). Vigil believes that to solve the gang problem, "shoring up and strengthening social control institutions should be our first priority" (2002, p. 175). He recognizes that school and the criminal justice systems are public institutions and should be the first place to start. In other words, what is needed to "address the gang problem is a balance of prevention, intervention, and law enforcement" (2002, p. 169).

As I read Vigil's writing, it was apparent to me that he provides a complete picture of gang life and the social attributes that lead adolescents to the gang. He never judges or blames the victims. He shares a world that few readers will ever experience. By showing us what the communities where gangs are found are like, he offers an understanding of why kids are left to the street and join gangs. He also believes it is time that the adults of society "think of the children of our society, particularly the less fortunate, as ours to care for at an early age" (2002, p. 168).

Joan Moore's (1978) research took place at the same time as Vigil's early work. She was part of the Chicano Pinto Research Project, which was founded in 1974-75 by the National Science Foundation and the National Institute on Drug Abuse. The research that led to the book *Homeboys: Gangs, Drugs, and Prison in the Barrios of Los Angeles* is a collaboration between the academic world and Chicano ex-convicts and gang members. Most of the research took place between 1974 and 1975. However, the actual collaboration began years earlier and continued long after the official research ended. One source of information gathered was surveys of the residents' perceptions of local problems related to gangs and to drugs. Interviews were also a principal way to gather data. Some data and small projects of an ethnographic nature were conducted.

Moore identified three general points about the subculture associated with the Chicano gang. First, the behavior and activity of the "gangs can be seen as a symbolic challenge to the world." Second, gang subculture is "innovative like any other live phenomenon and develops within its own logic." Third, "Chicano gang subcultures are consistently responsive to certain types of programs" (p. 36). Moore, at the end of her book, states, "There are few fresh ideas these days on the old problems of urban America; time and inertia have built a hard scab on conventional concepts and policy" (1978, p. 168). In other words, we need to look in different areas to find new fresh ideas.

Like Vigil and Moore, Sheldon, Tracy, and Brown in their book, *Youth Gangs in American Society* (2000), wanted to record a bigger and more adequate picture of the kids who join gangs and what is involved in the decision. They closely examined the gang literature to gain an "understanding of this cultural phenomenon" (p. xv). Their desire was to provide a "lens through which to view gangs and ... begin to answer the many questions pertaining to gangs" (p. xvi). They also admitted they could not survey all the literature. In their conclusion they state, "It is irrational to declare war on a symptom while the causes are ignored" (p. 229). To see all "gang members as garbage, scum, or other such epithets denies their humanity" (p. 229).

Sheldon, Tracy, and Brown (2000) state, "most kids who join gangs are the kids society has given up hope for—the bottom of the barrel" (p. 229). They are the throw-away kids. However, Sheldon, Tracy, and Brown remind us that they are also the kids "who want love, respect, responsibility, and friendship" (p. 229)—like all kids.

To better understand the role of friendship in kids left to the street, we can look at Greg Dimitriadis' (2003) book, *Friendship, Cliques, and Gangs: Young Black Men Coming of Age in Urban America*. He started conducting research on black vernacular culture and the reception practices of black youth at a community center in 1995–1996. At the center Dimitriadis became acquainted with Rufus and Tony. Over a 5-year period, he documented the struggles Rufus and Tony dealt with on a daily basis. He first highlighted the role of friendship in their lives and later looked at his role as he became a source of support for the boys. During this time period Dimitriadis volunteered at the community center, and then was offered a job because he was there so much it was decided he may as well be paid.

Dimitriadis first examines the friendship network between Rufus and Tony and how it was rooted in place and in family. He helps us understand the support this friendship provided for both boys. Because of their friendship they called each other cousins and saw each other as family.

Later, he examines the role of the community center where both boys work. The center provides Tony and Rufus an opportunity to validate their lives and provides a path to success. Dimitriadis also documents the obstacles that can subvert this success. During this time Rufus and Tony became part of the street life and then the gang. As Dimitriadis documents Rufus and Tony's move into adulthood, his goal is to help readers gain a better understanding of the life of a young black man. He provides a complete picture. He shares their stories and we hear their voices. Dimitriadis (2003) states, "I tried to tell a different kind of story about contemporary urban youth—one that challenges the way in which they have been pathologies in the popular imagination while speaking as honestly as possible about their brutal lives and everyday realities. Above all else, I try not to tell a simple story of good and bad youth, but of a relationship that transcends such directions, pointing to new and different ways to think about the young people and the institutions that serve them" (p. 16).

S. Beth Atkins is a writer and photographer. Her first book, *Voices From the Fields: Children of Migrant Farmworkers Tell Their Stories* (1993) led her to her work with youth who were in gangs, resulting in *Voices From the Streets* (1996). Atkins writes, "I wanted my book not to glamorize gang members but to portray them with respect" (p. ix). She also wanted her book to carry a positive message and bring hope. Atkins worked for 2 years conducting interviews and taking photographs. She spent time with the kids on the street, in school, at the programs they were a part of, and in their homes. She met their girlfriends, boyfriends, spouses, parents, and friends. Atkins focused on gang members who were out of the gang. She tells the stories, including some of the kids' own writing, that led them to the gang and what helped them get out. After her experience with gang members, Aktins writes, "They have taught me that being in a gang was a way for them to adapt to their neighborhood, homes, and families in a society that is just theirs, but also mine" (p. xiii).

Janelle Dance's (2002) research also took her to the streets to discover street culture and its impact on school culture. Dance worked 1 year in the Cambridge after-school program for at-risk youth. In her words, "before I asked the first formal interview question or took the first field note, I spent one year hanging out with urban students" (p. 3). Her research included 70 interviews and almost 4 years of ethnographic observations with middle and junior high school students ranging from 12 to 16 years of age from urban and inner city neighborhoods. Her research has three purposes. First, to better understand the experience of street-savvy students who act hard, like gangsters. Second, to explore the gangsta posturing in schools. And third, to share real students' lives in a scholarly debate about the state of urban public education.

Because Dance (2002) spent time first getting to know the young boys in her research, she was able to gain an understanding of what street life is like and recognize that there isn't a single "street-smart kid" but different degrees of street-smart kids. She asked the kids to define "the streets." She discovered that street culture refers "to the full range of patterned, recurrent social interactions typical to urban and inner-city streets, from hanging out with one's peers or shooting hoops to joining gangs or crews, dealing or using drugs and engaging in other violent, mobster like activities" (p. 38). This was their world. Dance also learned that there are three variations on the urban gangster theme or different labels to describe street-savvy youth: *hard* is a state of being a street-savvy and tough gangster who has committed criminal acts; *hardcore wannabe* is a state of acting hard because it is a way to gain social status; and *hardcore enough* denotes the state of being street savvy and tough enough to assure one's peers that one is capable of being hard, but chooses not to be.

The next level for kids socialized into the street community is the gang. Joining a gang takes place in high school or maybe junior high. Younger kids may associate with others who are part of the gang, but the initiation takes place when they are older. It is a small percentage of adolescents that join gangs and much of gangsta behavior is not much different from typical adolescents—if there is a typical adolescent; they spend time just hanging out with friends. One activity gangsters will participate in is tagging.

Urban and inner-city kids have been marginalized and are powerless. They seek what has been labeled "charismatic authority." Dance says, "An individual has charismatic authority when others view that individual as possessing exceptional or superhuman qualities that warrant deference and respect" (2002, p. 169). These individuals can command respect on the streets. Interestingly, a high majority of these students may present themselves as gangster-like, but do not actually wish to become part of the gang culture. They posture as tough at school because the word will get back to the street if they are not. Street-savvy kids who maintain gangster-like posturing at school keep the respect they earn on the street.

The authorities in this section provide an understanding of the life kids live on the streets and the need to be tough and respected. Many share how this life flows into the school. As teachers we need to see the whole pictures of our students to better understand them and, as a result, be better teachers. Part of the gang world is the literacy the members use to make meaning; a growing set of research, part of which is described in the next section, focuses on literacy issues.

IMAGES FROM RESEARCH ON GANG LITERACY

Susan A. Phillips, an anthropologist, found herself studying gangs in Los Angeles through their writings. Phillips documented and discovered the meaning behind the symbolic and visual expressions of gang graffiti. The book, *Wallbangin': Graffiti and Gangs in L. A.* (1999), is the result of her research which took place between 1997 and 1998. To build a link with the graffiti authors, or in other words, to gain entry to the research site, Phillips took pictures of the graffiti and gave the authors of the graffiti the pictures. Graffiti doesn't last long in its composed public state, so having a picture provided the authors with a lasting image of their writings. Phillips states, "[graffiti] was the thing that drew me. And this writing was the only way that I could study L.A. gangs honestly and with any degree of success" (p. 7).

Graffiti is the voice of people who are silent and is used differently by different people. This study suggests some major genres of graffiti: popular graffiti—the everyday stuff; community-based graffiti—graffiti produced by and for members of the community; gang graffiti—written by and for gang members; and political graffiti—that represents the voice of the discontented. Phillips claims, "Graffiti has provided me a special window into people's lives. This window has allowed me to see the positive in what is usually viewed as negative, to find morality in what is often considered depravity, and to discover a creativity and depth of history that makes me grateful to live in the time and place that I do" (p. 351). Graffiti "allows people to create identity, share cultural values, redefine spaces, and manufacture inclusive or exclusive relationships" (p. 46).

Phillips hopes "to teach people that learning to read graffiti is a process of empowerment" (p. 11). She believes that if one can understand the graffiti written on the walls around them, they may not be so afraid of the writers. She continues, stating, "I hope to combat some of the fears and resultant hatred that surrounds these topics and enable people to see gangs and graffiti in new light"(p. 11).

As I read *Wallhangin'* I could tell that Phillips was concerned about the picture her work constructs. She wanted readers to move beyond the simplistic view that comes from the media to what is real about gang members and their writings. She, like many other researchers, maintains the complex identities of the gang members and includes the voices of her informants.

Matthew Hunt's (1996) dissertation, *Sociolinguistics of Tagging and Chicano Gang Graffiti* provides another view and understanding of tagging and Chicano gang graffiti. Hunt interviewed taggers and Chicano gang members about graffiti and why they produce it. Observations, photographs, and videos were used to document the tags and graffiti text over a 2-year period. Hunt learned that for the tagger, the greatest accomplishment is to be well known for one's tag as achieved through graffiti production. Features associated with the tagger's tag are "either the tag or the crew" (p. 118), characters, dates, and numbers.

Hunt explores the basic elements in Chicano gang graffiti, including the variety of functions that "cross-outs" serve depending on where a tag is placed. Hunt says the main function of a Chicano gang's graffiti is to reflect the pride a gang member feels about his neighborhood and gang. Since the literacy found in gang community is designed to help gang kids make sense of the their world, graffiti is the voice of the silenced.

Elizabeth Moje (2000) also asks, in her 3-year study of literacy practices associated with gangs, what graffiti, as an unsanctioned literacy practice, accomplishes for its adolescent writers. Moje spent 1 year in two English classes, a second interviewing students, and a third hanging out with three focus students. During this time she took field notes in and out of school, collected daily audio and video tapes of classroom interaction, conducted informal and formal interviews, maintained e-mail communication with the teacher, collected artifacts, documentation and photographs, and most valuable, kept a researcher's journal of impressions and notes that were written after an activity. She used a comparative method of data analysis. Moje was interested in how adolescents learn or gain knowledge about unsanctioned literacy practices associated with gangs. She examined written and oral language, the style and color of clothing, and the gestures that are part of meaning making in the gang world. She discovered certain characteristics of gang literacy that supported a meaning making practice, such as crossing out letters that represent rival gangs and substituting certain letters. Moje then asked, how do new members become familiar with the practices associated with gangs? She discovered there is no formal teaching. As new members become part of the gang community they are apprenticed to become active members in the learning community. Moje believes we need to use the knowledge adolescents bring to the classroom and help adolescents learn to talk about and share their social and literate practices from outside of the classroom in school. She believes school literacy should no longer be the privileged literacy.

The specific focus of Phillip's, Hunt's, and Moje's research is the literacy used by gang members. Even with a specific purpose, these researchers acknowledge that they spent time with the gang members to gain a true understanding of the literacy in their world. They do not place blame or discount the gang members as menaces to society, but analyze how literacy is used in order to give voices to the marginalized kids. Jankowski, Vigil, Dimitriadis, and Dance moved beyond observing a distant community to become participants in the gang world with the hope of gaining a truer understanding of the gang phenomenon. Jankowski states that as he became a part of the community, the newer gang members were not aware that he was a professor. "I had proven to be no threat or hindrance to them" (p. 13). These researchers make no judgments about gang members' "choice" (which was never actually there) to join a gang. In these studies, if there is blame to be placed it is named as the racism, poverty, and prejudice that results in the social conditions found in minority communities.

Nonetheless, these researchers would be the first to say that to understand the gang, we must turn to the experts—those who live within the gang subculture—to see what gangs are all about. A few examples of available writing by former gang members are described next.

IMAGES FROM GANG MEMBERS

Sanyika Shakur, aka Monster Kody Scott, says, "There are no other gang experts except participants." In his book, *Monster: The Autobiography of an L. A. Gang Member* (1993), we learn that gangstas are not born bad. This is evident in Monster's account of his first drive-by. After the shooting, Monster went home and sat on the bed in a daze, unable to make sense of what had just taken place. He writes:

> The seriousness of what I had done that evening did not dawn on me until I was alone at home that night. My heart had slowed down to its normal pace and the alcohol and pot worn off. I was left then with just myself and the awesome flashes of light that lit up my mind to reveal bodies in abnormal positions and grotesque shapes, twisting and bending in arches that defied bone structure. The actual impact was on my return back past the bodies of the first fallen, my first real look at bodies torn to shreds. It did little to me then, because it was all about survival. But as I lay wide awake in my bed, safe, alive, I felt guilty and ashamed of myself. Upon further contemplation, I felt that they were too easy to kill. Why had they been out there? I tried every conceivable alibi within the realm of reason to justify my actions. There was none. (p. 13)

If Monster was born bad or had some sort of innate sociopathic personality, he wouldn't have experienced the confusion and guilt he felt. He wouldn't have given his actions a second thought.

Stanley Tookie Williams is the co-founder of the Crip gang and a death row prisoner. He shares his life story in his book, *Blue Rage, Black Redemption: A Memoir* (2004). In the chapter titled, "The Art of Dys-education" that tells about William's schooling experiences, he writes,

> I was a darn good reader for my age. At home there was a box filled with books. Sometimes I would dump the books on the floor and sit in the middle of the pile trying to read everything. Often my mother would help me with the spelling and pronunciation of words. One of my favorite books was an encyclopedia on dogs, with numerous color photos …. Reading was a pastime I truly enjoyed and a way of escaping from my often-riotous thoughts. In my reading world there was no poverty, no discrimination, no violence, no racism, no pain …. (p. 27)

He goes on to tell how one of his teachers was more about punishing children than teaching, that books were placed on shelves and no one was allowed to read them, and that in his class "[p]encils and erasers were nowhere to be found" (p. 26). Williams was smart enough to be successful in school and he did have his moments, but he also had times when teachers seemed more like "school police." Not all his teachers were this bad, and he has some good memories. He writes, for example, that "Miss Johnson made learning so interesting that I didn't want to leave" (p. 52). Having good and bad experiences, Williams did in fact graduate, but his path was set. He wrote, "I never harbored dreams of becoming a president, astronaut, banker, millionaire, doctor, fireman, or lawyer. I was conditioned to anticipate a living hell" (p. 36).

Williams describes a world that is real for many children. The book ends with Williams' Protocol for Peace. He writes so others can learn from his mistakes. He states, "My former image is unworthy of emulation, I only reflect on undying determination under fire. This is why I find comfort in knowing that these children can triumph over adversity—and that they will not follow in my footsteps" (p. 336).

Another book that contains the stories of several gangbangers is *Do or Die*, by Leon Bing (1992). On the front of the book is the following quote: "For the first time, members of American's most notorious teenage gangs—the Crips and the Bloods—speak for themselves." Bing's purpose for going to Watts was to interview an 18-year-old member of the Grape Street Crips in 1986. He shares his first impression of Watts:

> [A]s I passed the welfare office on my way to the probation offices, I didn't know then that I would be better off if I did not make eye contact with many of the people standing there. I didn't know that when I did, I would see so much anger, so much fierceness, so much love and pride dribbling away in the face of poverty and despair. (p. ix)

Bing gathered and selected short stories by members of the gang that are designed to help readers better understand what life is like for the young kids who join gangs.

Finally, Ramon Serrano (1999) tells his story of how school aimed him toward gang membership. Serrano describes his early life. His mother dropped out of school to take care of the family after her mother died and his father, who graduated from college, moved his family to America for the dream of a better life for his family. Reality set in and he could only get a job working in a factory. Serrano remembers starting school in one class and being moved to the higher level class. This happened every year. Serrano was known as a good kid until the ninth grade. Like before, Serrano was moved from the low group to a higher group. He was nervous and in retrospect called the first day he met his new teacher his "living hell." "... my new teacher could not accept that a Puerto Rican would be placed in his classroom ... because the Puerto Ricans in this school did not have the brains it took to be placed so far ahead" (p. 228). This was said in front of him and the class. After 3 weeks of put-downs and embarrassing statements, the teacher said something about Serrano's mother. Serrano threw a chair at the teacher.

He began hanging out with the kids in the hall, who let him know he had done the right thing. He was accepted as one of them. Serrano remembers, "I felt like one of them because I was treated like one of them .... What I learned from the people I met made me feel important and superior to other students. It was a new sense of power and control which I had never before experienced" (p. 229).

Serrano only remembers one teacher in his high school career who made a positive difference. This teacher was young and from the ghetto and not well liked by the senior teachers. According to Serrano, this teacher "talked with us not just to us" (p. 232). Serrano moved back to Puerto Rico and things changed. In his last year of school, his attitude changed toward school and he credits this change to the teacher.

Reading life stories of Sanyika Shakur (1993), Stanley Tookie Williams (2004), the storytellers in Leon Bing's book (1992), and Ramon Serrano (1999), we hear the voices of the gangsters as they lived the gangster life. They tell us of the prejudice, the fears, and the hurt that is a natural part of their lives. Such writing makes it possible to see a world that, like Bing stated, we may not really want to see, because if we look carefully we may see the beliefs, courage, and desire of young kids who want a better life. We will no longer be able to walk with eyes closed and blame the victim.

IMAGES OF GANGS

Some researchers who study the gang phenomenon stand on the outside and look in. They find what they expect and thereby verify the beliefs they held before they entered. Other researchers are more invested. They become volunteers in the community and workers in recreation centers. They choose to live within the community rather than standing away, separated from the events and experiences of the gang. These researchers don't want to fix the gang members. They want to understand. They don't intend to only

take away their new understanding from the community they are research-
ing, they want to give back.

Like many of these researchers, as Debbie conducted her study and became a part of her boys' lives she grew to understand their worlds. She
could no longer stand by as she saw and experienced the injustice they experienced. She needed and wanted to help. She became their advocate. In
the next chapter, Debbie reflects on the experiences she had as an advocate
for Lil Boy Blue, Smurf, Juice, and Lil Garfield and other students in the
School (I) and Juvenile Court Communities. She describes her perspective
as a participant in the communities of practice and outlines the lessons she
learned about advocacy. We suggest her advocacy was a form of critical
ethnography.

Living on the Boundaries of School: Advocacy and Research

In this chapter, Debbie reflects on her experience as she shifted from Lil Boy Blue, Smurf, Juice, and Lil Garfield's teacher to their advocate. The group had been working together for four semesters at Nuestra Casa, an alternative high school program. Since several of the students, including Smurf, were exceeding their eligibility for the program and were required to return to traditional public high school, and others had met graduation requirements, Debbie decided to resign her position as their teacher, concentrate on her graduate studies, and advocate for the boys. She became the boys' advocate with the full support of their families. The stories in this chapter show how difficult it was for Debbie to gain permission from school officials to advocate and how nearly impossible it was for the boys to graduate and experience commencement with their class. Debbie offers readers lessons she learned about advocating. We join voices at the end of the chapter to discuss how Debbie's advocacy and research methods coalesced into a powerful form of critical ethnography.

WHAT IS ADVOCACY?

My advocacy story, as told in this chapter, undoubtedly reveals my early naiveté. When the study that generated the stories in this book began, I believed strongly that the educational system is designed to help students. I believed everyone should be allowed a choice to belong in school, not be forced out against their will. I knew there would be problems as I discovered what my role as an advocate would be, but I had been a public school teacher for 15 years and was a part of the system. I adamantly believed in the system. I understood it as an insider. At the outset, I believed my new role as an advocate would be simple: I would offer the students the kind of emotional support and insider knowledge that would tip the scales of potential success in their favor. Over the period of 2 years in which I was a full-time advocate, I learned just how hard it is to advocate for students no one wants in school. I learned some harsh lessons about "the system" as I worked to secure permission to advocate for my students and as I helped my students achieve graduation. I learned that sharing too much information with school officials was harmful and that fighting for the right to be included is important, even when parents and students say they don't want to fight. I discovered what it was like to be "invisible" and to talk but not be heard. My experiences as an advocate in educational and judicial institutions taught me that my students didn't really have access to an education or much hope to graduate with a diploma. I tell my story here with the hope that my experience might help other researchers and teachers who want to advocate for marginalized students have more realistic expectations.

According to Webster's Dictionary (1981), *advocacy* is "the act of pleading for, supporting a cause or course of action," and an "advocate is a person who speaks or writes in support of a cause." The Court Appointed Special Advocate Association states that an advocate is a volunteer "who speaks up for the best interests of a child—ordinary people who care about kids." Debbie Coughlin (1997) says her work with a young child named Valerie wasn't named *advocacy* until there was a controversy and that "advocacy on any level is political" (p. 12). Denny Taylor (Taylor, Marasco, & Coughlin, 1997) introduces "teaching as advocacy" as central to research in which intensive analysis is completed about (a) personal literacies and (b) the official version of these literacies in bureaucratic documentation. Taylor says advocates need more than personal opinions or expertise as teachers. Advocates "have to be able to deconstruct the official texts and build alternative explanations that we can document in more authentic texts" (p. 4). She describes her teaching and research as participatory, activist, and transformative:

> Participatory because each one of us believes in working closely and sharing problems with people. Activist because we are convinced that to make a positive and lasting difference, we must engage in activities that help people help themselves overcome the difficulties they face in their everyday lives. And transformative because we believe that to foster opportunities for our students, it is essential that we identify the problems

existing resources have overcoming the barriers that make us unresponsive to peoples' needs. The transformations we are seeking are in the situations in which people find themselves. (p. 8)

In the Gang Community, the concept of "having one's back" is about members protecting each other. I knew I had to let my gang member students know I would be there for them like they were for each other. An opportunity arose one time when my students asked me what I would do if I were with them and someone started a fight. I looked at them and thought, I don't believe in fighting. I responded, "I would be there to help you, and if that meant fighting, I would. But I would hope I could stop the fighting. I would have your back." When my students decided to go back to traditional school, I told them I would not leave them alone, that I would help them. This seemed to relieve their fears. For me, advocating meant I would be there to help my students navigate a system that kept them outside. For my students, an advocate was someone who had their backs.

ADVOCACY AND RESEARCH

Becoming an advocate layered a new perspective on my concurrent role as a researcher. As a qualitative researcher using ethnographic methods of data collection and analysis (Bogdan & Biklen, 1998; Merriam, 1998) and a teacher who believed relationships between home and school are paramount to positive educational experiences, I participated in many of the boys' family activities and heard Lil Boy Blue's, Smurf's, Juice's, and Lil Garfield's stories of their family, gang, and school experiences. I audiotaped the stories when possible and systematically wrote field notes after events. I collected artifacts from the Family, Gang, School, and Juvenile Court Communities. I conducted formal and spontaneous interviews with the parents and my students. I kept a researcher's journal. My goal was to do interpretive fieldwork, which Erickson (1986) defines as follows:

Interpretive fieldwork research involves being unusually thorough and reflective in noticing and describing everyday events in the field setting, and in attempting to identify the significance of actions in the events from the various points of view of the actors themselves. (p. 121)

Figure 8.1 summarizes my data collection methods.

I knew that by listening carefully to my "informants'" voices I could develop an understanding that was different and deeper than one based solely

---

PARTICIPANT OBSERVATION

Participating in family activities such as birthday parties and baby showers.

Literacy events in school and out of school.

Attending court sessions and school hearings. Wrote notes after event.

Transcribed audiotape of hearing.

IN-DEPTH INTERVIEWS

Four individual interviews were conducted with each participant. Questions concerning their gang activities, school, and literacy were asked. A total of twenty sessions were audiotaped and transcribed.

One in-depth interview with parents. A total of three sessions were audiotaped and transcribed. Many informal conversations with Lil Boy Blue, Smurf, Juice, and Lil Garfield and their families. Field notes were written after the informal conversations.

WRITTEN FIELD NOTES

Notes written after informal meetings with participants and families.

Field notes taken while teaching participants and while acting as an advocate.

Notes written after social events.

Notes taken after each interview session.

COLLECTION OF WRITTEN AND VISUAL ARTIFACTS

School texts and written assignments, leisure reading, letters, journal entries, official documents, tagging, music.

Photographs taken by participants.

School records.

FIG. 8.1. Data collection methods.

on my observation and interpretation of the same event or statistics. But as the students' advocate, I actually experienced—*lived*—the stories that they told me about school, the court, their families, and the gang. I no longer gathered data as a participant observer, but experienced the same events. I felt, on a personal level, what my students felt as students in the education system, and I came to know firsthand their parents' frustration as they tried to help their children. The artifacts I collected were forms I helped complete alongside the parents and students. My voice was silenced during the events I transcribed as well as those I was "studying." When the boys said no one heard them, I knew exactly what they meant. In short, as Kathy and I discuss at the end of this chapter, becoming an advocate turned a conventional ethnographic study into a critical ethnography.

ADVOCATING IN THE SCHOOL COMMUNITY (I): THE IMPOSSIBLE DREAM

My official advocacy role began as I drafted a letter and secured parents' signatures for permission to communicate with the students' teachers and to have access to classwork and records. I optimistically delivered the letter to the Brighton High School office secretary, who talked with the principal, Dr. Thompson. As she closed the principal's office door, the secretary informed me, "The letters cannot be accepted."

"What is wrong with them?" I asked.

She would not give me any specifics; the district would not accept them. I thought, "Why will they not let me help my kids? They have more than 2,000 students in this school. You would think they would want help."

I knew some people working in the district office and asked for suggestions. We decided that I should use language familiar to the district, so I scoured the district handbook and rewrote the permission letter using its formal language. I took the new letters to the parents, who happily signed permission for a second time, but warned, "This will never happen, Debbie. They will never let you help the kids." The students' fear and lack of trust in the education system was their parents,' as well. They had their own horror stories. They believed the school didn't want their children. I kept reassuring them that I would be able to work with the kids. "I am a teacher. I understand the system and I know how to work it. Trust me, it will work," I told them. I had to acknowledge to myself, however, that fear and doubts were surfacing for me, too. Not wanting to take any chances, I had the letters notarized.

I made an appointment with the principal. I wanted to share my story of working with these kids and their parents for 2 years. I wanted her to know the fear and mistrust my students and their parents had in the education system. I believed if she understood I was there to help the students be successful and that I was working with the parents, she would be receptive. I still believed in the system.

The principal and I sat at a round table in her office. I shared my background, handed her the letters, and waited for her reaction. To my astonishment, with no more than a quick glance, she slid the letters back. She rejected the letters. In my personal journal I wrote about the experience:

Today I met with the principal. What an eye-opener that was. I talked. Did she listen? I don't think so. I had no evidence of it. I walked out of her office shocked. In fact, I wanted to turn around and make sure she was in the room. The principal had no emotions, no reaction. I felt nothing from her. She asked me no questions and she made no comments. The wall gave me more of a response. I literally felt no emotions.

Believing that through tenacity I would gain access, I retained my faith in the system and returned to the district office. This time I went to the department concerned with equity in the school. I shared my story with a Mr. Parrson of the equity office. He acknowledged that I wanted to do a "good thing," but said advocating was something new in the district. He suggested we talk with Assistant Superintendent Lee and escorted me to his office. I was confident this time I would be allowed to advocate for my students. Mr. Lee was unavailable, but one receptionist and four secretaries outside his door said, "Those kids are lucky to have someone like you." One secretary took notes on my problem and another secretary photocopied the permission letters. They said the assistant superintendent would contact me.

On the way out I started to feel nervous about going to the district office for help and having the letters photocopied. I asked Mr. Parrson, "Will there be any problems with the principal? I did go over her head." My past experiences as a teacher taught me this could be a problem. He said, "There could be, but you never know. You might want to let her know."

While I was struggling to secure permission to advocate for all my students at Brighton High, I did have permission to visit Smurf in the alternative program. I was careful not to break any rules. I visited once a week and talked with the teacher before I talked with Smurf. Smurf's teacher kept telling me that things were fine. No problems.

Every Friday, I picked Smurf up at the alternative school and the other kids at Brighton, and we went to lunch to celebrate the completion of the week. Although everyone seemed to be adjusting to school, they told me over and over, "Miss they really don't want us here." Trying to build their confidence, I said, "Things are going to be different, but you need to give school a fair chance."

Sadly, the students were soon to prove me wrong and I was to learn an important lesson. Three days after I left the information with the assistant superintendent's secretaries, Smurf was told he had until Monday to acquire 500 points in the alternative program or he would be dropped from school. As I explained in chapter 4, the students started out with F's, and getting D's required 500 points. Although I talked him into a plan to get the points done quickly to save his enrollment, on Thursday Smurf was dismissed.

Smurf didn't want me to fight to get him back in school. His father, Felipé, didn't trust the schools and no longer wanted to deal with them. My hands were tied. Felipé didn't want to put Smurf through the same emotional trauma Lil Boy Blue had experienced.

Was it a coincidence that I allowed the secretaries of the assistant superintendent to photocopy the letters the parents had signed? Smurf's teacher had consistently reported that he was doing well. What else could explain it? With a sick feeling in my stomach, I knew I had given out too much information.

Eventually, I learned that Smurf wasn't totally removed from the school and was given the opportunity to go back to regular classes at Brighton. But Smurf had a full-time job that started at 12:30 pm. He had a baby coming, and he wanted to support that baby. School policy would not allow him to go to school for half a day because he was a junior. I still hadn't heard from the assistant superintendent.

Advocating was not going to be as easy as I thought.

I called Mr. Lee once, sometimes twice, a week. Every time I was promised he would call me back, but he never did. It was more than 2 months before I received a return call and was allowed to make an appointment.

I arrived a little early that day. One of the four secretaries said Mr. Lee had just been called to an unexpected meeting and gave me two choices. I could call and make another appointment (not a choice because by the time I waited another 2 months the semester would be over) or I could come back in about 30 minutes. I decided I would return in 30 minutes. I returned to the office in 15 minutes and finally had my opportunity to meet Mr. Lee, but it was to no avail. Mr. Lee commended me on my desire to help "these" kids, and said they were "lucky" to have "someone like me" help them. But, he said, I was an "outsider—not part of the system." There was nothing he could do.

My hopes were crushed. I wanted to believe I would be able to help my kids; I wanted to believe in the system. I thought he would make this possible. I was angry! This was *my* system. I wasn't a contracted teacher in the district, but I still believed I was a teacher. I would not be allowed to work within the system to help kids. In that moment, I learned that school was not about helping kids—at least not my Mexican-American gangster students.

I had to accept I was not going to be given official access to my students. I would be praised for my desire to help "these" kids. I would be reminded how lucky the kids were to have someone like me. But no access and no help. I was on my own.

By this time, four of my students were enrolled in the traditional high school and three were in the alternative program located on campus. I was determined to not leave them on their own. All of the students had my pager number and were instructed to call me whenever they were sent to the office or needed help for any reason. (Although many times they were not permitted to call). I hadn't achieved formal permission, so I had to discover an alternative way to gain access. While helping my seniors with graduation, I met a school counselor with whom my students were comfortable. This counselor became my alternative route for advocating and helping my kids. She helped me gain access to teachers so I could monitor their progress. She helped arrange schedules so they were placed with teachers who she felt would have more compassion for them. Often, my students and I sat together in her office to solve problems and overcome barriers. Eventually, the students learned to trust her. When they were called to the office they would first stop at her office and call me or just talk with her about their situation. I had been named an "outsider" by the assistant superintendent. I was pushed to find new and different ways into the system.

GRADUATION PROMISES
IN THE SCHOOL COMMUNITY

My advocacy activities had actually begun during my fourth semester teaching at the Nuestra Casa program, when five of my students saw the light at the end of the public school tunnel—high school graduation. As they moved toward completion of graduation requirements, I visited Brighton and met with vice principals, counselors, and school officials in charge of school transcripts to verify that my students' credits were correct and to provide the students opportunities to participate in the numerous social activities and rituals organized for graduating seniors. I gathered information and did exactly what I was told by the educational officials. Lil Boy Blue was one of the students who, after years of challenges and a roller coaster of successes and failures, had completed the requirements to graduate.

Just before graduation, I was informed that Lil Boy Blue would not be allowed to walk in the commencement ceremony with his class. I was ready to fight whatever battle was ahead to get Lil Boy Blue on that stage, but Lil Boy Blue didn't want to. Since I had decided my job as an advocate was to support, not to dictate, I didn't fight for Lil Boy Blue and he didn't participate in the commencement activities. Today, as I think about this experience, I regret not fighting for him to graduate from his home school. I discovered later that even though he seemed not to care, he and his parents were very upset and disappointed. I should have done more. Brighton High School never acknowledged what Lil Boy Blue accomplished academically.

Two other students were informed they were not going to be allowed the privilege of walking in graduation either, because they had book fines. I hadn't been told about any sort of fine as we completed the myriad forms and procedures necessary to graduate. The students knew nothing about the book fines either and claimed they had returned all their books when they dropped out of school.

It is important to realize that each of these students had to be officially withdrawn from Brighton before they could attend the Nuestra Casa program. The withdrawal procedure required checking on fines, at which time any past due fines would have been reported. Both students had been in my class for two semesters. During this time, they never received notices about book fines. Hoping for the best, the two students and I met with several administrators. We explained the books had been returned. One student claimed she never received a book, because she never attended the class. Our voices were not heard and the students were required to pay the fines or they would not be allowed to walk in the ceremony. The next problem was money. I explained to the administrators that in many families extra money doesn't exist and there wasn't sufficient time to plan for these unexpected expenses. Eventually, I was told about a program designed to help poor families provide books for their students. We received funding for half of the fines from this program and between the students and me, the rest of the fine was paid. Why hadn't I been told about this complication earlier? During this puzzling time, I kept wondering—why would a school stop students who had worked so hard to graduate from walking in their commencement ceremonies?

My first year of advocating wasn't all disappointment, though. I considered it a major success that four of my students were in traditional high school and three were in alternative settings. I learned new ways to get around some of the barriers built by the education system. One such strategy was to find a counselor who was willing to go the extra mile and help me get around barriers I couldn't eliminate.

Kids who don't trust the school system because of the injustice they experience find multiple reasons to drop out—to give up and quit. I believed that part of my responsibility as my students' advocate was to provide a safety net so they couldn't fail. Often I picked kids up and took them to school—walking them to class if needed. Schedules were adjusted making sure my students were placed in the best classes with good teachers. I sat with one student in McDonalds' and worked on packets and worksheets to make up 3 missing credits. I insisted they regularly request grade reports, throughout the semester, to document that they were being successful, just in case something should happen and they would get failing grades. (This indicates my own mistrust in the system.) When things went well, we celebrated. Three students graduated the first year. It was exciting. The families and I sat together in the bleachers. We screamed and hollered when the students' names were read and they walked across the stage. We knew just how hard they had worked to gain the privilege of walking across the stage and receiving their diplomas.

ADVOCATING IN THE JUVENILE COURT COMMUNITY

When I decided to advocate for my students, I never dreamed it would include advocating in the Juvenile Court Community. I became aware of Smurf's probation officer (PO) when he pulled Smurf out of my class at Nuestra Casa on several occasions. Smurf was on a strict schedule. If he wasn't where he said he would be, he could be in trouble. At first, I had to get permission for Smurf to participate in each Nuestra Casa field trip from his PO. As I built a relationship with the PO and he came to trust me, eventually, I didn't need to call. As long as Smurf was with me he could participate in all field trips and activities I organized at school. This negotiation was my first advocating experience in the Juvenile Court Community.

As described in chapter 3, Smurf was struggling with the death of his homie Oso when he was my student. When the other boys in the gang were mourning, he was locked up in juvenile detention. As memories were shared in class about Oso, Smurf felt angry and left out of the discussion. I called Smurf's mom and asked about counseling for Smurf. She said she and Felipé had tried to arrange counseling for Smurf, but were told it wasn't possible. I said, "If you don't mind I would like to call and see what I can find out." She was happy to get some help. Once again I called the probation office and talked with Smurf's PO. He said he would check into counseling for Smurf. After 2 weeks neither Smurf's mom nor I had heard form Smurf's PO. I decided to talk with the supervisor in charge of the probation officer. I told him what was needed and assertively asked for a date when he would accomplish my request. I told him I would call back on that date. Smurf came to school the next day and told me that his surveillance officer (SO) came that night with papers to arrange counseling and told Smurf and his family that he didn't know what I said, but everyone was jumping. There were times when advocating did work.

In chapter 6, I told the story of when Juice wanted to play on the Brighton High baseball team but his PO had him arrested on the day of tryouts. At that point, Juice's PO, who was a community officer, wanted to place Juice with the school officer who worked directly on the high school campus. Her reasoning was that the school PO could keep a closer eye on Juice. Juice was angry and fearful about the change and claimed he would run (go into hiding) if it happened. He didn't want someone watching him every minute of the day and would not go to school if the change took place.

I tried to help the community PO understand that before a child can learn in school they must believe school is a safe place. For Juice, the idea of having someone watching "24/7" would transform school into a juvenile detention center. School had to be a place where he could feel good and not worry. The PO told Juice's mother and me that we would have to speak to the judge at the upcoming trial about retaining her as Juice's PO. As instructed, before the trial was over, Diane asked the judge not to change Juice's probation officer. The judge informed her that he had nothing to do with assigning probation officers. He said we needed to take the issue up with the probation officer. Since none of the court officials would take responsibility for making a decision to change the practice that was already in place, Juice's PO was never changed. Juice stayed in school and finished that semester, passing four classes.

I began to believe that advocating in the Juvenile courts was easier than in the schools. My voice as a school teacher was heard by probation officers and it was respected. I wasn't invisible. I learned that I had to stick to my guns and "wear them down." If I did so, I was often successful advocating for the boys.

LIVING ON THE BOUNDARIES OF SCHOOL

My reputation as an advocate grew, and I was helping several students. I frequently attended hearings and meetings with school boards, principals, counselors, and teachers. I learned that revealing too much of my information could result in students being dropped from programs, such as in Smurf's case. I learned that school information was protected and/or limited, which constrained my ability to help. Most helpful was my discovery that I should think more like a lawyer than a teacher or an advocate. I learned how to approach every meeting and hearing with facts related to the school policies. No emotions. No personal stories. No justice. Just the facts! Most of the time, in order to succeed, my only recourse was to prove that the school hadn't followed due process.

A good illustration of my success, once I realized due process was key, occurred when Chris (another of the students for whom I advocated) asked me to advocate for him because he might be suspended for allegedly being abusive to a young female student. My first understanding of the story was the classroom teacher's version: He claimed Chris was hurting a girl in the hallway and when he called Chris on it Chris became abusive toward the teacher. The teacher referred Chris to the office reporting that Chris was hurting the girl. The teacher's complaint led to a possible suspension.

Chris, on the other hand, said the girl involved was a good friend of his and that although he was touching her, he wasn't hurting her.

I took the knowledge I'd gained in my previous experiences with Smurf, Juice, and Lil Garfield to Chris's suspension hearing. At this point, I knew the student handbook inside out. I was highly familiar with the policies and due process. I knew I needed to demonstrate how due process was not followed, but I was also determined that Chris's side of the story be heard. At the hearing, I learned the most critical missing piece of the story: The classroom teacher filed his referral based on the Brighton principal's declaration, at a school assembly, that students were not to touch each other. I realized that the "no touching" rule the teacher claimed Chris had broken wasn't in writing in the handbook. I knew this was my opportunity.

Using the handbook, I pointed out every step that was not followed in the suspension process. When invited, I also took the opportunity to ask the teacher who had written the referral a few questions. I asked the teacher to describe what he saw. He described exactly what Chris had told me with the exception of hurting the girl. I asked the teacher, "How did you know the girl was hurt? Was she crying? Was she withering in pain? Did the girl scream for help?" The teacher answered, no, he just thought she was hurt because Chris's hands were on her shoulder. The teacher had no real evidence of the girl being abused by Chris. Chris was being falsely accused. Chris was not suspended as a result of my participation and support. But this incident was still frustrating to me. The fact that Chris was falsely accused was never addressed by the school and didn't play a role in the decision. Chris wasn't suspended because the school failed to follow due process and because I noticed. They couldn't suspend Chris because "no touching" wasn't written in the handbook. The injustice Chris felt was not an issue.

I left the meeting with many thoughts in my head. We basically won, but it was a shallow victory. Why did policy and due process play such a big role and not the student or the student's voice? Were rules and regulations more important than the people they were made by and for?

No one heard my students' and my stories because bureaucratic policies controlled the system. Every time a student was removed from school or suspended it was because the policy demanded it. Every time we won in a hearing it was because the policies were abrogated. There was no person to whom we could appeal because administrators washed their hands of responsibility with the policy. The policies were responsible, not them. All doors were closed.

Davidson (1996) points to differential treatment and bureaucratized relationships and practices as factors that contribute to students feeling isolated. Rigid adherence to policy is most important in the School Community (I). When policies supersede the importance of people's lives, the people's stories are never heard (Taylor, 1996). When my students were forced to live on the boundaries of the School Community, they were no longer members of the community of practice. They were no longer important. They became invisible.

As an advocate, I was forced to live on the boundaries, too. I became invisible like my students. When I took students into the school office, I could stand for many minutes waiting for a secretary to acknowledge my presence. They looked right at me, yet acted as if I wasn't there. Phone calls to the district office were never returned. Were they hoping I would just slowly go away? As an advocate, my voice was silenced along with the voices of my students.

Living on the boundaries taught me that to want an education does not guarantee an education. Like my students, I lost trust in the education system and came to see it as an inhuman institution.

ADVOCACY AS A FORM OF CRITICAL ETHNOGRAPHY

Research expands knowledge. Through educational research, new ideas can be discovered that can shape theory and practice, and new potentials for teaching and learning can be imagined. But before this study, Debbie often wondered what better reasons for research might exist than just learning more. As this study began, Dell Hymes's perspective, which Debbie read in Figueroa (1994), offered a preliminary justification. Hymes posits that research "does not separate the role of the academic scholar from the role of the individual in a moral social role" and that "sociolingustic knowledge" should be used to solve "socio-political problems" (Figueroa,

1994, p. 32). For Hymes there is more than doing *research. There is more than discovery of the unknown. There is a need for discovery that brings about change. Research should—must—bring about social justice.*

At the beginning of the study, Debbie layered a researcher position onto her role as classroom teacher. She was a teacher researcher in her Nuestra Casa classroom and a participant observer in the boys' homes and neighborhood. She gathered data using traditional ethnographic methods. She sought to describe and interpret the boys' literacy learning and viewed them as her informants.

When Debbie added the layer of "advocate" to her positions as teacher and researcher, the study became a form of critical ethnography. According to Jim Thomas (1993), "conventional ethnographers study culture for the purpose of describing it; critical ethnographers do so to change it" (p. 4). Critical ethnography renders stories "problematic through cultural critique and by asserting multiple voices" (Britzman, 2003, p. 33). Both "pedagogical and political," critical ethnographies are designed to understand how and why societies, cultures, schools, etc. are inequitably structured and to "transform the relations of power that constrict people's lives" (Simon & Dippo, 1986, p. 196).

Advocacy meant not only describing and understanding, but interrupting *the traditions and cultural norms of the school and* challenging *power relations. In order to accomplish tasks that were within the cultural norm for many students, but systematically excluded Lil Boy Blue, Smurf, Juice, and Lil Garfield and their parents (i.e., school enrollment, participating in sports, graduation), Debbie had to examine the context of power and authority. She had to exercise resistance. The goal of the study was now to advocate for students who were marginalized by school in order to make the injustice of society visible and aid the students' emancipation (Thomas, 1993; Trueba, 1999; Carspecken, 1996). Critical ethnography is conventional ethnography with a conscience. Advocacy is acting upon the conscience.*

In the next chapter, we step away from the boys' stories to achieve enough distance to consider what they mean more abstractly. Clearly, the various communities in which the boys lived and learned were at once overlapping and distinct. In chapter 9, we open a dialogue about learners who live on the margins of schools and offer our interpretation of the stories told in the previous chapters through discussions about school failure, community, identity, and literacy. We suggest that literacy was one mechanism that excluded Lil Boy Blue, Smurf, Juice, and Lil Garfield from legitimate participation in the communities that count.

9

Literacy in Communities of Success and Failure

We've arrived at the end of this book, where readers of educational studies anticipate authors will declare answers to the research questions and offer solutions to classroom problems, not uncommonly under a heading titled, "teaching implications." So beware that we have no intention of projecting ourselves as holding "answers" to the "problems" described in the first eight chapters. Indeed, if we intend anything by way of a "conclusion" it is to highlight Lil Boy Blue, Smurf, Juice, Lil Garfield, and Debbie's story as one that confronts and complicates, rather than explains, failure (McDermott, 1997). In this chapter, we consider the constructs of community, school failure, literacy, and identity. We ask more questions. What are the boys' positions in each of their communities? How is the boys' School Community (I) a culture of failure? How does literacy contribute to the divisions that exist between the boys' communities and to their failures in school? How, in fact, is literacy a tool society uses to construct borders between communities of practice in order to fabricate failure? And finally, what might advocacy, as a form of critical ethnography, offer for shifting constructions of failure for marginalized kids?

In the introduction to the book *Naming Silenced Lives* (Mclaughlin & Tierney, 1993), William Tierney tells a story about Charles, a 40-year-old African American man who had AIDS, and how important memories were to him as he moved back to his mother's home to die. Tierney writes, "By telling Charles's story I move the memory beyond merely my own private reflection, and involve others in the retelling ... When we speak our memories and document them, we are engaged in an act of construction of our present worlds. Our individual and collective memories help construct the reality of our present" (p. 2).

In writing this book we intend to "involve others in the retelling" of Lil Boy Blue, Smurf, Juice, and Lil Garfield's stories to make them part of the "constructed reality of our present worlds." Telling the boys' stories makes possible a dialogue about what their real lives and experiences mean. We hope this final chapter inspires readers to initiate dialogue with others.

As we share our interpretation of the boys' stories, we recognize our limitations and worry about our positions. We realize that our life experiences as two middle-aged, white, and privileged women are about as far from the boys' realities as is possible. Our own identities and histories clearly limit and shape our understanding and the knowledge we produce (Simon & Dippo, 1986). We don't pretend to know the "truth."

Our identities as scholars and educators enable us to name the boys' experiences so their voices can reach a new audience, but create another concern. As we draw attention to the "plight" of Lil Boy Blue, Smurf, Juice, and Lil Garfield, we run the risk of contributing to the phenomenon of school failure (Smith, Gilmore, Goldman, & McDermott, 1996). We refuse to name the boys' story "failure," because to do so would accept failure as a fact when it is not. We will, however, couch their stories in a necessary theoretical discussion about school failure. First, we offer summaries of the perspectives of "clubs" and "communities of practice," two perspectives on learning that are driven by their focus on identity.

CLUBS, COMMUNITIES, AND IDENTITIES

We all move between communities as we go throughout our daily activities. Which communities we are members of contributes to the formation of our identities. How we participate in each community depends on our status. Our identities and our status in communities define what and how we learn and who we become.

Frank Smith (1998) refers "to communities of influential people as *clubs*" (p. 11). He draws an analogy between a child who must become a full member of the literacy club to be successful with reading and an adult becoming a full member of a fitness center. A full fitness center member has all the rights and privileges associated with the center and its resources. A full member can invite a friend to visit the club, but the friend will not have the same access to participation as the member. Smith's discussion of club identity invites obvious parallels to Lil Boy Blue, Smurf, Juice, and Lil Garfield's identities as Crips:

As we identify with other members of all the clubs to which we belong, so we learn to be like those other members. We become like the company we keep, exhibiting this identity in the way we talk, dress, and ornament ourselves, and in many other ways. The identification creates the possibility of learning. All learning pivots on who we think we are, and who we see ourselves as capable of becoming. (p. 11)

Critical to this perspective, learning for club members is effortless, inconspicuous, vicarious, and permanent.

The communities-of-practice perspective distinguishes the significance of membership and participation as related to learning. Jean Lave and Etienne Wenger (1991) define a community of practice as "a set of relations among persons, activity, and world, over time and in relation with other tangential and overlapping communities of practice" (p. 98). They describe legitimate peripheral participation in a community of practice as the central defining characteristic of learning viewed as situated activity and learning as "configured through the process of becoming a full participant in a sociocultural practice" (p. 29). Learning "implies becoming a full participant, a member, a kind of person ... becoming a different person with respect to the possibilities enabled by these systems of relations," In short, learning "involves the construction of identities" (p. 53).

To learn from and understand Lil Boy Blue, Smurf, Juice and Lil Garfield's stories, our challenge is to figure out how the boys' activity was situated in their communities. Was their activity legitimate? Peripheral? Were they full members? Were they left out? Frank Smith says, "We build our identity from the clubs we are excluded from as well as from those we join. We learn who we are as much from the people we don't want to be like as from those we do. And as we decide who we are, so we start to act those roles out" (1998, p. 21).

Legitimate peripheral participation is the trajectory of newcomers moving toward full participation in a community of practice. Newcomers and novices mutually engage in the practices of a community, building shared repertoires of knowledge and ways of being, and constructing identities of belonging already held by old-timers and full members (Wenger, 1998). "Viewing learning as legitimate peripheral participation means that learning is not merely a condition for membership, but is itself an evolving form of membership" (Lave & Wenger, 1991, p. 53). "Membership in a community of practice is therefore a matter of mutual engagement. That is what defines the community" (Wenger, 1998, p. 73).

Although Lave and Wenger (1991) suggest there may be no "illegitimate" peripheral participation, clearly Lil Boy Blue, Smurf, Juice, and Lil Garfield's four communities offered contrasting characteristics regarding their membership. Lave and Wenger elaborate:

> Peripheral participation is about being located in the social world. Changing locations and perspectives are part of actors' learning trajectories, developing identities, and forms of membership. Furthermore, legitimate peripherality is a complex notion, implicated in social structures involving relations of power. As a place in which one moves toward more-intensive participation, peripherality is an empowering position. As a place in which one is kept from participating more fully—often legitimately, from the broader perspective of society at large—it is a disempowering position. (p. 36)

The boys' positions differed in each community. They were *full members* in their Family and Gang Communities, with all rights and privileges. Although they were *legitimate peripheral participants* in the School (I) and Juvenile Court Communities, they were denied participating more fully and often left invisible on the margins.

As *members* of the Family Community Lil Boy Blue, Smurf, Juice, and Lil Garfield were expected to fully function within the community. A good illustration of legitimate peripheral participation as indicative of membership potential was when 4-year-old Anna was an equal member in the event of tamale making in the Espinoza household. She chose when to join the activity and when to exit. She had access to existing knowledge as her great grandma and grandma helped her learn. She was a member of the community. This was also true for Debbie during family events. Other members were more experienced and capable, but Debbie was afforded equal access and rights to engage productively. Newcomers had access to the same resources/knowledge/literacy events as existing family members. Some members had particular status granted to them by age and gender, but all rights and privileges belonged to all (even "adopted") family members who were expected to fully function within the community. Lil Boy Blue, Smurf, Juice, and Lil Garfield became members in the Family Community in the same ways.

Lil Boy Blue, Smurf, Juice, and Lil Garfield were *members* of the Gang Community. When they walked into the Nuestra Casa classroom, their ritual was to shake hands with everyone. They used their personal gang handshake with those who were part of the gang and a regular handshake with everyone else. Their blue clothes identified them as Crip. They greeted each other with "West up cuzz." "Cuzz" was a term that referred to other members in the Crip gang. "West" was a substitute for the word "what" and identified members of the westside. Their language carried the "meanings, symbolism, shared history, and experiences of people within a landscape" (Zepeda & McCarty, 1997, p. 2). The boys were a part of a history that began during neighborhood baseball games and evolved as they grew and shared experiences. Their behaviors proclaimed their intention to respect members and disrespect rivals. The gang was their way of life. They were members.

Lil Boy Blue, Smurf, Juice, and Lil Garfield were legitimate, but marginalized *participants* in the School and Juvenile Court Communities, with specifically and narrowly defined admission to the basic activities of the club, but without access to the power, knowledge, or information to completely belong (i.e., to learn) or to move toward more engaged participation. As marginalized participants in both school and the court, they and their families spent a lot of energy trying to figure out what was going on and how to get the information they needed to gain access to better understanding or making sense of the events in which they were participating.

Importantly, in the School (I) and Juvenile Court Communities, Lil Boy Blue, Smurf, Juice, and Lil Garfield's participation was simultaneously *required* and *denied*. Although the boys often wanted to attend school, they were also frequently required to attend according to court orders. Felipé waited for untold hours over numerous days to see a school district administrator and facilitate Lil Boy Blue's return to high school. When Kristina and he went to a school board meeting to advocate for their sons, they were denied the right to be heard because they didn't know how to act or how to obtain a turn to speak. Not only were access and knowledge not available to them, they didn't know where to go to access information that may have helped. Debbie was formally and overtly denied access and participation in the School Community (I) as an advocate.

Similarly, Debbie, the boys, and their families were given no opportunities to participate more legitimately in the Juvenile Court Community. In essence, their job in this community of practice was to sit silently and listen, to follow instructions, and to not object. The more compliant and unobtrusive they were with court officials like probation officers, the better. They had no say about any of the activities of the community and on occasion, when they attempted to provide information or ask questions, they were denied participation. When Debbie and Diane wanted to help Juice continue with his community PO rather than change to a school-based PO, they were advised to discuss the issue with the judge at an upcoming trial. They followed the advice and brought up the topic at the scheduled time only to be told it was not a topic for the judge or the trial. In many instances like this, Debbie and the others were challenged to make basic sense of the system and figure out how to play the game. They were still denied access to knowledge and resources.

The boys' various positions across communities of practice calls attention to the points of overlap between them. Clearly, the "boundaries" and "peripheries"—the edges of communities where they make contact with the rest of the world (Wenger, 1998)—are fundamental to understanding the four overlapping Communities of Family, Gang, School, and Juvenile Court. Wenger says boundaries are discontinuities and peripheries are continuities. "By weaving boundaries and peripheries," he says, "a landscape of practice forms a complex texture of distinction and association, possibilities and impossibilities, opening and closing, limits and latitude, gates and entries, participation and non-participation" (p. 121).

Much of the rest of this chapter explores these notions of boundaries and peripheries. Specifically, we consider Wenger's suggestion that boundary objects organize the overlaps and intersections between different communities of practice and investigate how literacy events and texts create boundaries, rather than peripheries, for gang members in school. First, however, our goal to better understand the boys' identities, and therefore learning, in each community necessitates a brief discussion about school failure.

SCHOOL FAILURE: CONSTRUCTED IDENTITY

Debbie's students were seen by most of the supporting characters in their stories as school failures. They were retained for at least one grade and maybe two, dropped out of school on several occasions, and were suspended and/or expelled. Paradoxically, they were also sincere when they expressed their desires to graduate from high school. Although getting a diploma was important to them, they seemed to sabotage themselves and their own stated ambitions by ditching class, refusing to do work, and pushing the limits legally and culturally at school. In *Lives on the Boundary*, Mike Rose (1989) describes his students' responses to school:

> No one could doubt the veterans' motivation; some were nearly feverish. But over my time with them, I had come to see how desire was only part of the equation. A number of the men—like me during my early schooling—had skated along the surface of true education, had read

too little, were propelling themselves forward on the jet streams of fleeting dreams. So they did all the things that learners, working class to upper crust, do when they lose focus or get scared or give up: They withdrew or faked it or cheated or got stoned or stayed home or blew up. (p. 154)

Debbie asked, "If you want a diploma so badly why don't you just do what you need to do to stay in school?" "I don't know, I'm just lazy I guess," was the boys' common response.

Many of the boys' comments confirmed the notion that students who fail/drop out of school often blame themselves. A closer look, however, reveals moments when the boys talked about teachers not being fair, not belonging, and school not wanting them—forms of bureaucratic and institutional "silencing" according to Michelle Fine (1991). Whether the boys realized it or not, they were "actually forced out because of unresponsive institutional arrangements" (p. 79). Fine says, "When the policies and practices of purging are rendered invisible, no one but the adolescent is held to blame" (p. 82). She asks, "What is obscured by a portrayal of dropouts as *deficient* in a *fair* system? If youths who drop out are portrayed as unreasonable or academically inferior, then the structures, ideologies, and practices that exile them systematically are rendered invisible, and the critique they voice is institutionally silenced" (p. 5).

Ray McDermott (1997) reviews three theories that explain school failure. The theory of Deprivation states, "Children not learning in school have been broken by impoverishing experiences: in addition to suffering a restricted environment, they are now restricted kids" (p. 125). This theory suggests that Lil Boy Blue, Smurf, Juice, and Lil Garfield, who were successful outside of school in the workplace and home, were damaged by childhood occurrences. The boys did face challenges—particularly Juice and Lil Garfield, when their mother was unavailable to them literally or emotionally. The boys were not broken, however, as their success in some of their communities demonstrates. We find no explanation inherent in the boys' abilities or intelligence that explains "failure."

The theory of Difference states, "Children not learning in school are not broken, although they can appear that way because of constant miscommunication organized by cultural and linguistic differences" (McDermott, 1997, p. 126). This theory suggests that the boys wouldn't know how to do school because their cultural and linguistic differences created "miscommunication." Although Lil Boy Blue, Smurf, Juice, and Lil Garfield's first language was English, their working class, Mexican American, and especially gang member identities and language meant they were defined by many school officials as culturally different.

McDermott's description of a "more Political account" is that "children are not so much broken or different as they are made to appear that way. Competition is endemic to our society, and the search for inherent intelligence organizes the school day and its children around the issue of successful and unsuccessful competence displays" (p. 127). This theory says that Debbie's students were failures because "school failure is a cultural fabrication and is constantly looked for, noticed, hidden, studied, and remediated" (p. 127). This theory rests the construct of school failure in the school rather than in the child.

School failure and school success are social creations. Much of school failure is constructed by and within the lessons that students complete in school (Bloome, 1989; Moll & Diaz, 1993) and according to students' access to the resources required to succeed (Toohey, 2000). Teaching to the test, tracking by ability, and standardized testing, among many other institutional commonalities, organize the system so that some kids will fail (Oakes, 1985; D. Smith et al., 1996). As long as these practices exist, students will have available two normal paths to travel through school: as successes or as failures. School failure is a strong option for many students.

Our society needs stories of students who fail in order to have stories of students who succeed. Schools need classes of remedial students in order to provide classes for the gifted students. Schools need the student who gets in trouble in order to have the students who shine as perfect. This dichotomy has become so much a part of our "common sense" that schools unknowingly create and promote a culture of school failure. Both are unavoidable when children are placed in a system designed to pit one student against the other. The students who lose at the game are denied the extra benefits associated with school. And once students are deemed "failures" in public school, their likelihood of moving up in the ranks toward success is virtually impossible (Allington, 1977, 1980).

Herbert Kohl (1991) suggests that what "is often disastrously mistaken for failure to learn or the inability to learn" is what he calls "not-learning " (p. 10). He continues, "because not-learning involves willing rejection of some aspect of experience it can often lead to what appears to be failure" (p. 13). This means that the students found in the culture of school failure are those who refuse to conform to the school's idea of what, who, and how they should be, who are labeled by the institution as not capable and placed in remedial classes. Kohl's position is that failure, or rather not-learning, becomes an identity for such students. "Not-learning produces different effects. It tends to strengthen the will, clarify one's definition of self, reinforce self-discipline, and provide inner satisfaction" (p. 15). Lil Boy Blue, Smurf, Juice, and Lil Garfield's identities as Crips were no doubt strengthened by their determination to not conform, particularly to gang-specific requirements like dress codes.

Schools are structured with regulations that make it "legal" to push kids out (Fine, 1991). Little Boy Blue, Smurf, Juice, and Lil Garfield's identity was not only Mexican American and working class, but "gangster." According to their school handbook, a gang is an illegal organization. As members of the Manzanita Lynch Mob Crips, Lil Boy Blue, Smurf, Juice, and Lil Garfield were "illegal students." They were designated as individuals who needed to be removed from the school so the good students wouldn't get hurt. Not-learning got them in trouble when it resulted in "defiance or a refusal to become socialized in ways that are sanctioned by dominant authority" (Kohl, 1991, p. 15).

In *Bad Boys: Public Schools in the Making of Black Masculinity*, Ann Ferguson (2000) examines the lives of 11- and 12-year-old African American boys in the school system to document how the school system constructs the sense of self in students. Her research determines that in order to be successful at school the young African American boys have to give up all or part of their self-identity. Once students are assigned the label "at-risk," they become more visible in the classroom and are singled out and punished for behaviors that are perceived as rule breaking. Students who don't have the label but exhibit the same behavior are ignored or their behavior is passed off as "just being kids." The at-risk students' behaviors are perceived as inappropriate, the children are viewed as troublemakers, and they are punished.

By the time Debbie worked with the boys, they had spent years sitting in spaces, hearing language, and seeing print that transmitted literacy, as well as "school" as a culturally defined authority. They had internalized the positions school assigned them (Street, 1995). Smith says, "Students who have 'failed' school literacy instruction for 10 years have learned that they can't read and write, that they don't want or expect to, that they are 'dummies'" (1998, p. 36). When Smurf returned to traditional high school, his teacher informed Debbie that he had scored poorly on a reading test. Debbie quickly responded with information about the quantity and quality of reading Smurf had done in and outside of her class at Nuestra Casa, but the information did nothing to alter the teacher's perception. The test said he was a poor reader, therefore he was a poor reader. Smurf made no effort to show her he could read better than the test score suggested. Why try, he may have thought, if the teacher already believes I'm incapable?

When Juice's teacher criticized men from the "southside" because of their language (see chapter 5), she chastised Juice. Juice analyzed the interchange. "Because everybody looks down on you. Like, not everybody, some teachers are cool, but some teachers talk about racist things. She doesn't know she's being racist, I guess. Everybody calls women 'Miss.' ... She always brings up the southside .... I was all like ...." Juice's voice trailed off and his head lowered as if in shame. "I go, 'yeah, I grew up there.' And she goes, 'See what I mean.' I go, 'Fuuuuck.'"

In order to learn from this teacher, Juice had to sell part of himself. He said, "The teachers can disrespect us because they know there is nothing we can do. This is Whiteman's school." For many students who find themselves members of the culture of school failure, not-learning is a means of saving one's integrity—a way to survive on the margins. Lil Boy Blue, Smurf, Juice, and Lil Garfield's refusal to do any work that looked like school gave them some power over the school that "didn't want them." Their refusal was a way for them to save face. They were in control for the moment.

LITERACY: IDENTITIES BUILT,
DESTROYED, FABRICATED

In today's world, all members of all communities are known to regularly participate in literacy events (Heath, 1982) and literacy practices (Street, 1995). Research and theoretical development in the past several decades has stretched and refined understandings about literacy "beyond knowing how to read and write a particular script [to] applying of this knowledge for a specific purpose in specific contexts of use ... it requires a shared cultural knowledge" (Scribner & Cole, 1981, p. 236). To understand the literacy stories of Lil Boy Blue, Smurf, Juice, and Lil Garfield, we conceptualize literacy as "an ideological practice, implicated in power relations and embedded in specific cultural meanings and practices" (Street, 1995, p. 1; see also Gee, 1987, and Luke, 1995, among others).

Members of clubs and communities interact with each other and produce varied forms of oral and written language texts: oral discourse, written documents, and nonverbal symbols and actions. These texts serve as "a historical trace of artifacts—physical, linguistic, and symbolic—and of social structures, which constitute and reconstitute the practice over time" (Lave & Wenger, 1991, p. 58). Literacy is a marker of identity and it constructs identity.

Lil Boy Blue, Smurf, Juice, and Lil Garfield's literac(ies) in their families and gang marked them as fathers, sons, and respected gang members.

The literacy they experienced in school defined them as not capable, drop-outs, and delinquents. The literacy they experienced in court defined them as illegal. As Street says, " ... the acquisition of literacy becomes isomor-phic with the child's development of specific social identities and posi-tions: their power in society becomes associated with the kind and level of literacy they have acquired" (1995, p. 110).

GANG MEMBERS' PERCEPTIONS OF THEIR OWN LITERACIES

Before delving more deeply into the critical argument of this study, we re-turn to the voices of the boys, themselves, to share their perceptions of their literacy. Were Lil Boy Blue, Smurf, Juice, and Lil Garfield literate? Did they consider themselves literate? Observers of the boys' outward behavior in Debbie's class might question if they could read or write. At the begin-ning, Debbie wondered herself. They fought reading and writing as if they weren't able. On one occasion Smurf explained, "Miss, we know how to read, we just don't want to."

Debbie asked Lil Boy Blue, "What do you read on a typical day?"

He thought for a while. "I don't read anything."

Debbie was startled. Lil Boy Blue's coffee table was littered with chil-dren's books, newspapers, and magazines; Dallas Cowboys posters and stickers decorated the walls; and newsletters, advertisements, bills, and schedules were stuck to the refrigerator.

"Do you consider yourself a reader today?"

"Ummm, yeah and no. I like to read, like I read the paper everyday. But I don't read any books."

Again, evidence existed to the contrary. Debbie checked out several books on Al Capone that Lil Boy Blue read and talked about at Nuestra Casa. When Debbie took her students to a big warehouse bookstore to se-lect books for the classroom, Lil Boy Blue didn't complain and knew what book he wanted to get—*Where the Red Fern Grows* (Rawls, 1981).

"What type of reading do you do at work?"

Debbie learned that in his role as supervisor at work, the first thing Lil Boy Blue did each shift was read the information left in a file from the pre-ceding shift. At the end of his shift, he wrote instructions for the next super-visor. Lil Boy Blue read and wrote every day at home and work. Yet, he refused to acknowledge any reading and writing in his world.

Smurf often said he didn't read, but Debbie persisted. "What reading do you do in a typical day?"

"Rap. You gotta know how to read to rap."

"Do ya?"

"Yeah, I mean, because rapping you got to use words. I mean, you gotta use different words. You can't just use … you can't use just regular words, Crip and Blood gang this and westside and south. You can't use just that all the time. You gotta come up with some other words that mean the same kind of stuff that you're trying to say, but it's a different word, you know, that's where reading comes in. You got to look through dictionaries and find words or thesaurus."

"Do you consider yourself a reader?"

"Yeah, I look through the dictionary to try to find new words to put in my rap. I don't, well, read. I don't consider myself a reader. I never, I'm really not one to sit down to read a book. Not me, I mean I'll do it. I mean, when I was locked up, of course. I'm not a reader."

"What are some of the things you read?"

"I don't … at work …. maybe on the computer. Naaaah, I really don't read."

With further conversation, Smurf admitted he read CD inserts, *Source* magazine, articles on the Internet, the newspaper, road signs and messages at work. At Nuestra Casa, Smurf willingly read out loud. Yet Smurf just couldn't say he was a reader.

"Do you consider yourself a writer?"

"Ahh, I do a lot of writing at work and then I write a lot of raps. The thing nowadays, I don't write my raps on paper. I … at work I make them up in my head and I memorize them. I'm very proud of myself. 'Cause of all those years of writing rap now I can just do it in my head. I can see it in my head."

Smurf did not consider the reading and writing he does every day to be "real."

Once in the Espinoza's living room, the family started talking about books. No one remembered how the discussion began, but Lil Boy Blue immediately shared books he remembered reading when he was in grade school. Smurf chimed in with titles of books he read. The room buzzed with energy. The boys lit up with excitement as they talked. Listening, Debbie wondered how and when their excitement about books was lost.

"Juice, do you see yourself as a reader?"

"Naah, I really consider myself a writer. When I get bored or when I get mad, I can sit down and tag. That be cool." Once, Juice sat in the front of Debbie's truck reading *Monster: The Autobiography of an L.A. Gang Member* (Shakur, 1998). As they walked into the mall, he was still reading. He always read the magazines or books he found on the front seat of Debbie's truck. He regularly read to his daughter. Why didn't he consider himself a reader?

Juice claimed when he was younger he wanted to read "real bad. I got mad because everybody would be reading signs and billboards. Little tiny things like that." Then in second grade he connected with reading. "I read everything I could get my hands on."

"Do you remember how you learned to read?"

"By reading. Looking at the letters. I think I had to learn to spell before I learned how to read to pronounce the words, the letters and everything cause we used to have spelling tests. I had to spell and then while I was spelling, like I kind of more or less like all of a sudden, when the year was over, I knew how to read."

"How did you learn to write?"

"Through the spelling test, I learned how to read. You have to learn how to write. To learn how to write, you have to learn how to read. Can't read without writing, because if you don't know what you are writing, then you know what I mean? You can't read it, you know what I mean?" For Juice, reading and writing went together.

"What do you like to read?"

"I like the book 'C-Monster.'"

"What else?"

Juice hemmed and hawed a bit. "I'm not really into reading. Miss, I hate reading."

"Why?"

He responded quietly, "I don't know, maybe I'm just lazy."

Juice put an end to the conversation. "Reading isn't my thing."

During Debbie's interview with Lil Garfield about reading and writing, he happened to be reading the chapter in her dissertation about the boys. He easily listed what he read as they chatted, but got frustrated when Debbie asked, "Do you see yourself as a reader?"

"Shit, I don't know," he said. "I fuckin' read. You know what I'm saying, but I don't read. I just skim through all the fuckin' pinpoint words. Like if you got an article on this sort of thing. I see what the question is, where is fuckin' Africa? I am saying I won't read the whole fuckin' paragraph that says Africa was discovered for this long and the first man came. I don't give a fuck. That's not what I am looking for. I'll just skim through it until it says 'Africa is.' You know what I am saying, 'in the east.' Oh, here it is."

Lil Garfield looked for clues in the paragraph to find the answer to the question, clearly a school task. Debbie knew he hadn't skimmed the dissertation, though. "Did you skim the dissertation or did you read?"

"I was reading it all because it interested me."

"Are you a writer?"

"I'm not a writer because I could never write well. I broke my arm several times while growing up and I never developed good penmanship." For Lil Garfield, bad penmanship meant he wasn't a writer, but he wrote in a journal and wrote raps. He wrote several letters while he was in rehabilitation. Like the other boys, Lil Garfield acknowledged the literacy events in his life, but wouldn't identify as a reader or a writer.

School literacy defined reading and writing for these young men. Street (1995) asks, "Among all of the different literacy practices in the community, the home, and the workplace, how is it that the variety associated with schooling has come to be the defining type, not only to set the standard for other varieties but to marginalize them, to rule them off the agenda of literacy debate?" (p. 106).

Lil Boy Blue, Smurf, Juice, and Lil Garfield didn't have permission to view their literacy as legitimate. Everyday reading: TV guides, magazines, CD inserts, bills and notes, checks, order forms, and poems to girlfriends, as well as reading and composing complex tags and raps, were dismissed as things Lil Boy Blue, Smurf, Juice, and Lil Garfield *did*, but not as reading or writing. Adapting findings from Knobel (1999), "These literacy practices involve much more than merely encoding and decoding (usually) written texts. Instead, these literacies are part-and-parcel of [their] everyday life and Discourse memberships which includes sets of particular social practices, ways of speaking about things, certain values and assumptions, and ways of interacting with others .... [They] constitute[d] significant aspects of [their] social identities" (p. 223). Why was acknowledging they were readers and writers so hard for Lil Boy Blue, Smurf, Juice, and Lil Garfield?

LITERACY: MEMBERSHIP DENIED

Each literacy event and literacy practice in a community is socially situated within multiple relations of power. The boys enacted literacy in each of their communities, but their shifting status in each context meant their actions as literates moved them along the trajectory toward membership or denied the legitimacy of their participation. The literacy artifacts in each of the boys' communities were "boundary objects" according to Wenger's descriptions. He says boundary objects are forms of reification that "both connect and disconnect. They enable coordination, but they can do so without actually creating a bridge between the perspectives and meanings of various constituencies" (Wenger, 1998, p. 107).

Because they were "inextricably linked to cultural and power structures in a given society" (Street, 1995, p. 161), literacy practices maintained boundaries between Lil Boy Blue, Smurf, Juice, and Lil Garfield's Family, Gang, School, and Juvenile Court Communities, rather than peripheries. Literacy was a vehicle used by full members to include or exclude, empower or disempower, newcomers to each community.

The boys were steeped in purposeful literacy events in the Family Community in which they fully participated, without fear of evaluation, to communicate, to play, and to learn. In "'ordinary' activities of everyday life, ... legitimate participation comes diffusely through membership in family and community" (Lave & Wenger, 1991, p. 92). Literacy contributed naturally and easily to the identity of belonging in the Family Community.

In the Gang Community, linguistically and conceptually complex tags were created to earn respect, raps were written to tell the story of the gang, and elaborate hand signs and oral language systems were developed to signify membership. Tagging, the predominant literacy event in the Gang Community, involved mutually engaged authors and readers and "... engagement in practice, rather than being its object, is a *condition* for the effectiveness of learning" (Lave & Wenger, 1991, p. 93, emphasis in original). Not every gang member could tag well—in fact Lil Garfield admitted he had a "sorry" tag—but *pee wees* (newcomers) were not excluded from gang practices because they couldn't, or were just learning to, tag. Power was appropriated according to the placement of the tags in the community, not according to gang members' facility with reading or writing. Literacy was a resource for accomplishing necessary and pleasurable purposes for legitimate audiences. In the Gang Community, the boys had power and their literacy was part of the shared repertoires of knowledge that contributed to their membership and status.

Literacy artifacts in the School Community (I), which took the shape of mundane classroom assignments, letters of reprimand from administrators, minutes from disciplinary hearings, and permission papers for parents to sign, systematically stripped the boys of their identities as readers and writers as their participation in the community of practice was reduced and eventually eliminated. Each of the boys had identified himself as a student, a reader, and a writer early on in school, but by the time they dropped out of high school all four came to believe they weren't readers or writers, weren't smart, and didn't deserve something better. The assignments at school reified their identities as failures. Such so-called "academic" literacy events of the classroom were, in essence, nonsense (Smith, 1998) that separated literacy from purpose and personal relationships. Labeled as the bad kids, or as the ones who were lazy and didn't care, they were told repeatedly that such work was all they were capable of. Their failure was constructed by their teachers, by the nature of the work they faced in their classrooms, and by their own decisions and actions of defiance. Refusing to do the work, or not-learning, actively took power away from the teachers and returned it to Lil Boy Blue, Smurf, Juice, and Lil Garfield—as if to say, "You may have the power to give me nonsense work, but you can't make me do it!" Literacy, as defined by the school, was a barrier to membership in the community.

Texts in the Juvenile Court Community constructed the boys as illegal. Their voices were absent in texts that reduced them from complex, real young men to compliant or noncompliant followers of "fill-in-the-blank" probation orders. Written orders in the Juvenile Court Community often complicated their opportunities for engagement in the School Community, and sometimes eliminated all opportunities for membership. Literacy kept the boys, their families, and Debbie powerless on the periphery.

Taylor (1996) says that without exception, there were times in the lives of the marginalized men and women with whom she worked when genuine opportunities to reconstruct their lives were denied. They, like Debbie's students, wanted to participate, but their lives were fabricated in toxic, official texts to fit the dominant ideologies of society. With each official document and artificial literacy exercise the boys experienced in public school, they identified less and less as "students" and more and more as "criminals." Literacy was part of what was done to them.

In the School Community (I) and the Juvenile Court Community, many participants were rendered invisible through literacy events that attributed all power and control to "the policy." Authority appeared to be in the hands of the teachers, administrators, or court officials, but policies (written texts) were actually in control. Written policy allowed full members of these communities of practice to wash their hands of decision making in the school and the court. Even when Debbie and the boys "won," victory occurred because due process wasn't followed. No one heard the injustices that happened. No one heard the participants' voices. How could students be expected to invest in school if there was no room for their voices?

And what about literacy in the School Community (II)? At Nuestra Casa, Debbie always viewed Lil Boy Blue, Smurf, Juice, and Lil Garfield as learners. They saw themselves as learners some of the time. Although they verbalized a value of learning and education, they all struggled to get the education they imagined and to include themselves in their descriptions of good students, readers, or writers. In their collective schooling histories, there were teachers who stood out positively and teachers who hurt them. They dealt with racism, stereotyping, and preconceived limits on their abilities and attitudes. They voiced responsibility for their actions and labeled themselves as lazy. They were the ones who "fucked up." The boys readily admitted to Kathy that they consciously tested Debbie to see how long it would take her to leave compared to her Nuestra Casa predecessors. Nonetheless, eventually, the "failing" students were observed actively engaged—even, on occasion, engrossed—in events in which they constructed meaning and purpose for reading and writing. Most of Debbie's students achieved conventionally defined success at traditional high school and received diplomas; many continued on to higher education or educational training programs.

Literacy events in the School Community (II) grew to be different from the boys' other school experiences. When Debbie assigned a writing assignment that was an exercise from the mandated curriculum, the students struggled and fussed. But when the students tagged, read gangster literature, or wrote poetry—in other words, when Debbie organized classroom activity as unlike traditional school as possible—the boys participated. Debbie removed competition. Everyone helped everyone else do the work, especially if "the work" was the mandated worksheets they all hated. The boys wrote what they wanted and how they wanted. They used their language. They censored themselves according to purpose and audience.

Most importantly, as a community of practice, the overlaps between Nuestra Casa and the other communities of practice were peripheries rather than boundaries (Wenger, 1998). Fine (1991) says, "If the lives and subjectivities of low-income adolescents are taken seriously, then the very boundaries and concerns of public school must stretch to incorporate that which is central to their lived experiences" (p. 221). Debbie didn't deny the students their identities, she learned about them. She learned about the boys' families, cultures, languages, and beliefs. As an advocate she strived to work with the Family and Gang Communities and against the School (I) and Juvenile Court Communities, thereby tipping the scales of power in her students' direction.

THE "CARING" TEACHER VERSUS TEACHER AS ADVOCATE

The last few paragraphs suggest a rosy, pat answer that is dangerously romantic and simple: provide students with choice, like them for who they are, encourage them to write the way they want, care about their lives outside of school, make school more social and fun, and success is around the corner. Not so. There were some successes, particularly within the dominant ideological stance that glorifies "graduation" as the finish line of public schooling. There are also plenty of loose ends for Lil Boy Blue, Smurf, Juice, and Lil Garfield. And several of their *homies* are dead.

Lil Garfield graduated, for example, but graduation didn't provide resolution to his story or the promised future the general public holds dear. Lil Garfield had been homebound since the shooting that left him disabled. A teacher came to his home to help him complete required credits to finish high school. Lil Garfield told us that at the graduation ceremony he was asked to sit (in his wheelchair) literally on the periphery of the stage (see Fig. 9.1). His family was nearly not allowed to attend. School officials were frightened that Lil Garfield would be "assassinated." According to Lil Garfield's interpretation, "They were assassinating my character."

Juice also graduated from an alternative school in the district (see Fig. 9.2). Juice confessed that his wife (with whom he now has three children) did the worksheets he was required to complete for him. He said he "learned how to survive school." Juice completed training in the Army Reserves in April, 2004, however, and in the top 10% of his class.

Smurf, who didn't graduate and is the father of two children, has returned to Kristina and Felipé's home to continue to sort out the direction his life should take. Lil Boy Blue, the father of two children, is in a training program to learn refrigeration, where he reports he's doing well (see Fig. 9.3).

FIG. 9.1.   Lil Garfield after his commencement ceremony.

FIG. 9.2   Juice after his commencement ceremony.

FIG. 9.3.   Lil Boy Blue and Smurf at Kristina and Felipé's home.

The boys are parents of a new generation of children in the public schools. There is nothing in their story or ours that suggests the children's futures will be less fraught with challenge than their fathers' were, either in school or in their neighborhood.

It is particularly dangerous to name Debbie a "caring teacher" as connected to these stories. Debbie shocked the boys when she asked them to read, write, and think about issues they cared about. Debbie shocked Kristina, Felipé, and Diane when she cared so much about their sons' participation in the School Community (II) that she called their homes to wake the boys if they were late for class. Many of the school officials Debbie encountered as an advocate labeled her as "caring," "good," someone the boys were "lucky" to have help them. But to frame Debbie as the good teacher, as Deborah Britzman (2003) describes, "positioned as self-sacrificing, kind, overworked, underpaid, and holding an unlimited reservoir of patience," would "subvert a critical discourse about the lived contradictions of teaching and the struggles of teachers and students" (p. 28). Debbie cared, and continues to care about the boys and their families. But it was Debbie's advocacy that interrupted the discourse of failure. She not only refused to allow Lil Boy Blue, Smurf, Juice, and Lil Garfield to be viewed as though failing school was their fault, she made the hidden agenda that was designed to make them look like they were "criminals" visible. She refused to let them be silent because she recognized the essentialness of their participation.

In a conversation with Denny Taylor about tagging at Nuestra Casa, Debbie described her role as a teacher and advocate:

Denny: And yet you have a track record for getting these kids into mainstream school and also into college.

Debbie: Yes. But I don't know what [other teachers] attribute it to. I know I attribute it to the fact that I accept the kids for who they are so that they can then accept themselves.

Denny: What would you tell an administrator?

Debbie: If I sat down with another teacher or an administrator, I would tell them first that tagging is language and that I don't advocate for destruction of property, I don't advocate for violence, but I do advocate for the student as a whole student. That it is part of their language. That it is part of who they are in everyday life, and if it is part of them then it has to be part of my classroom. Because they can only learn if they are accepted as a whole person in my room. I believe if I eliminate their language I eliminate their learning potential.

Denny: That's pretty profound.
Debbie: Well, if you silence them how can they learn? And by taking
             away their language and their tagging, you are silencing them.
             You can't learn when you're silent. (Taylor, Coughlin, &
             Marasco, 1997, p. 142)

Michelle Fine (1991) says classroom teachers of marginalized high
school students and their families are disempowered like those they serve.
"Those denied voice and power tend to reproduce this denial in their relationships with students" (p. 224). Teachers who move into the role of advocate, however, might accomplish the three "unequivocal beliefs" Fine
offers to create change:

[F]irst, that educators must reflect on practice critically, extract from it,
and innovate collaboratively; second, that this is possible only in radically
transformed educational settings; and third, that public high schools, as
they currently exist, mitigate the possibilities for teachers' collective reflection, active critique, or democratic participation. (p. 226)

From a communities-of-practice point of view, advocacy means creating
peripheries rather than boundaries. Debbie, as a teacher who was an advocate, was like teachers in apprentice settings that are communities of practice where "the issue of conferring legitimacy is more important than the
issue of providing teaching" (Lave & Wenger, 1991, p. 92).

Even in one of our final conversations about the boys and our determination to tell their story, Debbie wrote: "I would never say I was a caring
teacher in the typical way of using that word ... I believed Lil Boy Blue,
Smurf, Juice, and Lil Garfield had a right to an education—a fair and com-
petent education. Not only did they deserve it, they earned the right to have
it. I wanted them to have what was rightfully theirs. I didn't want them to
believe what the school and courts were saying about them ... they were
much more than what school and court saw. I don't want anyone to read our
book and say, 'that teacher' [meaning me] did a great job with 'those' kids. I
want the reader to hear my kids' stories. And hopefully start talking about
reform to stop the harm schools do."

We leave the last thought, appropriately, to one of the key characters in
this story. Lil Boy Blue wrote the words in Fig. 9.4 in school at Nuestra
Casa. They articulate the very real tension he experienced in gang life, but
they indicate that he, like Smurf, Juice, and Lil Garfield, will likely remain
"CRIP 4 LIFE."

4/6/95

My advice to someone
thinking about joining a gang is
not to cuzz its messed up. Ive
been running with a gang for almost
7 years and gain nothing but a couple
nights locc up and one of my closes
homie six feet under and other one
locc up un County looking at serious
time. I can't get out its too hard
too much Love for my homies but
yet I have its too crazy and I got a
2 month old baby girl. So I hope you
can see my point. As you can see I still
cross out my b's and put two c's
I guess you still got that crip in me.

boyblue 1

FIG. 9.4.   Lil Boy Blue's words of advice.

Appendix A: Timeline

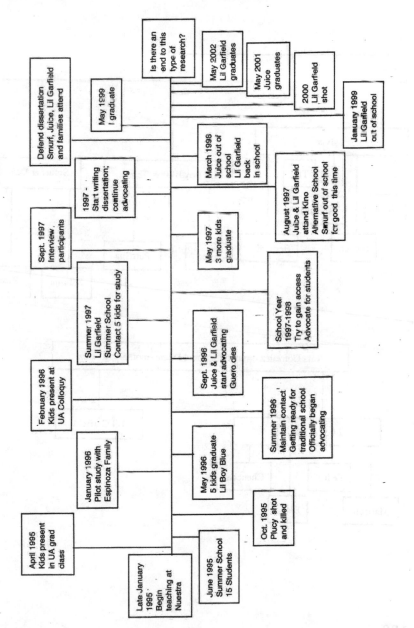

Appendix B: Family Trees

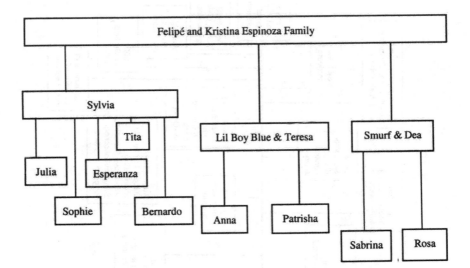

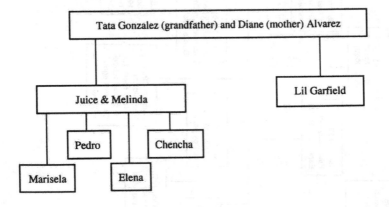

Appendix C: Glossary of Gang Terminology as Used by Lil Boy Blue, Smurf, Juice, and Lil Garfield

Claiming: Participating or being a part of a gang.

Down: With support, help.

EBK: Everybody killer.

Fools: People in general.

G: A gangster.

Gangbanging: Putting in work.

Gangbangers: A gang member.

Homie: Friend.

Hood: Neighborhood.

Jumped: Beaten up.

Jump you in: Initiation for membership in the gang.

Juvie: Juvenile detention center.

Locs: Friends in the gang.

Maza: Dough.

OG: Old gangster.

Padded down: Their body and pockets checked for anything in them.

Peewees: Youngest members in the gang.

Rock house: A partially torn down house made of rocks.

Roll call: A list of other gang members.

Represent: Participation in any activity that built the reputation of the gang.

Sagging: Pants riding very low on the hips.

Slobs: Crip name for the rival gang Blood.

Tagging: Graffiti.

Tail: A chunk of hair going down the back of the head.

Throw up: Showing signs.

Appendix D: Smurf and Sad Boy's Story

It was a dark blue night kiccin cacc on the 31 bloc, with some 40's of O'E, weed, and some homegirls that night was going well until a strange car full of slob's roll up. Smurf and I had two Desert Eagle's so you know we wern't slippin. The Lbb crew had two Sawed off Guage's with Shaggy on the side strappin a 45. The sound of screeching tires are coming on both sides of us. At least five heads in each car, slowing down as they pulled up slowly towards us. All of a sudden they stop, silence was all through the bloc, not a word said for atleast 10 seconds it seemed like the longest 10 seconds any one could ever go through. "Let's do this" was the words heard from the two cars as they opened there car doors slowly creepin out. Silent for another long 10 seconds exept for the clicc clacc of the cold steel hammer cliccing bacc. Eyes wide awake thoughts of death are going through our heads hoping we do die, but voices are telling us that every thing is gonna c alright. Different thoughts went through each one of our heads, about our kids, our parents, and thinking what a wonderfull future we would have had with our beautiful "ladies." But knowing if those triggers get pulled we'll never get to give our ladies a child or to have there hand in marriage. The first time that we ever cared and loved for a person were gonna loose it for our pride, and what we believe in. It's trippy how so much things go through your mind in such little time. I wish we could c our hynas once again "Till Times Ends." As we pull out our cuates were praying to god asking for forgiveness and asking if Mauricio to c with us the whole way, and to c waiting for us in that "GANGSTER LEAN." Should have been an "L O C" yelled out Shaggy as he started going cycso on the solo rampage. "Watch your cacc Cuzz" screamed out Bad Boy Pumping his guage like there was no tomorrow. Clicc clicc bang bang Linch Mob Crip Gang yelled Boy Blue dumping on fools like he was suposed to. I ran up to the car with plenty of fear in my heart "ah phuk" im hit said Shaggy. I turned around grabbed a slob by his throat with an evil mind "got any last words" I asked, well phuk your life bang, bang I started unloading my clip on his face. After I dumped my whole clip on his face I popped a new clip in, then I looked cacc and saw little SMURFY LOC pistol whippen some slop to death then I saw the slob fall to the ground and lil SMURF took to three to the chess but he was still shooting cacc. those lil PEE-WEEZ SMURF and SHAGGY went out like some real soldgers, at the age of 15. The sound of hot bullets go through your bodies but not giving a phuk cuzz Mauricio gots my cacc so we kept gunning yelling out "Crip for Life." all the girls are dead six slobz are down four are still fightin for their lives SMURF and SHAGGY are cacc on thier feet poppin in some new clippz the Lbb crew are still bustin on foolz when all of a sudden lil BAD BOY was hit in the necc but hez still gunnin, Lil BOY BLUE took a gage to the leg. then all of a sudden everybodys down silence is in the night once again flood and smoke is everywhere. All you can hear is an helicopter and the sirens of police cars. Before we continue my name is MR.SMURF LOC and ill -C- telling the rest of the story. The only ones still livin is those insane locstaz SAD LOC, SHAGGY, Lbb crew, and me. were all struglin half way dead runnin from one time. Hoping we dont get caught just RUNNIN, RUNNIN, and STRUGLIN. We -C- a house with no lights on so we think nobodys home so we brake in to that mothafuccer but what we didnt know is that there was a mother of two in there havin thier good night sleep. So we had to hold them hostage one of the motherz children was a 16 year old boy that tried to get brave so I hit him with my gun and knocced him out and SHAGGY started to kicc him Lbb tide them all up when all of a sudden the hoota surrounded the house CUZZ they knew were we had gone. Then next thing you know the pigs shooting the shit telling us to give our selfs up they know were injured so they broke the doors down and tried to rush us but we started to blast at those pigs we took down four of them fools but they taccled us LOCSTAZ and locced us the fucc up.

Two weeks in jail and we already run the joint. But we got to watch our cacc's CUZZ there is a mob of slob's tring to shank us, all. They were good friend's of the fools that we bucced on. But we aren't going out like a bunch of pussiez so we stay strapped with anything we coud find. Ice piccs, sharp sticks, or whatever the phuk. But Phuk this shit I can't take it anymore so I got up went to the spot where the slob's chill and started going cyscho, shanking fool's left and right all you could C was fool's dropping loosing there lives Cuzz I lost my mind, brain gone already Locced to the fullest hoping I die through all this drama. As the guard's rush me off to solitary. I think of how we used to get into all kinds shit and get rushed off to PCJCC. But this is the real deal doing two life sentences each, in FLORENCE there goes the rest of our lives but phuk it that's the way we choose to live. Three young killers ready to die point blank downer than phuk for one another. Solitary time is slower than slow it seems your never gonna C the light of day. All you can do is think of how you could change your life when you get out but with two life sentences all I can think of is how to make my life worse or maybe even taking my life by suicide.

References

Allington, R. L. (1977). If they don't read much, how they ever gonna get good? *Journal of Reading, 21*, 57–61.

Allington, R. L. (1980). Poor readers don't get to read much in reading groups. *Language Arts, 57*, 872–877.

Atkin, S. B. (1993). *Voices from the fields: Children of migrant farmworkers tell their stories.* New York: Little, Brown and Company.

Atkin, S. B. (1996). *Voices from the streets: Young former gang members tell their stories.* New York: Little, Brown and Company.

Bing, L. (1992). *Do or die.* New York: Harper Collins Publishing.

Bloome, D. (Ed.). (1989). *Classrooms and literacy.* Westport, CT: Greenwood Publishing Group, Inc.

Bogdan, R. C., & Biklen, S. K. (1998). *Qualitative research for education: An introduction to theory and methods.* Boston, MA: Allyn and Bacon.

Branch, C. W. (1997). *Clinical interventions with gang adolescents and their families.* Boulder, CO: Westview Press.

Britzman, D. (2003). *Practice makes practice: A critical study of learning to teach.* Albany, NY: State University of New York Press.

Carspecken, P. F. (1996). *Critical ethnography in educational research.* New York: Routledge.

Coughlin, D. (1997). Maybe I should have died: Learning from Valerie. In D. Taylor, D. Coughlin, & J. Marasco (Eds.), *Teaching and advocacy* (pp. 12–38). York, ME: Stenhouse.

Crutcher, C. (1983). *Running loose.* New York: Dell Publishing.

Dance, L. J. (2002). *Tough fronts: The impact of street culture on schooling.* New York: Routledge Falmer.

Davidson, A. L. (1996). *Making and molding identity in schools: Student narratives on race, gender, and academic engagement.* Albany, NY: State University of New York Press.

Dimitriadis, G. (2003). *Friendship, cliques, and gangs: Young black men coming of age in urban America.* NY: Teachers College Press.

Erickson, F. (1986). Qualitative methods in research on teaching. In M. C. Wittrock (Ed.), *Handbook of research on teaching.* (Vol. 3, pp. 119–161). NY: Macmillan.

Ferguson, A. A. (2000). *Bad boys: Public schools in the making of black masculinity.* Ann Arbor, MI: The University of Michigan Press.

Figueroa, E. (1994). *Sociolinguistic meta-theory.* Oxford, UK: Pergamon.

Fine, M. (1991). *Framing dropouts: Notes on the politics of an urban public high school.* New York, NY: State University of New York.

Friar, G. (1982). *Barrio warriors: Homeboy of peace.* Los Angeles, CA: Diaz Publishing.

Gardiner, J. R. (1980). *Stone fox.* New York: Scholastic, Inc.

Gee, J. P. (1987). What is literacy? *Teaching and Learning: The Journal of Natural Inquiry, 2*(1), 3–11.

Gillis, C. (1992). *The community as classroom: Integrating school and community through language arts.* Portsmouth, NH: Heinemann.

Goodman, K. S. (1996). Principles of revaluing. In Y. M. Goodman & A. M. Marek (Eds.), *Retrospective miscue analysis: Revaluing readers and reading* (pp. 13–20). Katanah, NY: Richard C. Owen.

Hagood, M. C., Stevens, L. P., & Reinking, D. (2002). What do THEY have to teach US? Talkin' 'cross generations! In D. Alvermann (Ed.), *Adolescents and literacies in a digital world* (pp. 68–83). New York: Peter Lang.

Heath, S. B. (1982). Protean shapes in literacy events: Ever-shifting oral and literate traditions. In D. Tannen (Ed.), *Spoken and written language: Exploring orality and literacy* (pp. 97–117). Norwood, NJ: Ablex.

Hunt, M. B. (1996). *Sociolinguistics of tagging and Chicano gang graffiti.* Los Angeles, CA: University of Southern California.

Jankowski, M. S. (1991). *Islands in the street: Gangs and American urban society.* Berkeley, CA: University of California Press.

Knobel, M. (1999). *Everyday literacies: Students, discourse, and social practice.* New York, NY: Peter Lang.

Knox, G. W. (1994). *An introduction to gangs.* Bristol, IN: Wyndham Hall Press.

Kohl, H. (1991). *I won't learn from you: The role of assent in learning.* Minneapolis, MN: Milkweed Editions.

Lave, J., & Wenger, E. (1991). *Situated learning: Legitimate peripheral participation.* Cambridge, MA: Cambridge University Press.

Lipsyte, R. (1993). *The brave.* New York: Harper Collins Children's Books.

Luke, A. (1995). When basic skills and information processing just aren't enough: Rethinking reading in new times. *Teachers College Record, 97*(1), 95–115.

Maguire, J. (1991). *Starting over.* NY: Ivy Books.

McCarty, T. L., & Zepeda, O. (1999). Amerindians. In J. A. Fishman (Ed.), *Handbook of language and ethnic identity* (pp. 197–210). New York: Oxford Press.

McDaniel, L. (1989). *Too young to die.* New York: Bantam Doubleday Dell Books for Young Readers.

McDermott, R. P. (1997). Achieving school failure 1972–1997. In G. D. Spindler (Ed.), *Education and cultural process: Anthropological approaches* (pp. 110–135). Prospect Heights, IL: Waveland Press, Inc.

McLaughlin, S., & Tierney, W. G. (Eds.). (1993). *Naming silenced lives: Personal narratives and the process of educational change.* New York, NY: Routledge.

Merriam, S. B. (1998). *Qualitative research and case study applications in education.* San Francisco, CA: Jossey-Bass.

Moje, E. (2000). "To be part of the story": The literacy practices of gangsta adolescents. *Teacher College Record, 102,* 651–690.

Moll, L. C., & Diaz, S. (1993). Change as the goal of education research. In E. Jacob & C. Jordan (Eds.), *Minority education: Anthropological perspectives* (pp. 209–231). Norwood, NJ: Ablex Publishing Corporation.

Moore, J. (1978). *Homeboys: Gangs, drugs, and prisons in the barrios of Los Angeles.* Philadelphia: Temple University.

Nichols, S. L., & Good, T. L. (2004). *America's teenagers—Myths and realities: Media images, schooling, and the social costs of careless indifference.* Mahwah, NJ: Lawrence Erlbaum Associates.

Oakes, J. (1985). *Keeping track: How schools structure inequality.* New Haven, CT: Yale University Press.

Peterson, R. (1992). *Life in a crowded place: Making a learning community.* Portsmouth, NH: Heinemann.

Phillips, S. A. (1999). *Wallbangin': Graffiti and gangs in L. A.* Chicago, IL: University of Chicago Press.

Rawls, W. (1981). *Where the red fern grows.* New York: Bantam Doubleday Dell Books for Young Readers.

Rey, H. A. (1941). *Curious George.* Boston, MA: Houghton Mifflin Co.

Rose, M. (1989). *Lives on the boundary: A moving account of the struggles and achievements of America's educationally underprepared.* NY: Penguin.

Schaafsma, D. (1993). *Eating on the street: Teaching literacy in a multicultural society (Pittsburgh series in composition, literacy, and culture).* Pittsburgh, PA: University of Pittsburgh.

Scribner S., & Cole, M. (1981). *The psychology of literacy*. Cambridge, MA: Harvard University Press.

Serrano, R. A. (1999). Schooling for gangs: When school oppression contributes to gang formations. In C. Edelsky (Ed.), *Making justice our project: Teachers working toward critical whole language practice* (pp. 226–241). Urbana, IL: National Council of Teachers of English.

Shakur, S. (1993). *Monster: The autobiography of an L.A. gang member*. New York: Penguin.

Sheldon, R. G., Tracy, S. K., & Brown, W. B. (2000). *Youth gangs in American society*. Albany, NY: Wasworth Publishing Company.

Simon, R. I., & Dippo, D. (1986). On critical ethnographic work. *Anthropology and Education Quarterly, 17*(4), 195–202.

Smith, D. (1997). Tagging: A way to make meaning. In D. Taylor, D. Coughlin, & J. Marasco (Eds.), *Teaching and advocacy* (pp. 125–137). York, ME: Stenhouse.

Smith, D., Gilmore, P., Goldman, S., & McDermott, R. (1993). Failure's failure. In E. Jacob & C. Jordan (Eds.), *Minority education. Anthropological perspectives* (pp. 209–231). Norwood, NJ: Ablex Publishing Corporation.

Smith, F. (1988). *Joining the literacy club: Further essays into education*. Portsmouth, NH: Heinemann.

Smith, F. (1998). *The book of learning and forgetting*. New York, NY: Teachers College Press.

Street, B. V. (1995). *Social literacies*. New York, NY: Longman.

Taylor, D. (1996). *Toxic literacies*. Portsmouth, NH: Heinemann.

Taylor, D. (1997). We *do* language: That may be the measure of our lives. In D. Taylor, D. Coughlin, & J. Marasco (Eds.), *Teaching and advocacy* (pp. 1–11). York, ME: Stenhouse Publishers.

Taylor, D., Coughlin, D., & Marasco, J. (Eds.). (1997). *Teaching and advocacy*. York, ME: Stenhouse Publishers.

Thomas, J. (1993). *Doing critical ethnography*. Newbury Park, CA: Sage Publications.

Toohey, K. (2000). *Learning English at school: Identity, social relations and classroom practice*. Clevedon, UK: Multilingual Matters.

Tovares, R. (1996). "Ganging up on the gang." In R. M. DeAnda (Ed.), *Chicanas and Chicanos in contemporary society*. Boston: Allyn & Bacon.

Trueba, E. T. (1999). Critical ethnography and a Vygotskian pedagogy of hope: The empowerment of Mexican immigrant children. *International Journal of Qualitative Studies in Education, 12*(6), 591.

Valentine, B. (1995). *Gang intelligence manual: Identifying and understanding modern-day violent gangs in the United States*. Boulder, CO: Paladin.

Vigil, J. D. (1993). Gangs, social control, and ethnicity: Ways to redirect. In S. B. Heath & M. W. McLaughlin (Eds.), *Identity and inner-city youth: Beyond ethnicity and gender* (pp. 94–119). New York: Teachers College Press.

Vigil, J. D. (2002). *A rainbow of gangs: Street cultures in the mega-city*. Austin, TX: University of Texas Press.

Vigil, J. D. (2003). *Barrio gangs: Street life and identity in southern California*. Austin, TX: University of Texas Press.

Wells, G. (1986). *The meaning makers: Children learning language and using language to learn*. Portsmouth, NH: Heinemann.

Wenger, E. (1998). *Communities of practice: Learning, meaning, and identity*. Cambridge, MA: Cambridge University Press.

Whitmore, K. F., & Crowell, C. G. (1994). *Inventing a classroom: Life in a bilingual, whole language learning community*. York, ME: Stenhouse.

Wiesel, E. (1982). *Night*. New York: Bantam.

Williams, S. T. (1996). *Tookie speaks out against gang violence* (a series of children's books about gangs and their danger). New York: The Rosen Publishing Group, Inc.

Williams, S. T. (2004). *Blue rage, black redemption: A memoir*. Pleasant Hill, CA: Damamli Publishing Company.

Author Index

Subject Index

A

Advocacy, 151–164
  at school, 155–160
  definition, 152–153, 185
  due process, 162
  gaining access, 155–158
  in court, 161–163
  research, 164
  teaching as, 152–153, 181–185

B

Bureaucratic literacy, 92, 112–113, 163, 180

C

"Caring" teacher, 156–157, 184
Co-researcher relationship, 12–13, 51
Community, 1, 96, 121, 166
  overlaps, 130, 170, 181
Communities of practice, xxiii, 2, 37, 68,
      114, 130, 163, 165, 167–170,
      180, 181, 185
  boundaries, 163, 170, 179
  definition, 167
  legitimate peripheral participation,
      68–69, 92, 114–115, 167, 178
  marginalized participants, 132,
      168–169, 178–180
  membership, 92, 114, 130–132, 140,
      167–169
  peripheries, 92, 170, 179–181

  texts as boundary objects, 170,
      178–181
Critical ethnography, 163–164

D

Diane, 28–32

F

Family Community, 6–7, 14–15, 168, 179
  Alvarez, 26–33, 52–53
  Espinoza, 18–25
  Juice's own, 36–37
  Lil Boy Blue's own, 34
  literacy, 25–26, 29, 33–34, 35–36, 37,
      179
  rituals, 21–25
  Smurf's own, 36
Felipe, 18–21, 47, 52, 77–80

G

Gangs
  autobiographies, 147–149
  causes, 139, 140–142, 143, 146
  culture, 143
  deficit research approach, 135–136
  definitions, 40
  ethnographic research approach,
      137–146
  involvement levels, 139–140, 143–144
  joining, 40–42, 47, 137, 138, 142, 144